GUERRILLAS

GUERRILLAS

War and Peace in Central America

DIRK KRUIJT

ZED BOOKS
London & New York

Guerrillas: War and Peace in Central America was first published in 2008 by Zed Books Ltd, 7 Cynthia Street, London N1 9JF, UK and Room 400, 175 Fifth Avenue, New York, NY 10010, USA

www.zedbooks.co.uk

Designed and typeset in ITC Bodoni Twelve
by illuminati, Grosmont

Cover designed by Andrew Corbett

Printed and bound in the EU by Biddles Ltd, King's Lynn

Distributed in the USA exclusively by Palgrave Macmillan,
175 Fifth Avenue, New York, NY 10010, USA

A catalogue record for this book is available from the British Library

Library of Congress Cataloging in Publication Data available

ISBN 978 1 84277 738 1 hb
ISBN 978 1 84277 739 8 pb

Contents

Acknowledgements

This book was written with the help of many people. The fieldwork and analysis that preceded the actual writing of this study took four years, but the genesis of the project dates back to the early 1990s. Between 1988 and 1992 I worked as a development diplomat in Central America, spending a great deal of time in El Salvador, Guatemala and Nicaragua. In Nicaragua, I advised the Sandinista government and, afterwards, the government of Violeta de Chamorro, on mass employment and social reconstruction. In Guatemala I worked with the Social Investment Fund, which addressed the problem of mass unemployment during the peace talks in that country. Shortly after the peace agreements were signed in El Salvador, I served as an adviser to the Secretariat of National Reconstruction. During these years, I became acquainted with the personalities and institutions directly involved in the peace negotiations and the post-war reintegration process.

After 1992 I also had the good fortune to work at the three research institutes of the Facultad Latinoaméricana de Ciencias Sociales (FLACSO) in San José, San Salvador and Guatemala City, where I collaborated on research projects with a number of this organization's distinguished scholars: Edelberto Torres-Rivas and Francisco Rojas, FLACSO's former and current secretaries-general, respectively; the late Rafael Menjívar and Carlos Sojo, former and current directors in Costa Rica; the late René Pointevin and Víctor Gálvez, former and current directors in Guatemala; and Héctor Dada and Carlos Briones, former and current directors in El Salvador.

Utrecht University provided the funding for the research that resulted in this book. I received invaluable suggestions from my colleagues and my Ph.D. students who participated in the university's postgraduate programme 'Political Conflict, Cultural Trauma and Social Reconstruction'. In 2004 I spent some months researching at ILAS, the Institute of Latin American Studies of the University of London, and at CEDLA, the Latin American Study Centre at the University of Amsterdam. I am grateful for the support of these organizations' directors, James Dunkerley and Michel Baud respectively, and for the assistance of library staff at the two centres. Most of the fieldwork for this study was carried out between 2004 and 2007.

In El Salvador, Carlos Ramos (FLACSO) and Luis González (Universidad Centroamericana) helped greatly in the interpretation of decisive historical events. Ruben Zamora was exceptionally generous in offering me free and unlimited access to his private archive of the wartime and post-war FMLN.

In Guatemala, both Rodrigo Asturias and Julio Balconi also afforded me access to their private archives and provided a helping hand in scheduling appointments and interviews. Their assistance is greatly appreciated. Héctor Rosada-Granados granted me access to his vast collection of books, reports and documents about the peace negotiations and the URNG.

I am indebted to the hospitality of Nicaragua's Instituto de Historia de Nicaragua y Centroamérica (IHNCA). I am especially thankful for the collaboration of Margarita Vannini, director general of this fine facility. It was only through her personal intervention that I was able to conduct a number of sensitive interviews. My compatriots Jan-Kees de Rooy and Jan-Kees Verkooyen provided helpful advice and information. Maritza Blanco was of inestimable assistance in scheduling appointments. Manuel Ortega Hegg (Universidad Centroamericana) offered dispassionate and incisive interpretation of election campaigns and outcomes. Marion and Mayela Fleuren, my research associates, supplied great help in documenting and cross-checking references, and in scheduling and rescheduling appointments.

Robert Molteno and Ellen McKinlay of Zed Books were of great help. Ellen McKinlay convinced me of the advantages of a thematic rather than a historical analysis of the guerrilla wars. Robert Forstag did sterling work in editing all the English and translating all the Spanish during the prepublication phase.

Finally, many thanks to Jorge Castañeda, Kees Koonings, Menno Vellinga and Edelberto Torres-Rivas, all of whom read and commented on various parts of the manuscript.

Foreword

Seven Points to Keep in Mind as You Read This Book

1. More of the same? So-called 'crisis literature' experienced a genuine publishing boom in Central America during the 1980s and part of the 1990s. The conflicts that broke out in quick succession in Nicaragua, El Salvador and Guatemala became the subject of descriptions, analyses and narratives. The majority of the works published back then had a rather journalistic flavour about them and – even more to the point – often owed their existence to the author's sympathy with the particular revolutionary cause discussed in the book. Emotion and immediacy were all the rage. Analytical publications with theoretical heft were also written as part of the effort to understand the history of Central American societies. It has been noted that it is often foreign intellectuals who have best 'pondered' Central America and its problems. The contribution of such scholars was highly regarded, especially when their works were published in Spanish.

The book introduced by the present essay belongs to that small group of works that aim to capture the reality of our region not only through the passions engendered by human solidarity but through the clarifying lens afforded by healthy distance and the exercise of sober analytical thinking. The last of the conflicts discussed in this volume ended more than ten years ago. As I write the text of this foreword, the twentieth anniversary of the signing of the Esquipulas Agreements – known as Esquipulas II – is being observed.[1] This was a landmark event that heralded the end of military conflicts in the region and began to steer a course towards democracy.

Guerrillas is most emphatically not more of the same. It is not merely a tired rehash of what is already known. Instead, it is more of something else – of what has until now either remained partially obscured or, in some cases, never seen the light of day. The events that together constitute a historical process are many, and this book is an insider's view of the events as they unfolded, revealing new and hitherto unpublished material.

2. The author. In stark contrast to those who write about a country after a single brief visit, Dr Kruijt is a social scientist with long years of experience in Central America. Writers of the former description, who pen their works on the fly, have produced books that can be called 'intelligent travelogues': they came, they saw, they wrote. This is far from being the case with the present author. I know this because I have witnessed it personally. I have also attempted to steer the same course that Dr Kruijt has successfully navigated: that is, engaging in the great issues that afflict our region while trying to maintain the perspective that is so essential to the work of a serious historian. The way that Dr Kruijt has managed to accomplish this is highly instructive, and might serve as a model for those – foreigners and native-born alike – who would hope to attain a profound understanding of our region.

A foreign researcher can be said to know a country when he reads its history, when he interacts with those who shape and experience that history, when he does these things time and time again, and, above all, when he harvests the fruits of these arduous efforts by writing with insight and passion about the key issues of that country's history. It was thus that I first came into contact with

Dirk, who has probably been the person who has interviewed me the most throughout my long life. He managed to accomplish this by employing a number of different strategies. We have co-authored various studies; I was the editor of two of his books; we have taken part in a succession of academic events, and we have eaten numerous meals together – meals that were always accompanied by fine wine. Last but not least, we have shared many of the same deep yet transient passions during our respective life journeys.

It is my great pleasure to write the foreword to a book by a Dutchman who without question is his country's foremost expert on Central America. Without any false modesty, I can claim to have read almost everything that has been published about the great crises of the region during the 1980s. On this basis, I can unequivocally state that Dirk's book constitutes a distinct contribution. Moreover, it is the first book on the region that was conceived in Dutch, written in English and – let us hope – will soon be published in Spanish.

3. The method. I will not attempt to write a methodological critique of the present book. Instead, I merely wish to emphasize what seems to me a substantive technique designed to do justice to the complex texture of a social phenomenon: this is the method of direct, repeated, in-depth interviews with the leading political personalities of those times. As Dr Kruijt puts it, he has had the opportunity to meet, speak and debate with many of the persons who have made Central American history. The testimonial method is very powerful but also very dangerous. The author needs to be wary that an interviewee may lie, and thus must know what kinds of questions to ask.

To live through an event is something different from remembering that same event. Boldness, joy, pain and fear are emotional filters through which personal actions are viewed. The fact that there has been deep personal involvement in the events recounted does not guarantee that, for example, a comandante's version of events is the correct one. This is the difference between a historical figure who writes a memoir and a historian who analyses it. The former writes from within the history of the events recounted, whereas the latter writes from a perspective distant from those same events. It is for this reason that the relationship between actor and author needs to be treated carefully by both parties. Dirk is without question an expert when it comes to both asking questions and discriminating fact from fiction. The interview method, as well as the discerning use of that method, lends weight to his research, for it is rich in detail, specific facts, anecdotes and quotations that clarify the familiar official version of events. Conducting ninety interviews is no mean feat.

4. The book sets out to examine one particular aspect of the history of civil war or armed conflict in three different countries. In short, this is *a book about guerrilla fighters and their comandantes.* It therefore is a book that discusses their lives, their dreams, their struggles and their failures. The testimonial value of the work is complemented by other primary and secondary reference material. There is a certain wisdom in the careful balance that Dirk is able to strike between analytical objectivity and an unmistakable sympathy. When one writes about this kind of subject, complete neutrality and disinterestedness are as out of place as blatantly partisan advocacy. In this work, there is a balance between facts and their meaning, and between references cited and their supporting documentation. There would be little point in presenting a summary of the book's content in this foreword. But it is useful to examine a number of features that illustrate the value of the information presented within these covers.

There are three features of this book that seem to me to constitute innovations, and that serve to complement the contributions of previously published research. There is, first of all, remarkable information presented regarding the genesis of radical opposition movements: the kind of youth who rose in rebellion, their indoctrination and their socio-economic background. One subject of particular interest that is examined is the financial and military assistance that the guerrilla organizations received at certain critical junctures. In addition, there is an endeavour to trace and to detail the development of strategies that shaped both the guerrillas' will to fight and their tactical decisions – decisions that led to victory in some cases, and to defeat in others. This latter feature represents an important contribution to the understanding of revolutionary movements in the region.

5. Bias in the present volume is, apparently, inevitable, and seems to function as a salutary corrective to what among many past historians has been a negative bias towards the Sandinistas. In fact, there is an entire chapter in this book that is devoted not to the country of Nicaragua, but to the Frente Sandinista de Liberación Nacional. Presented in that chapter are the conversations held with some of the most experienced political and military cadres – conversations that are as notable for their informative value as they are for their emotional intensity. The word 'bias' is used here not as a criticism and not as an indication of weakness, but rather as something eminently justifiable since the revolution in Nicaragua was the only one that can be termed a success. And, as I've pointed out in another context, the triumph of the Sandinistas prevented what appeared at the time to be the certain victory of the guerrilla forces in El Salvador. As an old wise man once said: two miracles cannot occur at once.

6. Omissions obviously refer to those things that I would have liked to see covered in Dirk's book. But, rather than being a criticism of what is missing, the mention here of omissions is rather an indirect acknowledgement of the comprehensive treatment accorded in this book to the subjects that he has chosen to focus on. In studying civil wars in Central America, it is impossible to ignore the pervasive and multifaceted influence of the United States. In fact, 'influence' is hardly a strong enough term, for US foreign policy has in fact been the decisive factor in our history, and to such an extent that I dare say that there was armed conflict in the first place and then subsequent peace negotiations only because each of these

phenomena was at the time in the interests of the United States. The documentation supporting this thesis is overwhelming.

In the armed conflicts of the region, the involvement of ethnic groups, either as passive bystanders or as active participants, was far from insignificant. In brief, there was active involvement on the part of the Miskitos-Sumus and Ramas of Nicaragua's Atlantic coast, to the point where they were incorporated into the military forces of the Contras. This involvement helped bring about the Atlantic Coast Autonomy Statute. In Guatemala, important Mayan communities pushed for inclusion in two of the insurgent groups: as a result, these communities were subjected to savage reprisals on the part of the army – reprisals that came to take on a genocidal character, and that had the unintended consequence of giving rise to the current indigenous movement. The passing references in this book to these events do not reflect the strategic importance of these sectors of society either during the war or in the war's aftermath, when these nations embarked upon an attempt to construct societies of a truly multicultural character.

The particular way in which peace was achieved in each nation is also open to question. In Nicaragua, a serious socio-economic crisis (1987–90) imposed limits on policy and forced the Sandinista government to the negotiating table: the calling of early elections in 1990 was the price paid by the Sandinistas for the chaos that they had not been able to avert. In El Salvador, military stalemate made negotiations unavoidable, which in turn allowed the modernization of the political system, introducing changes in the army, the establishment of a Truth Commission, and other reforms. In Guatemala, slow and protracted negotiations allowed for the signing of new agreements on substantive issues that today form the basis of what could be called a programme of national reconstruction – a programme that continues to serve as a point of reference for the nation's very weakened progressive elements.

7. Conclusions can be drawn from the analysis of civil wars in these countries. The most important conclusion is that these revolutions

did not bring about revolutionary change, and that they represented the uprisings of desperate people who had nearly lost all hope. The countries of Central America have had the experience of political democracy for the past two decades. For the first time, a generation has been born and educated without being subject to the dangers of state violence or the chaotic effects of civil strife. It is not possible here to address the question of whether democracy was born from the barrel of a gun. What we do know is that the deep structural causes that in part led to armed revolts are still with us, perhaps to a greater degree than was previously the case. Dirk devotes extensive space to a discussion of the legacies and ambiguities of the rebel leaders in each nation, and to other matters that are central to his stated purpose: to study the guerrilla fighters and their comandantes.

Another conclusion has to do with the changes experienced by oligarchic groups that formed the undisputed leadership of these nations for more than one hundred years. In Nicaragua and El Salvador, there were agrarian reforms and important attempts to foster participation of the masses in the political process, efforts that were aimed at creating vigorous civil societies. This explains why there are today powerful leftist political forces in these two nations. This is not what happened in Guatemala. This is the country where the war was the longest and most brutal, and where the conflict yielded the fewest dividends in terms of engendering political democracy. Land ownership did not change, and civil society was not strengthened.

Finally, *rebus sic stantibus*, I agree with Dirk: if the goal of reducing poverty is achieved and a voice is given to those who had previously been silent, these will be the fruit of the electoral successes of the moderates and reformers – of the generation that succeeded those comandantes who took up arms in pursuit of the selfsame goals.

Edelberto Torres-Rivas,
Guatemala de la Asunción, August 2007

Abbreviations and Spanish Terms

For more detailed information about the Central American guerrilla organizations, see Appendix 1.

ACS Asamblea de la Sociedad Civil; Guatemalan consulting body comprising civilian organizations.

AFA packet In Nicaragua, the government-supplied family food ration of rice, beans and sugar (in Spanish: *Arroz, Frijoles y Azúcar*) (Nicaragua).

AGEUS Asociación General de Estudiantes Salvadoreños; the National Students' Association in El Salvador.

AMNLAE Asociación de Mujeres Nicaragüenses 'Luisa Amanda Espinosa'; Sandinista women's association, successor organization of the AMPRONAC (Nicaragua).

AMPRONAC Asociación de Mujeres ante la Problemática Nacional; Sandinista womens' organization (Nicaragua).

ANE Asociación Nacional de Educadores; Sandinista teachers' association (Nicaragua).

ANN Alianza Nueva Nación; Guatemalan political grouping.

ARDE Alianza Revolucionaria Democrática; Contra forces headed by Edén Pastora (Nicaragua).

ARENA Alianza Republicana Nacionalista; Salvadoran right-wing political party (see PRUD).
ASTC Asociación Sandinista de Trabajadores de la Cultura; Sandinista cultural workers' association (Nicaragua).
ATC Asociación de Trabajadores del Campo; Sandinista rural workers' association (Nicaragua).
BIAS Batallones de Infantería Antiterroristas; Sandinista counter-insurgency forces (Nicaragua).
BIRI Batallones de Insurgencia y de Reacción Inmediata; Sandinista counterinsurgency forces (Nicaragua).
BPR Bloque Popular Revolucionario; confederation of popular organizations, associated with the FPL (El Salvador).
BPS Brigadistas Populares de Salud; Sandinista Youth Volunteer Health Brigades (Nicaragua).
CACIF Comité Coordinador de Asociaciones Agrícolas, Comerciales, Industriales y Financieras; Guatemalan national entrepreneurial association.
campesino Rural smallholders and rural workers, or rural low-income classes in general; the rough equivalent is 'peasant'.
CDCs Comités de Defensa Civil; Sandinista neighbourhood committees.
CDSs Comités de Defensa Sandinista; Sandinista neighbourhood committees, successor organization of the CDCs (Nicaragua).
CEDLA Inter-university Centre for Latin American Research and Documentation (University of Amsterdam).
CEH Comisión para el Esclarecimiento Histórico; Guatemalan Truth Commission.
CEPA Centro de Educación y Promoción Agraria (Nicaragua).
CEPAL Comisión Económica y Social para América Latina y el Caribe (ECLAC in English), with headquarters in Santiago de Chile.
COCEP Consejo Superior de la Empresa Privada; Nicaraguan national entrepreneurial association.
CIA Central Intelligence Agency (USA).
CNR Comisión Nacional de Reconciliación; Guatemalan National Reconciliation Commission.
comandancia general The guerrilla leadership (in the military and political sense), formed by the *comandantes-en-jefe* in El

Salvador and Guatemala. In the pre-1979 period in Nicaragua, each of the three FSLM wings was headed by three leading comandantes; this meant that the FSLN leadership was a collective of nine members.

comandante Highest rank within guerrilla forces; leader of a guerrilla battle group or *frente*.

comandante de la revolución Highest honorary guerrilla rank in Cuba and Nicaragua. In Nicaragua the nine *comandantes de la revolución* made up the *dirección general* between 1979 and 1990.

comandante-en-jefe Commander-in-chief.

comandante guerrillero Second-highest honorary guerrilla rank in El Salvador and Nicaragua.

combatientes (Revolutionary) fighters.

comisión política-diplomática The equivalent of a Ministry of Foreign Affairs of the FMLN, the FSLN and the URNG. The most influential members of this committee also acted as guerrilla negotiators during the peace talks.

Contra(s) The counterinsurgency forces in Nicaragua that fought against ('contra') the Sandinistas, trained and financed by the CIA. Their main supply lines and military bases were established in Honduras.

cooperantes People sympathetic to the guerrilla cause.

COPAL Colegio para América Latina (University of Louvain).

COPMAGUA Coordinadora de Organizaciones del Pueblo Maya de Guatemala; national confederation of Maya movements (Guatemala).

CST Central Sandinista de Trabajadores; Sandinista trade-union system (Nicaragua).

CSUCA Consejo Superior Universitario Centroamericano; the Central American system of public universities.

cuadros Cadres.

CUC Comité de Unidad Campesina (CUC); a mass organization of Maya *campesinos*, rural workers, landless indigenous and Ladino peoples, with strong sympathy for the EGP (predominantly) and ORPA (Guatemala).

DC Christian Democratic Party (Guatemala).

dirección nacional Formally the national guerrilla leadership

(El Salvador, Guatemala, Nicaragua). In fact, the real guerrilla leadership in El Salvador and Guatemala was formed by the *comandancia general*. The nine *comandantes de la revolución* comprised the *dirección general* in Nicaragua between 1979 and 1990; this was the group of leaders that ran the government in the country during those years.

EAP Economically active population (persons aged between 14 and 65).

ECA *Estudios Centroamericanos* (academic journal published by the Salvadoran Universidad Centroaméricana).

ECLAC Economic and Social Commission for Latin America and the Caribbean (CEPAL in Spanish), with headquarters in Santiago de Chile.

EGP Ejército Guerrillero de los Pobres; Guatemalan guerrilla organization.

EPA Ejército Popular de Alfabetización; Sandinista Youth Volunteer Literacy Brigades (Nicaragua).

EPS Ejército Popular Sandinista; the Nicaraguan army formed with Cuban technical asistance, and until 1984 a force of volunteers; in 1990 reorganized and transformed following the defeat of the Sandinistas in the presidential elections into the Ejército de Nicaragua.

ERP Ejército Revolucionario del Pueblo; Salvadoran guerrilla organization.

FAR Fuerzas Armadas Revolucionarias; Guatemalan guerrilla organization.

FDN Fuerzas Democráticas Nicaragüenses; Nicaraguan Contra organization.

FDR Frente Revolucionario Democrático; the umbrella organization of the non-military organizations of the FMLN (El Salvador).

FECCAS Federación Cristiana de Campesinos Salvadoreños; Christian rural workers' federation (El Salvador).

FER Frente Estudiantil Revolucionario (Nicaragua).

FETSALUD Federación de Trabajadores de la Salud; Sandinista health workers' federation (Nicaragua).

FIL Fuerzas Irregulares Locales; mostly Maya civilian groups supporting the guerrilla forces, generally associated with the

CUC and sympathetic to the EGP (Guatemala).

FLACSO Facultad Latinoaméricana de Ciencias Sociales; Latin American postgraduate research facility in twelve member states; the secretariat general is located in Costa Rica.

FMLN Frente Farabundo Martí de Liberación Nacional; Salvadoran umbrella guerrilla organization, comprising the Fuerzas Populares de Liberación 'Farabundo Martí' (FPL), the Ejército Revolucionario del Pueblo (ERP), Resistencia Nacional (RN), the Partido Revolucionario de los Trabajadores Centro-americanos (PRTC), and the Partido Comunista de El Salvador (PCS).

foquismo Guerrilla strategy advocated by Che Guevara that emphasizes the necessity of a rural *foco* ('flashpoint' or area of concentration of activity) of guerrilla fighters which would attract rural *campesinos* (peasants) and urban industrial workers joining them in a general uprising.

FPL Fuerzas Populares de Liberación 'Farabundo Martí'; Salvadoran guerrilla organization.

Frente Refers to the FMLN or FSLN, the Salvadoran or Nicaraguan umbrella guerrilla organizations, after 1994 and 1979 a political party.

frente Guerrilla battle group.

frente interno Urban guerrilla formation (Tendencia Tercerista, FSLN).

FSLN Frente Sandinista de Liberación Nacional; Nicaraguan umbrella guerrilla organization, formed by the Guerra Popular Prolongada (GPP), the Tendencia Proletaria (TP), and the Tendencia Tercerista or Insurreccionista; the last one formed the Frente Interno, the urban guerrilla forces, and acquired national prominence.

Grupo de los Doce Group of Twelve: civilian advisers to the Sandinista leadership before 1979. Many cabinet members and high-ranking government officials were recruited from this group between 1979 and 1990.

Guardia Nacional National Guard: US-created militarized police forces, the pillar of the Somoza regime (Nicaragua).

guerrilla, guerrilla warfare Literally 'small war', it generally refers to a kind of irregular combat, carried out by guerrilla fighters: partisan forces, resistance groups, irregular troops, or freedom fighters.

guerrillero guerrilla fighter.

HDI Human Development Index (UNDP).

HPI Human Poverty Index (UNDP).

IHNCA Instituto de Historia de Nicaragua y Centroamérica (UCA, Nicaragua).

ILAS Institute of Latin American Studies (University of London).

ILO International Labour Office.

internacionalistas International volunteers, generally citizens of the USA, Western European and Scandinavian countries and Latin American political refugees who participated, mainly in non-combatant roles, on the side of the guerrilla forces during the conflicts in Nicaragua, Guatemala and El Salvador.

JPT Juventud Patriótica del Trabajo; Guatemalan Communist Youth organization.

junta 'Ruling group', mostly used to denote a military or civil-military leadership group that as a collective assumes the role of chief of state after a military coup or popular uprising.

Juventud Sandinista 19 de Julio Sandinista youth association (Nicaragua).

KGB The Soviet Union's Committee of State Security.

ladino Guatemalan for *mestizo* (of mixed indigenous and Iberian descent); in spite of its mixed racial heritage, this population has, generally speaking, consistently identified itself as 'white', in contradistinction to the indigenous peoples of Guatemala.

Maya Indigenous population of the Maya language groups (more than twenty in Guatemala; the related Maya population in the southern region of Mexico speak other languages).

militantes Members of the (revolutionary) party.

Military Youth (Juventud Militar) Social movement led by young Salvadoran army officers.

MILPAS Milicias Populares Antisandinistas; Contra militia forces (Nicaragua).

MINUGUA United Nations Verification Mission in Guatemala.

MISURASATA Ethnic Contra forces of the Miskito, Sumo and

Rama Amerindian peoples of the Atlantic coast (Nicaragua). These indigenous peoples of Nicaragua were allies of the Contras against the Sandinistas.

Mossad Israel's intelligence service.

MPS Milicias Populares Sandinistas; Sandinista volunteer militia formations (Nicaragua).

MRS Movimiento de Renovación Sandinista; political movement of ex-members of the FSLN, comprising most of the prominent political Sandinista actors of the 1980s (Nicaragua).

OAS (OEA) Organization of American States (Organización de Estados Americanos).

ONUCA United Nations Observer Mission in Central America.

ONUSAL United Nations Observer Mission in El Salvador.

ORPA Organización del Pueblo en Armas; Guatemalan guerrilla organization.

PAC Patrullas de Autodefensa Civil; paramilitary forces, generally recruited from among the Maya population and controlled by the army (Guatemala).

PCS Partido Comunista Salvadoreño; Salvadoran Communist Party.

PDC Partido Demócrata Cristiano; Salvadoran Christian Democrats.

peón (Unskilled) farm hand.

PGT Partido Guatemalteco de Trabajadores; Guatemalan Communist Party.

PRTC Partido Revolucionario de los Trabajadores Centro-americanos; Salvadoran guerrilla organization.

PRUD Partido Revolucionario de Unificación Democrática; the military-controlled officialist party in El Salvador, in 1949 transformed into the Partido de Conciliación Nacional. ARENA is the successor party.

Resistencia Campesina 'Peasant Resistance'; the civilian wing of ORPA, one of the constituent guerrilla movements of the URNG (Guatemala).

RN Resistencia Nacional; Salvadoran guerrilla organization.

SINAMOS Sistema Nacional de Movilización Social; organization for mass movements (Peru).

STASI The East German state security apparatus.

UCA Universidad Centroaméricana (both in El Salvador and in Nicaragua).

UES Universidad de El Salvador.

UNAG Unión Nacional de Agricultores y Ganaderos; Sandinista small and médium-sized rural entrepreneurs' association (Nicaragua).

UNAN Universidad Nacional de Nicaragua.

UNDP United Nations Development Programme.

UNE Unión Nacional de Empleados; Sandinista white-collar union (Nicaragua).

UNO Unión Nacional Opositora (1972); Salvadoran centre-left political coalition.

UNO Unión Nicaragüense Opositora (1985); political organization of the Nicaraguan Contras, headed by Adolfo Calero, Arturo Cruz and Alfonso Robelo.

UNO Unión Nacional Opositora (1990); Nicaraguan anti-Sandinista political coalition, headed by Violeta de Chamorro.

UPN Unión de Periodistas de Nicaragua; Sandinista journalists' association (Nicaragua).

URNG Unidad Revolucionaria Nacional Guatemalteca; Guatemalan umbrella guerrilla organization, comprising the Fuerzas Armadas Revolucionarias (FAR), the Ejército Guerrillero de los Pobres (EGP), the Organización del Pueblo en Armas (ORPA), and the Partido Guatemalteco de Trabajadores (PGT) (the Guatemalan Communist Party).

USAC Universidad de San Carlos de Guate.

USAID United States Agency for International Development.

Xeljú Political movement of the (urban) K'iche' Mayas, the most important indigenous language group of Guatemala, in Quetzaltenango, the country's second largest city. Two-term mayor of Quetzaltenango Rigoberto Quemé Chay and Nobel laureate Rigoberta Menchú Tum are probably the best known K'iche's.

INTRODUCTION

Guerrillas and Comandantes

This is a book about guerrilla soldiers and their comandantes. It is a study of the aspirations and ideals, the dreams and achievements, the pride and shame, the successes and failures, the suffering and despair, the utopias and dystopias of an entire Central American generation and its leaders. In three neighbouring countries in the Central American isthmus – El Salvador, Guatemala and Nicaragua – three parallel wars were fought in the latter half of the twentieth century by three guerrilla organizations, each of which was led by a generation of young urban intellectuals. They aspired to overthrow military dictatorships in their countries and to establish socialist societies that would root out the corruption and inequality that had characterized the previous dictatorships and oligarchies that had long held political and economic power. The Central American guerrilla wars from the 1960s to the 1990s were not the first civil wars in the region, as the next chapter makes abundantly clear. Yet a number of features of these more recent conflicts were unique. First, there was their long duration as well as the level of their brutality. Second was the worldwide support of solidarity organizations in Western Europe and the sympathy of most

Latin American nations for the guerrilla movements, while the USA in general supported the dictatorial regimes holding power. Third was that one of these local conflicts, in Nicaragua, took on the aspect of a proxy war between the world's two superpowers, the USSR and the USA; it had far-reaching consequences for the guerrilla forces in the two other countries. In this book I present an in-depth study of three of the actors in the wars, namely the three Central American guerrilla movements and their members, focusing especially on the guerrilla comandantes.

The Central American wars are well documented in terms of political analysis, counterinsurgency campaigns and the outcome of formal peace negotiations. Yet the emergence of the guerrilla generation and its leaders has received scant attention, in spite of the recently published memoirs of some prominent leaders (works not generally known for their analytical rigour) and a handful of perceptive books like those of Montgomery (1995), Le Bot (1997) and Flakoll and Alegría (2004) on the Salvadoran, Guatemalan and Nicaraguan guerrilla wars, respectively. Even the official reports of the Salvadoran[1] and Guatemalan[2] Truth Commissions are relatively sketchy and generally reference secondary sources with respect to guerrilla groups and their leaders. By contrast, the present work has made extensive use of primary sources, including lengthy and in-depth interviews, unpublished private archives, scholarly studies and government reports, sympathetic and adversarial position papers and white books, published and unpublished memoirs, mimeographs and booklets distributed by the guerrilla movements. In addition, numerous secondary sources were consulted, including interviews conducted by other researchers and journalists.

This book is not meant to be a general history of the three guerrilla wars that took place in Central America in the last half of the twentieth century. The present work is instead an analysis of three different guerrilla movements: of their leadership, their rank-and-file membership, their ideological and organizational evolution, their military success and failure, and, finally, of what became of each movement in the aftermath of peace negotiations in the three countries. In addition, the present study is an analysis of the role of three different politico-military organizations: the Frente Sandinista de Liberación Nacional (FSLN) in Nicaragua, the Frente Farabundo Martí de Liberación Nacional (FMLN) in El Salvador, and the Unidad Revolucionaria Nacional Guatemalteca (URNG) in Guatemala. Each of these umbrella organizations comprised several independent guerrilla groups, each of them operating with several *frentes*, or independently operating guerrilla deployments. Each constituent group within the national umbrella organizations functioned under a unified military and political leadership but maintained considerable autonomy in terms of arms procurement, finances and logistics. Special emphasis is placed on recruitment of the urban and rural *guerrilleros*, their morale and discipline, their daily activities and their relations with the local population.

The leadership of the movements is another important focus. At a personal level, there is extended discussion of the sociocultural, ethnic, religious and ideological background and demographic profile of the guerrilla leaders. At the organizational level, a good deal of space is devoted to war and organizational strategies and tactics, the relationship between urban and rural guerrilla warfare, and counterinsurgency operations by the armed forces in Nicaragua, El Salvador and Guatemala. Special attention is devoted to the final stage of the guerrilla wars, the peace negotiations, the implementation of the peace accords, and the arduous transformation of politico-military organizations with a high level of centralized leadership into political parties fighting to establish what they saw as their rightful place within a pluralistic and democratic society.

Terminology

It is necessary to cut through a thicket of confusing terminology in order to properly clarify prevailing tendencies and typologies within the three movements. 'Guerrilla', which literally means 'small war', is used to characterize undeclared wars or covert military operations against an established regime. 'Guerrilla warfare' generally implies a kind of irregular combat, carried out by partisan forces, resistance groups, irregular troops or freedom fighters. Beginning in the 1960s, guerrilla forces (that were in some cases later transformed into regular standing armies after emerging victorious in their struggles) constituted the military arm of national liberation movements. This term refers to struggles carried out by guerrilla movements in prominent Third World countries which gained independence after an armed insurgence. Algeria and Vietnam are the classic examples; other famous movements were launched in East Timor, Mozambique, Palestine and South Africa. Cuba and Nicaragua are two Latin American countries where, after victorious wars, former guerrilla formations were quickly and successfully transformed into regular armed forces.

In Latin America 'guerrilla' generally indicates the existence of so-called 'politico-military organizations' with an ideology characterized by the following features: intense nationalism, anti-imperialism or anti-colonialism; the prospect of a socialist utopia; and overt preparation for social revolution by means of armed struggle. Nearly all such movements distinguish among *cooperantes* (people sympathetic to the cause), *militantes* (members of the revolutionary party) and *combatientes* (revolutionary fighters). The intermediate leadership is formed by *cuadros* (cadres), the top echelon by *comandantes*. Strictly speaking, comandante is a military rank, the highest officer's rank in a guerrilla formation, and generally refers to the leader of a guerrilla *frente* (a battle group like a regiment or a battalion). The top-ranking military (and political) leader of the Cuban revolution was Fidel Castro, *comandante-en-jefe* (general commander), who alone had the power to appoint combat commanders. In the Central American context, where the three guerrilla confederations were consolidated after the beginning of civil wars, the *comandantes-en-jefe* of the constituent forces jointly formed a unified multi-person military and political command structure.[3] Nicaragua was the first country to consolidate a nine-person *dirección nacional* unifying three separate wings of the Sandinista movement, each represented by three senior comandantes. The nine comandantes acted as the collective management of the FSLN (1979), exclusively holding all military and political responsibilities and privileges.

In El Salvador and Guatemala, a similar structure was created with the foundation of the FMLN (El Salvador, 1980) and the URNG (Guatemala, 1982). In El Salvador the leaders of the constituent organizations, four guerrilla movements and the nearly noncombatant Communist Party created a five-member *comandancia general*, with a *dirección nacional* serving as a kind of civil-military parliament. In Guatemala a four-member *comandancia general* was formed, which included the secretary-general of the Guatemalan Communist Party. By 1986 the *comandancia general* had unified its logistical and financial operations; the civil-military *dirección nacional* of the URNG played a secondary role until the peace agreements in 1996. In El Salvador and Guatemala (and in Nicaragua before 1979) each participating guerrilla movement maintained its own internal party organization and military command structures. In general the term *comandante* was reserved for the military leadership. Nicaragua followed the Cuban example of restricting *comandante* status to guerrilla leaders who had distinguished records of service to the revolutionary cause. In Guatemala and El Salvador, however, the rank of comandante was sometimes granted to senior civilian leaders of the *dirección general.*

The present study features extensive use of direct quotation gleaned from retrospective interviews with the leadership of the guerrilla forces, as well as with the political and diplomatic members of the *dirección general.* To a lesser extent, this study contains segments of retrospective interviews with those on the opposing side of the conflicts: government politicians (including presidents and cabinet members), field commanders of the armed forces, other military leaders, delegates of the national government, negotiators representing the guerrilla groups, and other significant actors such as religious leaders and UN representatives.

Throughout this study, I will restrict the use of the term *comandante* to the military leaders of the guerrilla groups.

Data

Both primary and secondary sources were utilized for the present study. Primary data comprise more than ninety interviews with political and military leaders on both sides of each conflict, as well as with social scientists and intellectuals. Most of these interviews were conducted between 2004 and 2007. In Guatemala, rounds of interviews were also carried out in 1994 and in 1999. Nearly all interviews were conducted as open-ended conversations of between one and three hours, with a number of individuals being interviewed more than once. In one case (with Rodrigo Asturias and Julio Balconi, both in Guatemala) the interviews took place over a period of several years. Sometimes the respondents also provided me their written reflections in the form of diaries, personal documents or formal memoirs.

Products of the literary imagination in each of these three countries were also consulted. El Salvador is probably the only country in the world where two adversaries, both poets, first conducted peace negotiations with one another from opposite sides of the table and then collaborated on the publication of a collection of poems.[4] Two scholar-politicians, Héctor Rosada-Granados in Guatemala and Rubén Zamora in El Salvador, the former a cabinet minister and peace negotiator between 1993 and 1996 and the latter a prime minister (*ministro de la presidencia*) during the first revolutionary civil-military junta of 1979 and later in 1994 the first post-war presidential candidate for the FMLN, provided me access to their private archives. I also benefited from listening to the taped interviews and reading the written sources that Tommie Sue Montgomery had used in her excellent study (Montgomery, 1995), which are housed in a special archive at the library of the Universidad Centroamericana (UCA) of San Salvador. Also indispensable were more than thirty taped interviews conducted by Luis González of the UCA of San Salvador. In El Salvador and Nicaragua, the archives in the special sections of the library of the two national FLACSO[5] institutions were consulted. In the spring and fall trimesters of 2006 I was a visiting scholar at Nicaragua's Instituto de Historia de Nicaragua y Centroamérica, an excellent research centre associated with the UCA of Nicaragua, where the private archives of Somoza and most of the archives of the Sandinista governments between 1979 and 1990 can be found. The political and military organizations mentioned within the present study are included in Appendix 1. Appendix 2 provides demographic data on Central America between 1950 and 2005. A list of interviews (including the place and date of each interview) appears in Appendix 3.

Structure of the Book

In this comparative analysis of the Salvadoran, Guatemalan and Nicaraguan guerrilla movements, the reader will notice both striking similarities and remarkable differences. The most noticeable similarity is the pervasive fear and stark socio-economic inequality common to all three societies. The three countries share the same social history of poverty and exclusion, the same political legacy of oppressive dictatorships and implementation of state terror against which the guerrilla leadership in each nation rebelled. This is the primary theme of Chapter 1. This chapter may be somewhat tough going for the reader not familiar with Central American history: it presents a condensed political history of dictatorship and repression and it portrays the emergence of a multiplicity of small leftist proto-guerrilla groups that afterwards became constituent elements of the three umbrella organizations FMLN (El Salvador), URNG (Guatemala) and FSLN (Nicaragua). If the chapter poses any undue difficulties, the reader may find it useful to consult Appendix 1 for basic information regarding the guerrilla structures and the social support organizations in all three countries from the 1960s to the 1990s. The chapter concludes with a brief overview of the three Central American civil wars.

Chapter 2 provides a portrait of the generation that produced the leaders of guerrilla movements within each of the three countries. Who were they? From which socio-economic strata did they arise? What was it that spurred their political dissent? What mixture of anti-imperialist sentiments, leftist tradition, and religious and moral convictions led them to decide to join the ranks of the relatively few who launched the armed insurrection? What elements of their personal histories enabled them to achieve positions of leadership within their respective movements? In this chapter I make use of the extensive life histories of the leading guerrilla personalities – life histories obtained, for the most part, through extensive and multiple personal interviews. There is abundant empirical evidence about their recruitment, mainly from the student movements and the religious groups that arose as an outgrowth of the wide popularity of liberation theology – a religious movement very much in vogue in Latin America during the 1970s – and to a lesser degree from among young revolutionary military officers or Communist Party youth movements. Unlike previous studies that have not moved beyond broad generalities regarding the genesis of the guerrilla movements, this chapter is very detailed.

Guerrilla strategy and tactics are generally created and re-created by guerrilla leaders in response to ever-changing circumstances. In Chapter 3, I provide an analysis of the strategic ideas and the implementation of the revolutionary tactics as used in El Salvador, Guatemala and Nicaragua. The Nicaraguan case is an example of guerrilla triumph by the FSLN. It occurred in the late 1970s – on July 1979 to be precise – whereas the guerrilla war in El Salvador was fought out in the 1980s and the Guatemalan civil war lasted thirty-six years, from 1960 to 1996. In El Salvador the guerrilla and state forces reached a military stalemate; the Guatemalan guerrillas were eventually defeated in their struggle. Chapter 3 contains an analysis of the strategy, logistics, finances and communication during the war years. In addition, the chapter focuses on activity of the guerrilla columns in the mountains or in the more stable bivouacs, the relations with the local population and, in general, the day-to-day challenges and the never-ending task of maintaining morale within the encampments.

Chapter 4 is devoted in its entirety to the Sandinista revolution between 1979 and 1990 and the fate of the FSLN. It is a history of exultant hopes and profound disillusionment. This chapter is an analysis of Nicaragua's ill-fated socialist experiment: the decade-long Sandinista government in Nicaragua following its victorious guerrilla war against a tyrannical government. The Sandinista regime was born as a 'real-life utopia' with the liberation of the former capital, León, and the successful insurrection in Managua. It died a bloody death after a second civil war against a CIA-sponsored and -trained counter-guerrilla movement of a rural resistance force (the Contra), a war accompanied by the economic disaster of rampant hyperinflation over the course of several years.

Chapter 5 examines the peace negotiations in Nicaragua (1989–90), El Salvador (1989–92) and Guatemala (1987–96). In Nicaragua, the Sandinista army, the successor institution of the former FSLN guerrilla forces, had won a civil war against insurgent counter-revolutionary forces – the so-called Contras – that were trained and financed by the USA. Peace and disarmament talks had already been accomplished in 1989 before the elections in 1990. The elections were lost by the Sandinista government and during the two months between the defeated Sandinista government and the victorious opposition alliance, both a formal peace accord and a gentlemen's agreement were reached between the new government and the Sandinista military establishment regarding the future of the army and the police as national security institutions. In the case of El Salvador, the military stalemate between the US-trained Salvadoran army and the battle-hardened guerrilla forces produced a series of pragmatic peace agreements which essentially consisted of political reforms, disarmament of the guerrillas, a radical restructuring of the military and the police, and far-reaching reform of both the judiciary and the electoral system. In Guatemala, where the guerrilla forces were losing the war, the comandantes tried to assure at least a far-reaching reform programme of the national economy and society. Peace negotiations were carried out between 1987 and 1996; the accords were reached in large measure by means of informal, secret discussions between the military establishment and the guerrilla leadership – in effect, a pact between establishment and revolutionary elites – arrived at in Cuba, where both delegations enjoyed the hospitality of Fidel and Raúl Castro.

The second section of Chapter 5 depicts the subsequent transformation of the guerrilla organizations into 'normal' political institutions within the context of pluralistic democratic societies. Both in El Salvador, where the former guerrillas had administered significant parts of the territory, and in Nicaragua, where the Sandinista government had been in charge between 1979 and 1990, the reconstituted guerrilla parties were able to maintain a substantial and loyal following. Guatemala's post-war guerrilla movement, however, ultimately splintered into small and ineffectual factions. After losing the war, the URNG lost its appeal to the newly emerging popular movements, leaving Guatemala's left in disarray.

The three guerrilla movements started as desperate efforts by small politico-military organizations to overthrow dictatorships that had endured for decades. They managed to obtain the support of a considerable part of the oppressed population. In Nicaragua, guerrilla activities resulted in a revolution in which the majority of the population eventually participated; but after ten years of government the Sandinista revolution was dealt a mortal blow in 1990 when the Sandinistas were defeated in the presidential election and a succession of three neoliberal governments adjusted the economy and society the hard way. In El Salvador an ample population segment supported the guerrillas until the very end of the war. But afterwards, four consecutive right-wing governments held power. In Guatemala the guerrillas represented the hopes

– hopes that would be cruelly frustrated, as it turned out – of a significant part of the indigenous population. But being forced into a fallback position of strictly military operations of a defensive character in the more remote regions of the country, they failed to retain their popular support. After the peace agreement, the country was administered by two right-wing and one populist – and very corrupt – government. In the three countries the guerrilla forces initiated revolutions that heralded very noble prospects but did not achieve radical and lasting transformations in the long run. Chapter 6, the book's final chapter, presents a short analysis of the achievements and failures of guerrilla groups in the three countries, while both reflecting upon the lessons learned from their experience and exploring their possible significance for today's social movements, not only in Central America, but within the wider Latin American context as well.

1

Dictators and Civil Wars

In its concentration of culturally and ethnically fragmented nations, Central America is to the Americas what the Balkans is to Europe. Enduring social and political divisions, which have tormented the Central American countries for centuries, will form the backdrop of the present study. In pre-Columbian times this region comprised, along with the Yucatan peninsula and Chiapas (both now part of Mexico), the heartland of the Maya peoples whose fascinating civilization once intrigued the conquistadors. After the Spanish conquest, the vanquished indigenous peoples of the region were incorporated into the lower strata of their respective colonial societies. Guatemala in particular bears the scars of the ethnic segregation that was imposed by colonial and post-colonial rulers. Under Spanish colonial administration, Guatemala, El Salvador, Honduras, Nicaragua and Costa Rica were unified under the Captaincy General of Guatemala. In 1823 they declared independence from Spain and Mexico, constituting a federal republic, the United Provinces of Central America.[1] Until the present, a vague though unmistakeable nostalgia has prevailed in the five Central American countries – Guatemala, El Salvador, Honduras,

Nicaragua and Costa Rica – about a common destiny. In contrast to the situation in other countries of Latin America, most citizens of these five countries retain a dual identity: as citizens of their particular nations and as *Central Americans*.

From a political standpoint, the original federation of the United Provinces of Central America was extremely unstable. It collapsed when Honduras left the federation in 1838. Two years later, Honduran president Francisco Morazán tried to reunite the fractured states. The Union dissolved again and a series of civil wars, secessions and reconquests followed. Independent republics, federations and confederations comprising three, four or five former provinces were first established and then dissolved during a span of several decades in the mid-nineteenth century. In the 1850s the five republics formed a military alliance to resist an invasion of Nicaragua led by US adventurer William Walker. Small armies were formed under the command of local potentates who pressed the peons of the indigenous villages into military service, sometimes within private militias, sometimes under the banner of the national armed forces. This kind of activity occurred in all of the Central American republics except for Costa Rica, governed by civilian presidents and maintaining a small army limited to 1,000 enlisted men. In the other Central American countries, however, a long succession of dictators, militia leaders, civilian-military juntas, war heroes, guerrilla leaders, separatist colonels and republican liberals served as president for longer or shorter terms of office. Military commanders were especially predominant as heads of state or leaders of violent revolution. In the early 1920s Guatemala, El Salvador and Nicaragua made the last attempt to form a Central American federation. In the meantime, Chiapas was incorporated into Mexico, the Guanacaste peninsula was transferred from Nicaragua to Costa Rica, and the English acquired British Honduras (later Belize) from Guatemala.

Costa Rica in many respects constitutes an exception to the turbulence and instability that plagued its Central American neighbours. After a short civil war in 1948, victorious president José

Figueres formally abolished the national army. In the decades that followed, the country evolved into a relatively prosperous and democratic welfare state with high standards of education and public health. Sadly, however, the long-standing tradition of harsh dictatorship and bitter repression continued in the other Central American countries throughout most of the twentieth century. Brutal repression, mass poverty, ethnic cleavages (most notably in Guatemala), large-scale social exclusion and religious division have been the characteristics of the other member states of the former federation. These societal fissures constituted fertile ground for the resentment and despair that eventually found expression in revolutionary movements. Again with the exception of Costa Rica, the countries of the Central American region were organized during the 160 years following independence as oligarchic economies whose cohesion was maintained by means of repression rather than participation. El Salvador, Guatemala and Nicaragua were strongly divided societies where an economy of poverty and a society of exclusion were maintained by long periods of military rule.

The guerrilla movements of the 1960s and 1970s were thus launched in a context of transgenerational resentment against a seemingly eternal regime of military domination and dictatorship, within societies permeated with repression and fear. When guerrilla groups emerged as armed actors it was against military-controlled regimes that fought back by means of organized brutality and indiscriminate terror in counterinsurgency campaigns directed against small bands of rebel fighters and their actual or potential bases of support – the rural peasants and their ethnic and economic organizations. Within a few years, the military governments were at war against a very considerable segment of their populations, whom they defined as 'terrorists' and 'communists'. Repression of dissent and indiscriminate persecution of the peasant population would later be accompanied by urban terror campaigns, organized against 'communists, future communists and potential communists': politicians, journalists, intellectuals, priests, student and union leaders, and those who led popular organizations. Political murders of those who were part of this broadly defined network of enemies became quite common, resulting in what might be termed a banality of bloodshed among dissenting activists.

El Salvador, Guatemala and Nicaragua were in the last part of the twentieth century centres of low-intensity warfare and counter-insurgency operations. From 1970 until 1994, parallel and partially interrelated civil wars were fought in these three countries. The numbers of dead and disappeared, along with the internal and external refugees created because of the wars, are very high in relation to the countries' total populations. The Salvadoran and Guatemalan truth commissions (Comisión de la Verdad, 1993; CEH, 1999) provide minimum estimates of 70,000 and 150,000 deaths respectively. The total death count for Nicaragua, including both the guerrilla campaigns of the late 1970s and the Contra War in the 1980s, is 110,000. That means a minimum of 330,000 deaths out of a total population in the three countries of some 15 million people in the early 1980s. These prolonged civil wars had a devastating impact on national and regional societies. Torres-Rivas, author of the analytical first volume of the report of the Guatemalan Truth Commission, remarks that the army's counterinsurgency offensive of 1980–83 'did not annihilate the guerrillas but forced their retreat while physically destroying 440 indigenous villages, murdering 75,000 *campesinos*, and displacing 100,000 to 500,000 people' (1993a: 125).[2]

The Central American economies were, even in comparison with those of other Latin American countries, characterized by a stark contrast between a small number of the very rich and masses of the desperately poor, and displayed features of a harsh and unmitigated capitalism reminiscent of mid-nineteenth-century Europe. The labour force was brutally exploited and trade unions as well as organizations dedicated to protecting the rights of workers and peasants were fiercely repressed. In terms of poverty and exclusion, Central America was a vast area of misfortune, suffering and economic hardship. Symbiotic relationships between economic oligarchies and military regimes were a distinctive feature of the socio-political order of the region, creating societies of repression and fear. Law and order were generally represented by death squads or militarized police who, weekly or monthly death lists in hand, marched into villages to restore respect for *de facto* law and reactionary order. Calls for unions, social reform and revolutionary justice were silenced by bloody gunfire. In the 1930s social revolts in both El Salvador and Nicaragua ended in massacres and led to the return of dictatorial regimes that ruthlessly repressed any social change or reformist movement for the next forty years. After decades of anachronistic dictatorship in Guatemala, the successive democratic governments of Arévalo and Árbenz between 1944 and 1954 seemed to herald a future of economic progress and political participation. Nevertheless, the announcement by the Árbenz government of progressive social policies and of a land reform that envisioned the expropriation of US properties led to a CIA-organized coup against his government, which was followed by thirty-five years of dictatorship and civil strife. The combination of shattered hopes, political backwardness, and the brutal repression of the military regimes, along with the perceived impossibility of peaceful and democratic change, are all part of the economic, social and political context of the emergence of the guerrilla comandantes who would later lead *frentes*, and of the soldiers who followed their orders.

In the next two sections of this chapter this socio-political background will be examined in more depth. The next section presents an overview of the socio-economic situation in each of the three countries. This is followed by a description of the Salvadoran, Guatemalan and Nicaraguan societies of repression and fear. The chapter then concludes with a short chronology of the Central American civil wars that were fought in the last half of the twentieth century.

Poverty and Exclusion

Nicaragua's surface area is 130,000 sq. km, Guatemala's is 110,000 sq. km and El Salvador's is 21,000 sq. km. All three countries are small in terms of size and population. Upon gaining independence in 1823, Central America's total population did not exceed 1.25 million persons. By the outbreak of the First World War the region had 5 million inhabitants. In the early 1980s Guatemala City had a population of 1.2 million (15 per cent of the national population), San Salvador 500,000 (10 per cent of the national population), and Managua 650,000 (21 per cent of the national population).[3] The capital cities of these countries are the centres of each nation's economic, social, cultural and political activity. During the civil war decades, Nicaragua was the most urbanized of the three countries, followed by El Salvador (see Appendix 2). Guatemala, on the other hand, preserved its rural character. Between 1960 and 1980 the population per km^2 grew from 10 to 20 in Nicaragua, from 36 to 67 in Guatemala, and from 116 to 226 in densely populated El Salvador (Vilas, 1994: 16).

In all three countries, tiny oligarchic elites, consisting of a relatively small number of families related by blood and marriage, exercised economic power through ownership of vast tracts of rural land, large-scale coffee and sugar production, banking and financial services, and construction companies. Central America has never been an industrial stronghold and thus never developed a large, highly organized urban-industrial proletariat. Dunkerley (1988: 207) has provided rough estimates of an urban-industrial proletariat in the 1960s and the 1970s:[4] El Salvador, Guatemala and Nicaragua had an apparently stable proletariat, oscillating between 9.3 and 11.6 per cent of the economically active population (EAP) between 1962 and 1975. Unemployment estimates in the early 1970s are 13 per cent in El Salvador and Guatemala and 19 per cent in Nicaragua. International Labor Organization (ILO) estimates of the total unemployment affecting the EAP during the 1980s are more than 20 per cent in Nicaragua, more than a third in Guatemala and 42 per cent in El Salvador.[5] The professionals and public employees of the urban middle classes had their own *colegios* and trade unions (of schoolteachers and medical personnel, for instance). Organization among the peasant population, the older generation of which still remembered the bloody repression of the *campesino* unions in the 1930s, was 'discouraged' by the authorities. Those who persisted in their efforts were reminded to avoid dangerous associations by vigilant militarized police forces in all three countries.

The Human Development Index (HDI) profiles of the UNDP reports classify El Salvador, Guatemala and Nicaragua, together with Bolivia, Haiti and Honduras, as the poorest countries in the western hemisphere. In Table 1.1. poverty data for the mid-war period, before the HDI profiles had been published, are summarized.[6] One telling indicator of rural poverty is that, in 1975, 41 per cent of El Salvador's rural families were landless and 34 per cent of rural families had farms smaller than 1 hectare. In 1979, 55 per cent of Guatemala's farms were smaller than 1.5 hectares; collectively, these farms comprised a mere 4 per cent of the nation's rural area. In 1976, 61 per cent of the farms were smaller than 7 hectares and these 61 per cent accounted for 4 per cent of the national farmland (Dunkerley, 1988: 183). It is also important to remember that in the decades preceding the conflicts, and during the conflicts themselves, the relatively attractive option of escaping to the formal and informal job market in Mexico and the USA did not yet exist.[7]

The present-day pattern of urban poverty that characterizes the urban and metropolitan cityscape in the form of *barriadas*, *tugurios* or *barrios populares* was largely unknown before the early 1960s in Central America. From that time forward the scarred landscape of urban poverty became evident in each of the capital cities. Mixco, a shanty town inhabited by poor rural-to-urban migrants, arose on the outskirts of Guatemala. Managua was similarly swollen by the ranks of very poor rural peasants. Newly formed slums cropped up in San Salvador's poor inner city, which abutted the well-to-do middle-class suburbs. The effects of this concentration of urban poverty were not strictly limited to the physical landscape of these cities. The presence of densely populated urban pockets of poverty also had political consequences.

Table 1.1 Poor households in El Salvador, Guatemala and Nicaragua, 1985–86 (%)

	Nationally	Capital city
El Salvador (1985)	86	42
Guatemala (1986)	83	64
Nicaragua (1985)	64	43

Source: Menjívar and Trejos, 1992: 60, 66.

Rural poverty had been a reality from time immemorial but had always remained relatively hidden; the reality of urban poverty within the shadows of the seat of national government, however, was impossible to deny. The middle classes and especially the urban student population of the national and the private (Jesuit) universities in the capitals were confronted on a daily basis with the presence of large and generally unorganized contingents of second-class citizens who were victims of poverty, exclusion and discrimination.

Societies of Repression and Fear

Guatemala

With only two exceptions, Guatemala was governed by military putschists or military presidents from the 1920s to the mid-1980s.[8] The despotic presidencies of General Estrada and General Ubico in the 1920s and 1930s served as models for the character in *El Señor Presidente* (1946), the widely acclaimed novel by Nobel laureate Miguel Ángel Asturias, whose son Rodrigo would become the *comandante-en-jefe* of one of the three Guatemalan guerrilla movements. The decade of democratic government enjoyed by Guatemala between 1944 and 1954 ended with a coup against President Árbenz after the landholdings of the United Fruit Company were threatened by confiscation and 'communism'.[9] Árbenz had indeed legalized the Communist Party (the Partido Guatemalteco de Trabajadores [PGT]) in 1952 but the party never had more than a couple of hundred members at that time. From 1954 to 1985, Guatemala's head of state was, with a single exception, always an army officer. This one exception was the formally civilian government of Méndez Montenegro (1966–70), during which the military established a level of repression that would endure for several decades after making a secret pact with the old guard of fiercely anti-communist colonels. Using the threat of a communist overthrow as a pretext, the military institutions began to acquire disproportionate power in relation to the public sector, political parties and social movements, a dynamic that gradually led to a hybrid civilian-military regime of violence and repression. An alliance between the military and the civilian political leadership became the modus operandi of any new government, whether constitutional or imposed. General Gramajo, who later served as minister of defence in the civilian cabinet of democratically elected President Cerezo in the late-1980s, described the situation as follows:

> And afterwards there were the president-generals who were elected, either fraudulently or otherwise. But in any case it was no big deal, because any fraud committed was at the expense of some other general. Any political party that wanted to take part in the political process had to have a general as their candidate. We thus came to the point where there was a knot – a knot where all differences between the military, political and administrative hierarchies were nothing more than one indistinguishable tangle.[10]

The armed forces expanded their control over key segments of the public sector. Military intelligence acquired an undisputed monopoly when it came to matters of security. The CIA, along with Israel's Mossad, provided support in such sensitive areas as counter-intelligence and intelligence processing.[11] The police forces were subordinated to the army at both national and local levels; local police had to coordinate their activities in minute detail with the local army commander and were completely dependent on information and intelligence supplied by the army. A military presence was established and consolidated in the rural departments of Guatemala where the armed forces began to behave, first *de facto* and then *de jure*, as the only legitimate representatives of the central government. However, the most violent institutional change that occurred as part of the transformation of Guatemala into a society of fear was the construction and implementation of a machinery of control, oppression and murder.[12] Intimidation, attacks, torture and other random violence were the tactics employed in the service of this machinery. In the mid-1980s, an independent US-sponsored study group portrayed the state of affairs as follows:

> To the list of the assassinated were added labor and peasant leaders, party officials, student activists, lawyers, doctors and teachers. And their number grew alarmingly: In 1972, 'political' deaths averaged 30 to 50 a month; by 1980, 80 to 100 a month; by 1981, 250 to 300 a month.[13]

The military targeted communists and suspected communists not only in civil society but also within its very own ranks. Aggrieved officers twice staged a coup against General Gramajo, then minister of defence, because they saw him as being soft on communism. On one of these occasions, they kidnapped his wife and children and surrounded the minister's residence with troops. Only intervention by Colonel Balconi, at that time commander of the capital's military elite Mariscal Zavala Brigade, who sent troops and tanks against the insurrectionists, prevented further action against Gramajo and his family. The attitude of some within the military towards Gramajo was most clearly on display during a lecture he gave to fellow officers that he recalled many years later.

> Even as a cabinet member, I was put on the list, along with religious leaders and other politicians, as communists condemned to death.... And, for example, when I spoke, say, in a hotel in the capital, and I began to discuss the thesis of national

> stability, and I began to talk about Guatemala being a society that was stratified, fragmented, etc., and that we needed to have a more tolerant culture, a professional army, greater political participation, and so on – what did people in the audience say? 'The minister is feeding us a line of bullshit. He came here to bullshit us.'[14]

El Salvador

Military dictatorship was institutionalized in El Salvador in the 1930s.[15] Sharp wage reductions for coffee workers in the western part of the country resulted in widespread discontent, leading to rural strikes in 1931 and culminating in open rebellion in early 1932. The rebellion was launched by the Communist Party, whose Central Committee dispatched Farabundo Martí to lead the uprising.[16] Martí, who had previously been the private secretary of revolutionary General Augusto Sandino in Nicaragua, was arrested and executed by a firing squad. General Martínez, dictator from 1931 to 1944, then ordered what in effect were state-sponsored pogroms against communists, targeting the rebel leadership with devastating effect. Estimated deaths resulting from this counter-insurgency range from 4,000, according to the government, to the 30,000 of subsequent historians.[17] The aftershocks of this crackdown reverberated within the Salvadoran Communist Party (PCS) until 1980, when it reluctantly joined the unified guerrilla forces that had been named after Martí. This sustained and brutal repression also helps explain why the western part of El Salvador largely sat out the guerrilla campaigns and civil war of the 1980s (Dunkerley, 1988: 97). Martínez set the tone for forty years of military rule that followed: rule characterized by repressive measures, carried out by vigilantes, paramilitary death squads, militarized police forces and the national army. Martínez was ousted in 1944 by a group of antifascist Military Youth. There were several more coups carried out by young officers during the decades that followed.[18]

The military rulers deserve credit for possessing a strong sense of realpolitik. They reached a modus vivendi with the Salvadoran oligarchy, whose economic interests they left untouched. The military also initiated some cautious reforms like the creation of a social security system and the recognition of urban trade unions, although rural unions and independent *campesino* organizations remained prohibited. Short-lived civil-military juntas of a more reformist character sometimes interrupted the long decades of purely military rule but, in general, national politics was dominated from 1931 until 1979 by officially sanctioned pro-military parties.[19] While military rule prevailed at the national level, army politicians did make concessions at the local level. Municipal elections were open to participation by middle-class parties like the Christian Democrats (PDC) and smaller parties of the far right. The general tendency of Salvadoran politics was in fact so right wing on the whole that it can justly be argued that the Alianza Republicana Nacionalista (ARENA), established by ex-major D'Aubuisson in 1981, represented a natural evolution of the nation's previous political parties, even taking into account its deployment of death squads.[20] Repression by the military, the police and paramilitary forces were constant companions to those who dared to test the limits of military rule. Samayoa, who in January 1980 resigned as minister of education in the government of the first civil-military transition junta of 1979–80 in protest against increasingly repressive measures on the part of the military, remembers one particularly violent episode of this era:

> The turning point probably came in July 1975 with the massacre of students. At that time, I was the administrative director of the Externado, a Jesuit day school, and the demonstrators were marching in front of the school. I was standing on the top floor of the building watching. I couldn't believe what I was seeing. I saw military units posted behind the National Social Security Institute on Calle 25 and they were actually shooting as if they were hunting animals. I gave the order to open the gates so that the students could enter the school grounds.... There is no question that the massacres were organized by the military establishment. Generally speaking, it was security forces that carried out such massacres – either the National Guard or the

> National Police. It was all expressed in terms of the security doctrine of those days – the whole business about Soviet-Cuban communism, etcetera.[21]

In 1972 a centre-left coalition, the Unión Nacional Opositora (UNO), under the leadership of José Napoleón Duarte, himself the head of the Christian Democrats, won the elections. A recount that was ordered by the ruling military government deprived Duarte of his victory. This blatant electoral fraud led to an attempted coup, popular uprisings and the formation of several politico-military organizations, the forerunners of the united guerrilla movement of the 1980s. Government repression increased steadily during the 1970s. In 1977 the UNO, still in opposition, replaced their civilian leadership with a respected retired colonel, Ernesto Claramount, gaining the support of members of the Military Youth and part of the officer corps. Once again, electoral fraud deprived the UNO of the victory that was rightfully theirs, leading to violent repression of popular protests that resulted in as many as fifty deaths. The fraud and subsequent repression represented a watershed in Salvadoran politics. The far left began to arm itself, and membership in the officially banned rural peasant associations rose spectacularly. Equally dramatic were the anti-communist activities of the death squads after 1977. Roberto Cañas, then a student member of the Resistencia Nacional and later a member of their peace negotiating team, explains how the Christian Democrats (PDC) were viewed by the military regime holding power at the time:

> It was the role of the Christian Democrats – a role it paid for with exile, murder and persecution – to be in the opposition. How the right viewed the Christian Democrats was best summed up by Roberto D'Aubuisson: 'The Christian Democrats are like a watermelon: green on the outside and red on the inside.' They were seen as communists by the right. The truth is that they were Christian Democrats: Catholics who respected papal encyclicals and who followed the social teachings of the Church, began a movement that guerillas used for their own purposes. There's no doubt about it: many of the Christian Democrats later joined the guerrillas. They took up arms.[22]

A dirty war was started against all possible perpetrators: Catholic priests, particularly the Jesuits, trade-union leaders and of course the hitherto small guerrilla bands, which in those days primarily attacked (and extorted) members of the economic elite and military hierarchy. In all interviews with ordinary people and rank-and-file members of the FMLN guerrilla forces the following picture emerges of military and police activities: shootings during general and student-led demonstrations in the streets of San Salvador, helicopter assaults on small villages, and nightly murders of priests, schoolteachers and labour leaders. Rubén Zamora, prime minister during the junta of 1979–80, who in 1994 became the first presidential candidate of the FMLN, remembers a junta meeting that he convened after the Christian Democrats had begun to sustain heavy casualties among their ranks:

> January and February [of 1980] came, and repression began to focus on the ranking cadres of the Christian Democrats. I think that this was a decision, a military strategy devised at the highest levels of the armed forces. It was a two-pronged operation: first, to bring the Christian Democrats to their knees and, second, to cut off all political support to the guerrillas at its source. I began gathering all the facts [regarding the recent repression]. After I had summarized my findings, we held a meeting of the Junta, the Army Command and the Military Youth. My brother Mario led the meeting. ... After the document was read, there was a deafening silence. A silence you could cut with a knife, as the saying goes. An unbearable tension. Nobody looked at anybody else. Everyone looked down at the floor, in total silence. Minister of Defence Garcia finally took the floor and said: 'Gentlemen, this is a very serious matter. The armed forces are unable to deal with this right away. We need time in order to evaluate it.' Hearing this, I thought, 'We've already won', and made a sign to Mario that we should leave. ... But [another Christian Democrat] asked for the floor and said, 'Look, I think that we have to be very careful about this statement. It may contain errors. This isn't a basis to take action; the document may contain errors.' ... And as soon as the military men saw that we were divided among ourselves, poof! They said the document was unacceptable, with the vice-minister, who was in charge of the death squads, even saying, 'I want to ask who it was that wrote this document?' ... The meeting

> then ended and it was at that point that the Christian Democrats capitulated to the military men and were defeated. Because if there's one thing that the military will never accept it is weakness and submission. They are military men: what they understand is orders, not arguments.[23]

From the end of the 1970s and the early 1980s the US embassy was reporting more than 800 [political] murders of civilians per month (Corr and Prisk, 1992: 237). Another event that shook the conscience of the world was the murder of Oscar Romero, Archbishop of San Salvador, by a death squad during the celebration of a Mass, and the subsequent shooting of hundreds of mourners during his funeral.[24] Death squads continued to operate until 1984 when, under strong US pressure, they formally disbanded.[25] The Report of the Truth Commission, whose mandate was restricted to the period between 1980 and 1991, notes:

> [the] undeniable impact of the incontrovertible evidence with regard to the death squads.... These consisted of organizations comprising groups of people who were usually dressed as civilians, were heavily armed, acted secretly, hid their association with the death squad and concealed their identity. They kidnapped members of the civilian population and rebel groups. They tortured hostages, concealed their whereabouts, and usually executed them.... The squadrons, who were tied to state organisms through the latter's active collaboration or silent acquiescence, achieved a level of power that transcended that of an isolated or marginal phenomenon and became an instrument of terror and of the systematic physical elimination of political opponents. During the 1980s many civilian and military authorities participated in, promoted and tolerated the actions of these groups.[26]

Nicaragua

Both the nature of Nicaragua's ruling governments and the character of their repressive actions were of a somewhat different order. Nicaragua was ruled by a family dynasty whose actions were not generally speaking as brutal and murderous as those of the regimes in San Salvador and Guatemala City. Instead of institutional rule of the military hierarchy, Nicaragua was from 1933 on governed by successive generations of the Somoza family: Anastasio and his sons Luis and Anastasio, whilst grandson Anastasio was in charge of some counterinsurgency operations during the regime's final years.[27] The power base of the Somoza dynasty was fourfold: first, direct control over the National Guard, a combined military and police force created by the USA;[28] second, gradual control over the country's economy, the basis of the economic empire of the family; third, an ongoing accommodation with the national opposition, finally resulting in a pact between (Somoza's) Liberals and (the opposition's) Conservatives of a fixed 60:40 distribution of congressional seats and a flexible system of appointments in the public sector; fourth, steadfast US support of the regime.

US military influence had been pervasive in Nicaragua for decades. In the case of El Salvador direct military, political and economic involvement of the USA was minimal until the outbreak of the civil war. In Guatemala the ten-year period of democracy and development was ended by the US-sponsored coup of 1954.[29] It was here that the CIA cut its teeth with respect to the implementation of covert operations by US-trained forces, later repeated with calamitous results in the failed Bay of Pigs invasion and later still, on a much larger scale, with active support of the Contra forces against Nicaragua's Sandinista regime.[30] In Nicaragua, the USA provided both financial and military support. During a civil war in 1927, 2,000 US Marines occupied the country's Atlantic and Pacific port cities and established control over the entire country. A pact between the different disputing factions was agreed, but one of the local commanders, General Sandino, refused to sign the accord and for six years carried out a guerrilla campaign in the north-eastern region of Nicaragua against both the National Guard and US forces.[31] After the withdrawal of the US Marines Somoza personally ordered Sandino's execution by guardsmen in 1934. Somoza García, head of the National Guard, and in US government circles referred to as 'the last marine', was for the next eighteen years Nicaragua's undisputed dictator.[32] Governing either directly or via puppet presidents, forming economic and political alliances and even co-opting workers' unions, the Somozas always retained direct control over the National Guard, which functioned as a nationwide military police. The Guard was established in every urban centre as well as in the larger rural municipalities and was responsible for both military and civil security. The National Guard was relatively small and never exceeded 9,000 effectives.[33] The Guard repressed all political dissent with an iron fist. The 1960 murder of thirty student protesters was one of many instances over the course of decades of lethal government action by armed troops against peaceful demonstrators and individual political dissidents. Fear and resentment resulting from such actions built up over a period of more than forty years and help to explain the national jubilation that erupted when the National Guard headquarters were overrun by the Sandinistas in 1979.[34]

It is instructive to compare the political culture of Nicaragua during the Somoza decades to the 35-year rule of Stroessner in Paraguay. The dictatorships of the Somozas and of Stroessner were relatively refined in comparison with the most brutal governments in Latin America, at least in terms of total deaths relative to the population. Having eliminated all potential political rivals the dictatorial regimes in Nicaragua and Paraguay evolved into regimes of political attrition rather than states characterized by continuous violence. The National Guard was known more for its intimidation and corruption than for its wanton violence. The 'mature' dictatorship of the Somozas was a combination of relative economic development and political authoritarianism that took a variety of more or less punitive forms: social and political ostracism, imprisonment of actual and potential adversaries, exile and political murder. During the 1950s and 1960s, overt hostility against the regime was expressed by relatively few adversaries. The national economy was in good shape; the regime had perfected its control over the legal opposition. There were small-scale guerrilla activities; periods of labour unrest were few and far between. Nicaraguan society was without a doubt marked by sharp antagonisms, although its socio-economic cleavages were less severe than those in El Salvador and Guatemala. The overthrow of the Somoza regime is to be explained more by the stifling political order and the effect of decades of political attrition than by the direct consequences of economic exploitation, deep-rooted ethnic resentment or ruthless transgenerational repression and massacres.

Son Anastasio Somoza Debayle tightened his grip on the national economy following the devastating Managua earthquake in 1972. In the aftermath of this natural disaster, he indirectly controlled the banking, financial, insurance and construction sectors of the nation's economy. These actions caused bitter resentment among the economic elite and middle classes, whose interests were now being directly and adversely affected. At the same time the student protest movement rapidly expanded in numbers and influence. The suffocating political culture, the denial of access of new political (student) opposition movements to any legally authorized form of political expression, and the growing popularity of the hitherto small guerrilla bands, whose bold actions captured the popular imagination and who enjoyed widespread support among youth in the cities, were all part of a complex dynamic that led the regime to increase repression of any and all dissent, feeling that it had no other alternative.

In the final phase of the Nicaraguan guerrilla campaigns, then, it was the following factors that played key roles in setting the stage for the urban uprisings of 1978 and 1979: the merciless repression of students and their leaders, and of urban youth in general; the loss of support among increasingly growing numbers of the political and business elites; the growing uneasiness among the middle classes; and, finally, the large-scale popular support for both guerrilla fighters and the independently organized urban militias that suddenly appeared in the major cities. During these two years the latent brutality of a regime that had in previous decades achieved its ends mainly through the non-violent coercive mechanisms discussed above, erupted in full force. During these two years of insurrection, 50,000 people lost their lives.

Chronology of the Guerrilla Wars[35]

In Guatemala and Nicaragua, guerrilla movements were formed in the late 1950s and early 1960s, strongly influenced by the success of the Cuban Revolution and by Che Guevara's writings on guerrilla warfare. In El Salvador the guerrilla movements launched in the 1970s were influenced by the Cubans and the Nicaraguans as well as by the strategy and tactics employed by the Vietnamese.[36] The unification of the five Salvadoran and the four Guatemalan guerrilla forces into the FMLN and the URNG respectively was influenced by the 1979 reconciliation of the three separate factions of the reconstituted FSLN. The triumph of the Sandinistas meant the establishment of a strategic rearguard for the FMLN in Managua. A tacit understanding, however, between the USA and the Sandinistas that the latter would not provide arms to the Guatemalan rebels was honoured until 1990.

Guatemala

The coup against the government of Árbenz in 1954 had at least two consequences in terms of the theory and practice of guerrilla warfare. For young Che Guevara, a political tourist in Guatemala at the time of the coup itself and then a refugee at the Argentine embassy in Guatemala City during the counter-revolution that followed, it carried a lesson that was at once painful and salutary. He never forgot the lukewarm defence of the Árbenz revolution and it influenced his writings on guerrilla warfare.[37] After 1959 he personally supported the revolutionary efforts of the first Guatemalan and Nicaraguan revolutionaries to launch guerrilla movements in Central America modelled on the Cuban example.[38] Guatemala's subordination to US interests after 1954[39] alienated not only the generation of revolutionary officers that had supported Árbenz but also a group of young nationalist lieutenants who attempted a coup in 1960; 44 officers and 2,000 soldiers participated. After the failure of the coup several junior officers, among them Yon Sosa and Turcios Lima, initiated guerrilla movements in the eastern (Ladino, mestizo) region of Guatemala. Along with Colonel Paz Tejada,[40] these two men led groups comprising former soldiers, students and *campesinos* that altogether totalled 400–500 insurgents. In 1966 the Guatemalan army started a counterinsurgency offensive with the support of US military advisers and right-wing paramilitary 'self-defence militias' recruited from the local population. The campaign crushed the guerrilla *frentes* in two years at a cost of 300 dead *guerrilleros* and 3,000 fatalities among the *campesinos*. The campaign leader, Colonel Carlos Arana, after being promoted to general and serving as ambassador to the Somoza government in Nicaragua, became president of Guatemala in 1970.

The guerrilla leaders of the 1960s were either killed or had escaped to Mexico. Of the remaining cadres, some junior officers went to Cuba for training. These survivors, joined by a cadre of fresh revolutionaries, generally recruited from the student population and indigenous peasants, formed the nucleus of three successor guerrilla organizations: the re-institutionalized FAR (Fuerzas Armadas Revolucionarias), the EGP (Ejército Guerrillero de los Pobres) and the ORPA (Organización del Pueblo en Armas). Merging to form the URNG in 1982, these movements' heyday was between 1978 and 1983. During these years substantial segments of the Maya population, especially the peasant movement CUC (Comité de Unidad Campesina), joined the guerrilla fighters. The urban guerrilla forces of the three movements comprised several hundred persons, recruited from the public sector, professionals and the student organizations. At the Ministry of Defence, commanding officers were deeply concerned about the possibility of encirclement of the most important urban areas. They estimated a total of more than 70,000 supporters among the Maya population (the so-called FIL or Fuerzas Irregulares Locales).[41] In a series of brutal counterinsurgency campaigns between 1980 and 1985, the armed forces enlisted whatever recruits they could find as a 'force multiplier'; intensified their counterinsurgency operations;[42] and organized an enormous paramilitary force – 1.2 million[43] mostly indigenous auxiliary troops with a licence to kill, rape, burn and destroy. The Truth Commission used the term 'genocide' to characterize the strategy employed.

By 1985 the guerrilla forces had been significantly weakened. The guerrilla *frentes*, now on the defensive, were forced to operate in increasingly remote areas. The *comandancia general* relocated to Mexico City. In the meantime, a generational change within the army leadership was in process. Twice – in 1982 and 1983 – the younger military had organized a coup against successive extremely hawkish dictators, first against Lucas García and then against Rios Montt. These younger officers had come to the realization that the war would never end without a political solution. They prepared a transition from military rule to civilian government, albeit under the tutelage of their military advisers. In 1991 the government, the army and the guerrillas initiated peace negotiations (1991–96), first under the aegis of the Archbishop of Guatemala City, then under the auspices of a UN delegate. These negotiations led to a final agreement in December 1996.

In the late 1970s the Guatemalan army had 27,000 officers and enlisted personnel. In the mid-1980s this number was increased to 55,000 (without counting the militarized police forces and the paramilitary forces). After the peace agreements the army was considerably reduced, from 46,500 in 1997 to 31,425 in 1998, 27,214 in 2003 and 15,500 in 2004. In 2005 the total armed forces numbered 15,000.[44] When it was demobilized in 1996, the URNG had less than 3,000 military personnel, in addition to another 2,800 international and political cadres. The official number of UNRG members demobilized was 5,750.[45]

Nicaragua

The first to participate in the emerging guerrilla movement in Nicaragua were some veterans of the campaigns of Sandino in the 1930s; they and a few ex-Guards provided the first military training of the new generation of *guerrilleros*. Between the end of the 1950s and the end of the 1970s nearly all guerrilla recruits came from student movements, dissidents of the traditional political parties and the religious left-oriented Christian Base Communities. Contrary to the Guatemalan experience where disparate guerrilla movements did not form a united front until 1982, Carlos Fonseca, a charismatic leader, succeeded in unifying the movement quite early. Fonseca was the vital link between the old Sandino Guard and the new breed of Sandinista revolutionaries. The strong patriotism and anti-imperialism of the FSLN stems in part from the legacy of Sandino himself. Veteran comandantes Tomás Borge and Edén Pastora were, along with Carlos Fonseca, founding members of the FSLN.[46] However, lack of military experience and a blind adherence to the Guevara doctrine of rural guerrilla warfare led to a long sequence of defeats at the hands of the highly trained National Guard and the death of almost all of the movement's leaders in the 1960s and 1970s. In 1967 the Guard carried out a search-and-destroy mission in the Pascarán area near Matagalpa and killed most of the FSLN cadres, including some of the founders of the movement.[47] Most of the succeeding comandantes were young, of urban and middle-class background. This pattern remained unchanged throughout the 1970s: younger subordinates replaced ageing leadership and there was an orderly transition of command functions whenever someone died or retired. The *dirección nacional* of the FSLN was thus continually renewed.[48]

In the early 1970s the movement was so small that all members of the *dirección nacional* participated in officer training courses, with graduates of these courses immediately becoming trainers of new recruits. In December 1974 the FSLN carried out a spectacular operation that boosted the stature of the movement and discredited the Somoza regime. An FSLN commando conducted a raid on a party at the home of 'Chema' Castillo attended by members of the economic and political elite, holding the attendees hostage. Somoza had to give in to the FSLN demands: freedom for a number of political prisoners – Daniel Ortega was one of those liberated – and the broadcast of Sandinista communiqués. In 1978 another commando unit raided Congress and captured approximately 1,500 persons, including 50 deputies and several relatives of Somoza.[49]

In this case also, the Somoza government ended up capitulating to the captors' demands.

Meanwhile an ideological dispute on strategy and objectives had split the movement into three separate factions: one that favoured a strategy of long-term popular warfare, another that insisted on an alliance with 'proletarian forces', and a third, the *terceristas*, that was opposed to the Guevara thesis of rural guerrilla warfare and instead favoured urban guerrilla and popular uprisings in alliance with non-FSLN 'progressive forces'. The ideas of the *terceristas* proved to be the most successful of all. First, they dissolved their rural *frentes* and formed urban guerrilla commands that took the lead in subsequent urban insurrections in Matagalpa, León, Masaya, Chinandega and Managua.[50] Second, they formed an alliance with a group of twelve prominent civilian leaders[51] whose support was crucial in securing international support and, especially, an accommodation with the Carter administration in the United States. Third, the *terceristas* succeeded in obtaining both arms and financial support from four Latin American heads of state: Omar Torrijos in Panama, Fidel Castro in Cuba, Carlos Andrés Pérez in Venezuela, and Rodrigo Carazo in Costa Rica. Fourth, they commanded the Frente Sur on the border with Costa Rica. This was the most formally organized force maintained by the FSLN, with 1,000 armed personnel.[52]

In 1979 the three guerrilla groups reconciled their differences and merged, their leaders forming the nine-person *dirección nacional* of the FSLN. Meanwhile the National Guard had launched a campaign against the Nicaraguan rebel forces and other opposition elements, attacking the FSLN guerrilla fighters and the newly formed urban militias with tanks, planes and helicopters. The often indiscriminate nature of the Guard's operations resulted in both high civilian casualties and widespread damage to infrastructure, especially in urban areas. This campaign resulted in 50,000 deaths, 100,000 wounded and widespread destruction in several of Nicaragua's major cities. The regime eventually lost popular support within Nicaragua and the Carter administration pressed for Somoza's resignation. After unsuccessful negotiations on a transition government and the fusion of the National Guard with the Sandinista military, the guerrilla forces finally liberated Managua and a couple of days later a new revolutionary government was formed. The 9,000-member National Guard was disbanded. The hundreds of officers who fled the country at that time later formed the nucleus of the CIA-sponsored counter-revolutionaries – the Contras. The guerrilla columns of the FSLN had comprised approximately 2,800 persons. There were probably at least another 15,000 adolescents and young men in the spontaneously formed militias, many of whom were incorporated into the newly created Ejército Popular Sandinista after the Sandinistas took power.[53]

El Salvador[54]

Salvador Cayetano Carpio (Marcial), then the secretary general of the Communist Party of El Salvador, broke with the party because of what he saw as its excessive timidity. In 1970 he constituted the Fuerzas Populares de Liberación Farabundo Martí (FPL) as a vanguard party of armed resistance; after the fraudulent elections of 1972 he opted for a strategy of guerrilla warfare. The vanguard had to lead strong mass organizations that would support the revolutionaries; that was the reason for the creation of an institutional framework of popular organizations and trade unions, the Bloque Popular Revolucionario (BPR). His second- and third-in-command were the leaders of the schoolteachers' federation, Mélida Araya Montes (Ana María) and Salvador Sánchez Cerén (Leonel González). In the years to come three other politico-military organizations with a nearly identical organizational pattern of vanguard and associated mass organizations would emerge,[55] headed by leaders of the student movements and the Christian Base Communities, whose significance will be examined in the next chapter. Political differences and personal disputes divided the four organizations. In 1979 a small detachment of the Communist Party, with Schafik Handal as its secretary general, joined the league of proto-guerrilla formations. After several three- and four-member federations the unified FMLN was established in October 1980 with its own *comandancia general.*

In October 1979, amid a rising tide of popular protest and growing sympathy for the armed left, the Military Youth staged a coup that brought three consecutive civil-military juntas to power. The first two of these juntas, which represented last-ditch efforts to avert a civil war, were of a reformist stripe and neither lasted more than two months. The increasing influence of the military hardliners in the juntas and the intensified repression on the part of the government drove many of the local leaders and large numbers of people living in both the urban slums and poor rural villages – in almost every case these were all unarmed civilians – into the arms of the guerrillas.[56] Facundo Guardado, in 1977 secretary general of the Bloque Popular, explains:

> The guerrilla groups themselves were small – each consisted of a few dozen members. They were lightly armed: a carbine, a pistol, hardly anything really. Grassroots organizations were the heart of the resistance.... Whether people thought of themselves as being on the left had no bearing. Instead, people chose to defend what was fundamentally important: the right to life, to defend their children. These were fathers, mothers and brothers who said: 'Okay, let them kill me. But I have to defend my family.' During many of the manhunts throughout the country, one's remaining time on earth was counted in terms of hours. To survive, to live another night, to see the sun rise the next day – these were the kind of things that people considered an accomplishment. It was under these conditions that the 1981 offensive took place. These were not acts that were coldly planned out beforehand, but actions by people defending what was most precious to them – their very lives. This also explains why so many people in El Salvador became involved in the conflict ... It was a matter of arming and preparing tens of thousands of people. It was also the case that if you give them something, you could end up getting lynched yourself, for example. I'm talking here about the leaders of the movement. So you had to say, 'Okay, here is your first shotgun, here is the first rifle, I'm bringing over the first carbine. There will be more.' And that's how arms were obtained for the first offensive.[57]

The civil unrest that began in 1978 flared into full-scale civil war with the 1981 guerrilla assault on the capital city of San Salvador. The guerrilla forces expected to ride a wave of popular support to a victory reminiscent of the 1979 Sandinista triumph in Managua. Neither the army of 12,000 enlisted soldiers nor the two militarized police corps were prepared for guerrilla warfare and tended to retaliate indiscriminately, resulting in high casualties among the civilian population and widespread panic. The revolt by largely unarmed masses thus ended in failure and the guerrilla forces retreated to the northern and eastern regions of the country, administering swathes of land that they termed 'controlled territories'. There the FMLN built up between 1982 and 1984, increasing its total force to 12,000 combatants deployed in more or less well-organized military units. In the first years of the war the guerrillas sometimes fielded battalion-size units against the battalions of El Salvador's armed forces. The Reagan administration, however, intervened on the side of the government with massive military aid.[58] The number of US advisers in El Salvador was never more than a couple of hundred but entire battalions were trained and equipped for counterinsurgency operations in the USA or in Honduras.[59] USAID provided extensive assistance with respect to the repair of damaged infrastructure. US support built up a 60,000-strong fighting force that retook some territories, such as the strategic Guazapa region, between 1986 and 1988. During this time, the FMLN reverted to more traditional guerrilla operations conducted by small-scale units.

The conflict ended in a military stalemate. The electoral victory of the moderate Alfredo Cristiani as president paved the way for a peace dialogue that had previously failed three times under the Duarte administration. But before this happened the FMLN launched a second offensive on San Salvador in November 1989, occupying large sectors of the city. In retaliation, the armed forces bombarded sections of the capital. In addition, a special detachment of the army's elite Atacatl battalion murdered six Jesuit priests of the Universidad Centroamericana (UCA). This indiscriminate response led to national outrage and international condemnation. Even the USA distanced itself from the government and the army. Both belligerent parties now came to terms with the reality of a military impasse and agreed to a peace agreement. A UN mission supervised the negotiations that lasted nearly two years, and that concluded with the 16 January 1992 agreements signed at the Chapultepec Castle in Mexico City.

The size of the army was immediately cut in half. Afterwards, further reductions of El Salvador's armed forces brought it back into line with the size of other Central American post-war armies (13,000 officers and troops).[60] There was a thorough overhaul of the officers' corps in order to make room for a new generation of post-war commanders. In addition, the military training institutes were entirely reorganized and a new police force was created, with a third of its members coming from the former guerrilla forces. The 15,000 members of the FMLN were demobilized in five successive stages, in each of which 20 per cent of the total force was relieved of its duties.

2

Genesis of a Guerrilla Generation

Revolutions are made by revolutionaries who come of age in a rebellious generation: a generation of dissident intellectuals, renegade clergy, radical ideologues, and committed political organizers, along with their loyal followers and devoted young disciples. This chapter will focus on the leaders, not the followers; that is, on those who would become the strategists and political guides who would later chart the course of the guerrilla movement. They attracted, shaped and guided the small vanguard groups of revolutionaries who exploited a social undercurrent of indignation and resentment resulting from decades of discrimination, exclusion and neglect of the masses of poor and underprivileged. What is the social, religious and educational background of these revolutionary elites? Who were their intellectual mentors and role models? What kinds of experiences helped shape their moral and ideological convictions? This chapter will trace their religious background and their ideological roots, the influence of their teachers and icons, the evolution of their own vision of the world and the paths that led each of them to embrace a strategy of armed revolutionary struggle. Essentially, this chapter will attempt to identify similarities with respect to both socio-economic context and personal experience that can be said to have shaped the quintessential commander.

Leiden and Schmitt (1973: 78–89) have researched the social and psychological characteristics of revolutionary leaders. They describe as typical revolutionaries those leaders who are rebellious, audacious and loyalty-inspiring – and who are extremely devoted to the cause. Revolutionary leaders, even those who rise to prominence only after spending many years in the ranks, are comparatively young men. The average age of the Bolshevik Politburo in 1917 was 39. The leadership of the three Latin American rebellions of the twentieth century that preceded those under discussion here – those of Mexico in the 1910s and 1920s, and of Bolivia and Cuba in the 1950s – came for the most part from the educated middle classes of lawyers, schoolteachers, bureaucrats and small landowners. In each instance, students and other young adults played a prominent role. In the case of Central America, the role of students was far greater. Wickham-Crowley (1992: 20, 327–39), whose definitive study supplies biodata of Latin American guerrilla leaders between the mid-1950s and the early 1990s, reported an average age of between 25 and 30 during the 1960s. In comparison, the members of the Sandinista *dirección nacional* were around age 25 when they defeated the Somoza regime in 1979; the only exception was middle-aged Tomás Borge. Most of the Salvadoran leadership was even younger. A politically restless generation seemed to be emerging in Guatemala, El Salvador and Nicaragua in the 1970s. Many of the young people of this generation found an outlet for their discontent with the established order in student movements at secondary educational institutes and universities, and some of these students were recruited by the guerrilla movements. The key role of students within the emerging dissident movements in Central America was identified by Roque Dalton as early as 1966.[1]

In all three countries, another revolutionary cohort emerged from the religiously inspired Christian Base Communities, which supplied much of the leadership of the popular organizations in the

1960s and 1970s. These groups drew ideological sustenance from Roman Catholic liberation theology, which also gained significant influence in student movements.[2] Probably half of the Nicaraguan comandantes had been associated with both the Catholic study groups and the FSLN-inspired student unions before being recruited as clandestine FSLN members. A smaller number of leaders were drawn from other sources: trade unions; grassroots organizations in the urban barrios; and associations of *campesinos*. The cadres of the left-wing parties, mainly the Communist Party, also provided some of the revolutionary leaders. Finally, young military officers sometimes changed sides and joined the underground, with veteran officers serving as military instructors of young guerrilla recruits. Before the Salvadoran and the Guatemalan armies were transformed into counterinsurgency machines, a certain proclivity to rebellion had existed among the young cadets and junior officers from the mid-1940s to the late 1950s.[3]

The background history of three leading guerrilla comandantes, one from each country, is presented here below. The three individuals started out as activists in the student movement, a Christian social action organization and the Communist Party respectively. As an example of the student leaders turned guerrilla comandantes I chose Francisco Jovel, member of the Salvadoran *comandancia general* and secretary general of the Partido Revolucionario de los Trabajadores Centroamericanos (PRTC):

> It started when I was young, during my middle school years, always with the idea of serving others – more concerned with being a leader in the student movement than I was about myself. One year after entering the university, I was elected representative of the general student union there [1971]. I was nominated vice-president of AGEUS and this led to some form or other of conflict with the government. Later we became targets of oppression when we were still in university; it got so bad that I had to live as a resident on the university grounds. Because outside the university the risk of being captured or of suddenly disappearing was much greater. Under the government in power after the failed coup attempt of 1972, I had to go deep into the

political underground. And we worked with other comrades, students as well as workers and *campesinos*, on forming an underground political organization. This organization was called the Organización Revolucionaria de los Trabajadores, ORT. And in 1975, formally in January 1976, this organization changed into a political party and took the name of the Partido Revolucionario de los Trabajadores Centroamericanos, PRTC.[4]

Monica Baltodano, *comandante guerrillero* of the Frente Sandinista de Liberación Nacional (FSLN), who in 1979 was in charge of the liberation of Granada, Nicaragua's southernmost important city, represents the case of a religiously inspired youth:

Already during my middle school years I had my first encounter with political ideas as a result of a concerned nun, who was a sociology teacher.... A group of students from both religious and public schools formed a secondary school movement of young Christians who questioned their Christian faith in such an unjust and unequal society. I remember [Father] Fernando Cardenal well, you know. These were not large groups: 15, 20, perhaps at formal gatherings there were as many as 70 or 80 people. Once I joined these movements we were involved in struggles that brought us into contact with the Sandinista Frente, which had a student organization called the Frente Estudiantil Revolucionario (FER). When I entered university, during my first year I was nominated to run for president of my class. And someone from FER also ran, and I won the election. He said to me: 'You shitty little Christian' [laughs]. But afterwards I asked them to recruit me; they didn't initially recruit me. [They] said to me, 'Your work will consist of staying in the Christian Movement and of working in an FER cell, in a study cell.' That's how, by 1971, in this world of students and of the Christian movement, I became involved in the Frente. And they [also] named me the Central American coordinator of the Christian Movement. The person who had held this post before me was Ana Margarita Peña, of the Salvadoran Fuerzas Populares de Liberación (FPL) ... And I got involved in what the Frente was doing, while continuing to do work for the Christian Movement. And my primary responsibility consisted of community work. In addition, a part of our mission was winning over more Christians. And also doing community organizing under the cover of the Christian movement. Because the [Sandinista] organization was completely banned, you know.[5]

The recruitment history of Celso Morales (Tomás), the second-in-command of the Guatemalan Ejército Guerrillero de los Pobres (EGP), is representative for those who passed through one of the Communist Youth organizations:

> I was born on 2 September 1946 in the small village of Morazán, in the Department of El Progreso. My father was a farmer whose crops had failed. So he became a day labourer. In 1951 everyone knew that there was a lot of work for poor people on the banana plantations of the United Fruit Company. My father began working as a *peón* until 1958, when the company let him go because he had a work accident. I was in elementary school when I had to leave school because of this. Through family connections, my father was able to find work with the Guatemala City government as a floor sweeper in a market. I was the oldest son, and my father tried to make sure that I studied something or learned a trade. He spoke to a friend of his who was a tailor – he had a small shop and he taught me the trade. I continued to go to school at night and that was where I was recruited by the revolution. A comrade in the PGT [Partido Guatemalteco de Trabajadores] who was a neighbour of mine began talking to me ... and passed my name around as a recruiting prospect. Then one day he said that he was inviting me to a meeting, if I was interested in coming. I told him that I was. I still didn't know that he was inviting me to the Youth Section JPT [Juventud Patriótica del Trabajo] of the PGT. I discovered this later. I was the youngest one there ... We attended meetings, trying to recruit new comrades, performed some minor tasks, moved things from one place to another – generally propaganda materials. We painted graffiti on buildings. At night, we surreptitiously passed out flyers in the streets. ... As early as 1964, they asked me one day if I'd agree to take military training. And I said yes. There was a ten-day training course in a house in the city for fifteen to twenty comrades, both men and women ... So this was the first military training that I received. It consisted of learning about handguns, 22-calibre rifles – about guns that were used in the military. We were taught about explosives and topography from a military point of view. In addition, there was a political aspect to the content of the training. They talked a lot about class struggle, about just and unjust wars. Some of us wanted to go off and join the guerrillas. ... They told me – because I used to nag them so much about going into the mountains – that they were

getting me ready to go into the mountains. So that was what was going to happen. Passports were obtained and finally, on 2 November 1965, all of the comrades from around here, from both the city and the country, gathered together. There were 20 or 25 of us. There was only one woman, Lola [Alba Estela Maldonado], who is currently a UNRG deputy. They put us up in cheap little hotels in Mexico City. The next stop was Cuba.[6]

Student Movements

Central America's university system grew considerably during the 1960s. The number of students increased, new departments were created, and campuses expanded in size. The influx of students naturally led to the growth in size and influence of the student organizations. Dunkerley (1988: 353) has described the evolution of this process in El Salvador. At the Universidad de El Salvador (UES) the number of students jumped from 3,000 to 30,000 in less than a decade. By 1972, more than half the student population was studying in humanities and social sciences departments. Moreover, the university was administered by progressive rectors like Rafael Menjívar.[7] Guatemala and Nicaragua both experienced a similar boom in their university systems. Public universities in Latin America are generally autonomous and neither the military nor the police can enter their buildings without the permission of the academic authorities. Even under the highly repressive climate of Central America's dictatorships, the military continued to respect academic autonomy in the universities. The faculties of the humanities and social sciences departments, as well as law schools and medical schools, became highly radicalized during these two decades. The following two interview fragments provide illustrative snapshots of this process. Edelberto Torres-Rivas, one of Latin America's leading social scientists, remembers the situation at Guatemala City's University of San Carlos (USAC), in the early 1960s:

I was the leader of the Communist Youth – I was secretary general. At the law school, we had a cell for many years, a core group of seven. It was never larger – there were seven, eight, five of us, and in the university as a whole there were no more than forty. By March and April [of 1962], there was such a chaotic influx [of new recruits] that the core group at the law school had swollen to 280 people. Things were getting out of hand. There was exponential growth. The fervour, the revolutionary enthusiasm untempered by any coherent ideology – it was all more of an emotional reaction to the political situation of the times. Everyone wanted to organize. The group started carrying out several operations on its own: disarming military policemen and stealing their weapons. And that's how the FAR [Fuerzas Armadas Rebeldes] came into being – built up from a core of communist youth.[8]

Santiago Santa Cruz, a doctor who as Comandante Santiago later led the Frente Unitario, the only military battle group of the URNG where members of the four constituent organizations fought together, describes the situation in the late 1970s:

You had to do your residency in public hospitals, where extreme poverty and gross inequality were always evident. In addition, many of the professors were active in the ranks of ORPA [Organización del Pueblo en Armas]. This was true in the case of the [coordinator of the] programme of the supervised professional internship, our rural residency programme. There were other doctors who were also active. Thus, the entire infrastructure of the San Carlos Medical School was put at the disposal of ORPA in order to supply its *frentes* – the cars, the land, the school were on. Many doctors who were sympathetic to the cause and who came to supervise the students in the different towns out there carried arms and ammunition, and transported other material needed by the guerrillas.[9]

It is undeniable that the three national and the three Jesuit universities in El Salvador, Guatemala and Nicaragua all provided large numbers of guerrilla recruits.[10] Many of those in El Salvador and Nicaragua who later rose to prominence in the revolutionary movements – Cañas, Gutiérrez, Jovel, Ortiz, Sancho, Villalobos, Zamora and at least half of the FMLN peace negotiating team in El Salvador; nearly all the founding members of the FSLN and most of the nine *comandantes de la revolución* plus a very considerable portion of the *comandantes guerrilleros* in Nicaragua – had previously been leaders in the student movements. The situation in Guatemala was somewhat different. There, the first guerrilla leaders like Yon Sosa and Turcios Lima, the founder of the FAR, had a military background, and had distinguished themselves as cadets. They had both been sent to the USA for additional anti-guerrilla training. Some of the first civilian comandantes were self-educated men like Jorge Soto (Pablo Monsanto) of the FAR, who received his formal education at the Asilo Santa Maria, and Celso Morales (Tomás), second-in-command of the EGP [Ejército Guerrillero de los Pobres], who joined the guerrilla forces in his second year of the *secundaria*. On the other hand, Ricardo Ramirez de León (Rolando Morán), *comandante-en-jefe* of the EGP and Arnoldo Villagrán (Ruiz), second-in-command of the FAR, had been student leaders and had studied at the USAC, as had Rodrigo Asturias (Gaspar Ilóm), *comandante-en-jefe* of the ORPA. As in the case of the FMLN in El Salvador, a considerable part of the *comisión político-diplomática* of Guatemala's URNG had acquired experience as leaders in student organizations. Sergio Ramirez, Nicaragua's vice-president during the Sandinista government (1979–90), had been the secretary general of the CSUCA, the Central American system of public universities.

A number of guerrilla leaders had either held academic posts prior to assuming positions of leadership or would do so at the end of the conflicts. Rodrigo Asturias had been in charge of a research institute at San Carlos University. Exiled in Mexico after his initial attempt to form a guerrilla force, he was appointed the associate general manager of Siglo XXI, one of Latin America's most prestigious academic publishing houses, before he created his own guerrilla force. He lectured at several Spanish universities in the 1990s, before and after the peace agreements. Jaime Wheelock (FSLN) obtained a grant from the Ford Foundation to earn an M.A. in Public Administration at Harvard. Salvador Samayoa, Eduardo Sancho, Maria Marta Valladares (Nidia Díaz) and Joaquin

Villalobos (FMLN) managed to find time during the war to publish in academic journals like *Estudios Centroamericanos* (ECA, published by the UCA) or in *Foreign Policy*.[11] Villalobos went to live in Oxford in the 1990s and he still enjoys life there on the fringes of the university as an independent scholar. He is not the only one of the former FMLN leadership to maintain relations with academia. Roberto Cañas is the director of postgraduate studies at the Universidad Evangélica; Dagoberto Gutiérrez holds a chair at the Universidad Luterana; and Eduardo Sancho is a professor of sociology at the Universidad Francisco Gavidia.

When I interviewed Pablo Ceto and Arnoldo Villagrán in 2005 they were finishing their professional (*licenciado*) theses at San Carlos University. Dora María Tellez, the youngest female Nicaraguan *comandante guerrillero*, went back to the UCA as a research professor in the 1990s. Invited to Harvard as a visiting professor, she was denied a visa by the US government. Rubén Zamora, coordinator of the Frente Democrático Revolucionario that during the war represented the FMLN to third parties, is now an outstanding social scientist who lectures periodically at Columbia University and at institutions of higher learning throughout Latin America.[12] I met in 2006 both Comandante Humberto Ortega and Antonio Lacayo (who between 1990 and 1996 was Nicaragua's prime minister) at the UCA where, within a single week, each man read from his recently published memoirs while sharing the stage with the other.[13]

Liberation Theology and Base Communities

Catholic social action movements were also an important proving ground for guerrilla leaders, their followers and sympathizers. These grew out of the pastoral work of Roman Catholic priests and laity at the local and national levels, which had far-reaching effects in El Salvador and which were also important, though to a lesser degree, in both Guatemala and Nicaragua. These movements were especially active in the universities, but their influence was also felt in the wider society of each of the three nations.

In the 1970s the intellectual climate at many universities throughout Latin America, and certainly at those in Central America, was strongly influenced by two intellectual currents: liberation theology and dependency theory. The scholars who developed dependency theory (including Fernando Henrique Cardoso [who later became Brazil's president], Enzo Falletto, Osvaldo Sunkel, Theotonio Dos Santos, and Edelberto Torres-Rivas) elaborated ideas of ECLAC economist Raúl Prebisch regarding the structural dependency and exploitation of Latin America's poor peripheral and underdeveloped economies by wealthy central and economically developed countries. Poverty, exclusion and social conflicts in Latin America were ultimately explained by the 'dependent integration' of Latin America in the capitalist world economy. Liberation theology established the relationship between (Catholic and Christian) religious ethics on the one hand and political activism on the other, interpreting the Bible in a way that engendered both compassion for, and practical action on behalf of, those who are poor and victims of injustice. As a consequence, themes of social justice, human rights and the alleviation of poverty were strongly emphasized by Latin American theologians like Hélder Câmara (Brazil), Gustavo Gutiérrez (Peru), Fernando and Ernesto Cardenal (Nicaragua) and Óscar Romero, Ignacio Ellacuría and Segundo Montes (El Salvador, all three of whom were later murdered).

Roman Catholicism is woven inextricably into the social fabric of Latin America and it was thus natural that the student movements drew ideological nourishment from liberation theology, which in turn was influenced by the Vatican Council II (1965), and the Latin American bishops' conferences in Medellín (1968) and Puebla (1979). This new orientation had both Latin American roots and European antecedents. In the late 1950s and early 1960s, for instance, in a branch of the theological seminary at Belgium's University of Louvain, the Colegio para América Latina (COPAL), directed by François Houtart, began experimenting with an approach to the region's history and social problems that combined theology, philosophy and sociology. Camus, Marcel and Sartre, influential among the leftist European intelligentsia, were closely studied and extensively discussed by COPAL faculty and students.[14] One can trace COPAL's influence upon a generation of Latin American progressive Christians like the left-wing Peronists in Argentina, the Chilean Izquierda Cristiana, and the intellectuals of SINAMOS during the Revolutionary Government of the Armed Forces under Peruvian General Juan Velasco Alvarado. Camilo Torres, Colombian priest and liberation theologist turned *guerrillero*, had been a lecturer at COPAL; Msgr Romero's auxiliary bishop Gregorio Rosa Chávez, secretary of the Medellín bishops' conference, was a COPAL alumnus as well. In the mid-1960s this cross-fertilization of modern sociology, European political philosophy and Latin American theology was adopted in Brazil, Chile and Peru, as well as in Central America. The ideas of the Brazilian social thinker Paulo Freire about emancipation through grassroots organizations and literacy campaigns had become influential. Latin American sociology in those days was strongly influenced by dependency theory as well as the early philosophical writings of Marx. The adherents of liberation theology interpreted the gospel as Christ's demand to liberate the masses from poverty and repression.[15] Radicalizing priests included in their analysis a comparison between Christ and Che Guevara, asserting that 'liberation and revolution are a legitimate extension of the gospel'.[16]

At Medellín the bishops called upon the Church and its priests to defend the rights of the oppressed, to promote grassroots organizations and to make ministering to the poor a priority.[17] A means to achieving these ends was the creation of Christian (i.e. Catholic) Base Communities, working groups of lay people who applied progressive interpretations of Church teachings to the political and social issues of the times. In El Salvador the movement proclaimed a shift 'toward the church of the poor and popular organizations'.[18] The Base Communities movement grew explosively in the 1970s. An important segment of the movement radicalized, a process reinforced by the murder of Archbishop Romero. Base Communities were composed of small groups of twenty to thirty people who met regularly for Bible study and a discussion of the nation's current events and social problems. They elected from among their ranks *delegados de la palabra* (i.e. 'Messengers of the Word'), who were trained lay preachers and religious instructors. In El Salvador alone, 15,000 *delegados* were trained between 1970 and 1976 (Montgomery, 1995: 87). Father Gerard Potter, a German priest who worked in the refugee camps in Honduras and among the poor in El Salvador, remembers:

> The *delegados* did not celebrate mass, although they did hold religious services. But they were lay people, *campesinos*. There was a severe shortage of priests and the *delegados* assumed the role of community leaders. They led the first meetings of these communities – which consisted of perhaps five to ten people and one of the things that seem important to me was that everyone spoke. Those present took everything that was said very seriously; everyone paid attention and showed respect. The Bible was a part of it all, but the Word of the Bible was always set against the daily experience of those present. [Many] priests took a radical stance, although these clergy faced opposition within the Church, as well as persecution by the state. A number of priests were murdered as a result of their activities. This didn't happen everywhere – only in places with priests that showed a new way of thinking. And those areas where there were priests were regions that later became guerrilla strongholds. Because the stages were as follows: first, Base Communities; then joining a grassroots organization like FECCAS [Federación Cristiana de Campesinos Salvadoreños] – and these organizations were persecuted by the military and by the authorities, leaving no choice but to head to the mountains. That is how people ended up joining the guerrilla struggle. Many priests became radicalized after the murder of Msgr Romero. And a lot of people who were organized in the parishes where liberation theology held sway also joined the guerrillas.[19]

The organization of peasant communities was officially prohibited and that explains the enormous success of rural associations that were formed by cadres of the Base Communities under the flag of the Catholic Church. Cabarrús (1983) relates in detail the explosive growth of the *campesino* organizations over a period of several years. The organizational efforts of the priests and lay preachers were matched by those of the leadership of the politico-military organizations. The majority of the popular organizations that later joined the guerrilla forces directly descended from the Base Communities.

A similar symbiosis between leftist radicals and disciples of liberation theology materialized in Nicaragua, where many religiously inspired middle-class students eventually joined the clandestine FSLN organization. Father Fernando Cardenal, member of the Grupo de los Doce[20] and minister of education between 1984 and 1990, explains:

> The Christian communities here played an important part in the Nicaraguan Revolution. We founded the Movimiento Cristiano Revolucionario here in 1973. It was a youth movement that had a strong influence in the FSLN.... There were also, among the *campesinos*, [lay] leaders of churches that had no priests. These people were trained and they were called Messengers of the Word [*delegados de la palabra*]. I was very involved with an organization called CEPA [Centro de Educación y Promoción Agraria], which had the goal of providing religious and political training to the Messengers of the Word who were working in the field. CEPA was a group of the Society of Jesus in Nicaragua. So the Sandinistas were advised to approach those leaders in the community who were especially well trained and politically committed – to recruit them for the Sandinista Frente.... Of course the time came when, for example, Carlos Fonseca Amador, founder of the Sandinista Frente, met one night with my brother Ernesto, who was also a priest. We talked all night. In that conversation, Carlos Fonseca imparted the following reflection to Ernesto and me: 'If we were orthodox Marxists, we would be obliged to say that, in order to make revolution, we would first have to strip all of the common people – the workers and peasants – of their religious beliefs, so that we could make revolution once they became atheists. But I'm telling you that this is impossible.... Since we know that the majority of Nicaraguans are Christians, we mustn't take their Christian faith away from them. Instead, we need to turn these Christians into committed

> revolutionaries as well. Thus we can have a popular revolution with the entire population that is Christian but who can also, having undergone this process of raising awareness, participate in the revolution.' He then said to Ernesto and me: 'Those of us in the Sandinista Frente expect a lot from the two of you. You have to help us turn Christians into revolutionaries.'[21]

In Guatemala, the direct influence of Christian religious elements was perhaps not as great. Yet in Guatemala's indigenous highlands, the influence of liberation theology cannot be denied. American missionaries of the Maryknoll Society introduced the new theology in Quetzaltenango and Huehuetenango in the late 1960s and formed discussion groups with local student leaders similar to the Salvadoran and Nicaraguan groups described above (Murga Armas, 2006: 79–84). Le Bot (1997: 146–52) mentions the activities of Spanish and Guatemalan Jesuits in Guatemala City, Chimaltenango and El Quiché. Liberation theologians were influential in the founding years of the EGP, when guerrilla leaders and Jesuit priests encountered two radicalized Spanish youth while assisting the victims of the earthquake in 1976:

> Among the most radical elements, two young Spaniards who had acquired Guatemalan citizenship stood out. From the very first stages, to the formation of a Comité de Unidad Campesina [CUC], to their openly recognized inclusion in the EGP, they were the vital yet invisible link to the rank-and-file fighters. Both rose to positions of leadership within the guerrilla organization and were the two persons who were in large part responsible for integrating Christian and Marxist-Leninist perspectives – an integration that affected both the doctrine and the practice of the EGP.[22]

An exclusive emphasis on the influence of Marxism and the Cuban Revolution upon the Central American guerrilla movements ignores the fact that radical elements within the Catholic Church had at least as much of an impact. Daniel Ortega emphasized the importance of the influence of his Christian (Catholic) upbringing in 1997 in not unclear terms:

> The Cuban Revolution hadn't triumphed yet. My idol was Sandino, and also Christ. I was brought up a Christian but I regarded Christ as a rebel, a revolutionary, someone who had committed himself to the poor and the humble and never sided with the powerful. I had a Christian upbringing, so I would say that my main early influences were a combination of Catholicism, which I saw as a spur to change, and Sandinism, represented by the resistance against the Yankee invasion. Later, the triumph of the Cuban Revolution was very influential, and Fidel, Che and Camilo [Cienfuegos] became our main role models.[23]

Contrary to what one might think from hearing the incessant railing of the Reagan administration against godless and wicked communism in Central America, the reality was that Catholic priests, as well as ministers and lay persons from various Protestant denominations, entered the ranks of the different guerrilla movements in considerable numbers. One of them is Salvadoran comandante Dagoberto Gutiérrez:

> I received a Christian education. But I am much more of a communist than I was before, and I'm more than 60 years old now, you know. Because at that time I didn't know anything about politics, except what I had learned from Jesus Christ. And I knew nothing about communism and capitalism. I learned about that from Marx. Afterwards, I discovered an affinity between Jesus and Marx ... If you look at those of us who led the war, you see university graduates, professionals, priests. This marriage between the resistance and the churches was inevitable. It was a wedding that had been foretold. Why was this the case? Our movement was never either anticlerical or atheistic. Never. Even the Communist Party had Bible-toting priests in its ranks. We communists had our own pastors to explain the revolution. There was no anticlericalism, no atheism ... And I'm talking about all of the churches. That relationship is very important – it was ecumenical. Both the Catholic and Protestant churches were committed. There were never any wars here between the two parties. The clueless gringos never knew who they were fighting. The evangelical sects – the most conservative of them – were also part of the guerrilla movement.[24]

Marxism-Leninism and the Cuban Revolution

During the war years, nearly all guerrilla movements professed their Marxist-Leninist purity in published interviews. One may wonder why this point was so heavily emphasized. The commitment to socialism and communism cannot be explained by the inherent appeal or influence of the existing communist parties in the region. The communist parties in all three countries were timid, led a semi-clandestine existence and were largely free of ideological control by either the Soviet Union or Maoist China. We must therefore look elsewhere to explain the appeal of the Marxist classics to the guerrilla generation.

The students at Central American universities who came of age during the 1960s considered Soviet Communism bleak, bureaucratic and boring. As Roberto Cañas explains:

> In El Salvador, my generation, which is to say this [student] movement of the 1960s and the first part of the 1970s, drew its inspiration from the 1968 experiences in Paris and Chapultepec, Mexico. This was also the expression of a rebellious generation, of the young rebels of the 1960s, rebellious in every aspect of social life: the music of the Beatles and the Rolling Stones, there was the war in Vietnam, there was Che Guevara. Because revolutionary change was in the air – in music, the way people dressed, the young people of that time glorified rebellion and were heirs to a tradition of rebellion. ... I was brought up with the idea that to be part of the left meant belonging to an intellectual aristocracy. You were part of the future of humanity. You were the precursor of the New Man. This was who we were. The most prestigious and superior people of all. We weren't followers like people in the Soviet Union. No, we were more interested in the Paris of 1968. We loved slogans like, 'It is forbidden to forbid.' We are the legitimate heirs of that current of the left. Of that generation. ... Roque Dalton said that poetry is the gateway to revolution.[25]

Similar assertions were expressed by the FSLN leadership in Nicaragua, despite the fact that Carlos Fonseca and some others had studied in Moscow or East Berlin. Some important FMLN leaders had previously been party members; Cayetano Carpio had even been the secretary general of the Salvadoran Communist Party. Leaders of the communist parties in El Salvador and Guatemala, Schafik Handal of the PCS and Carlos Gonzáles of the PGT served in the *comandancia general* of the FMLN and the URNG respectively, but only because of eleventh-hour conversions to the guerrilla cause. The military significance and the overall status of the party both remained low throughout the war years.

The adherence to Marxism and Leninism – namely, Lenin's version of doctrinaire Marxism that envisioned the revolutionary overthrow of the capitalist system led by a 'vanguard party', followed afterwards by the 'dictatorship of the proletariat' – of the young leadership of the guerrilla movements can probably be attributed to a combination of factors. For most of the comandantes the notion that revolution and socialism are two sides of the same coin was an article of faith. Marxism was an integral part of 'revolutionary theory', a sometimes voluntary, sometimes prescribed programme of study whose required readings included the writings of Marx himself, books by Marxist political and social theorists, and, perhaps most importantly, the military writings of strategists like Karl von Clausewitz, and of revolutionary heroes such as Che Guevara, Carlos Marighella, Mao Zedong, Sun Tzu and Vo Nguyen Giap. Apart from Marx himself, Lenin was the most widely read Marxist author. Gramsci, a highly regarded Marxist whose work was widely influential among radical intellectuals during the second part of the twentieth century, received somewhat less attention, and Trotsky, Russia's first successful revolutionary and the founder of the Red Army, was largely ignored altogether. Gramsci and Trotsky were probably regarded as renegades, a vision shared by the Cuban revolutionaries, who quickly had fallen under the influence of the official Soviet version of 'revolutionary thinking'.[26] A few Salvadoran guerrilla leaders had studied Marx's *Capital*.[27] From Lenin the comandantes adopted the notion of the critical importance of a small elite vanguard leadership and the planning of revolutions by central leadership. Scholarly reading of Marxist theory was sometimes replaced by scattershot perusals of popularizations by Marta Harnecker, whose *Conceptos elementales* served as a bible for several generations of Latin American student radicals.[28] Hugo Torres (2003: 355–8) reports in his memoirs a vibrant debate between guerrilla members on the ethics of using the pages of this book to make cigarettes. After remembering that they had already used the bible, most members voted in favour. To characterize the guerrilla leadership as 'popular intellectuals', as does Torres-Rivas (1996: 42–4), may be going too far.[29] Be that as it may, there should be no illusion as to the depth of Marxist knowledge or convictions on the part of most of the Central American revolutionaries.[30] As Jaime Wheelock, the foremost intellectual of the Nicaraguan comandantes, remarks:

> Our knowledge of Marxism was not very deep – I really don't think it was. In the Frente there were maybe two or three who had read, applied, or knew something about it. Remember that the majority of us were students, that we had been involved in the struggle since we were 18 or 19 years old. And the struggle was an underground struggle. Nobody could go around carrying books – reading something when you were trying to avoid being massacred. It was a very practical struggle. There wasn't a lot of time for that sort of thing.[31]

The general quality of guerrilla Marxism could probably be called 'communism with a Cuban face'. The influence of the Cuban Revolution and the Cuban example were without a doubt irresistible. While the young revolutionaries were also inspired by other rebel movements like the FARC in Colombia, the MIR in Chile, the urban guerrillas in Uruguay and Brazil, and insurgent groups in Peru and Venezuela, the Cuban Revolution and two of its protagonists, Fidel Castro and Che Guevara, towered above all other personalities and movements in terms of importance. Nearly all Central American comandantes had been in Cuba more than once for one reason or another: military training, consultation with the Cuban leaders, medical treatment, study, rest and relaxation. With a few exceptions, the only victorious post-revolutionary society they knew from direct experience was Cuban socialism.

Che Guevara's early affinity with Marxism-Leninism and Fidel Castro's post-1959 communism (and dependency on Soviet aid and support) had greatly influenced the course of the Cuban Revolution.[32] Che Guevara had been in charge of the political education of the guerrilla forces and also served as a field commander of the Cuban revolutionaries. The guerrilla campaign with Fidel as strategist and Che Guevara as campaign hero, along with Raúl Castro's rapid forging of the Fuerzas Armadas Revolucionarias into a formidable military force, generated a profound respect for Cuba among successive generations of leftist-nationalists throughout Latin America.[33] Castro's routing of US forces at the Bay of Pigs confirmed his iconic status. Guevara was a prolific writer who published extensively on guerrilla theory and who became the venerated guru of insurrectionist strategy. The high regard of Latin America's revolutionaries for the Cuban leadership meant that the Cuban model served for two decades as the living image of an ideal society for every leftist-nationalist insurgent. Being a revolutionary and identifying yourself as Marxist-Leninist thus came to be seen as one and the same thing.

Cuba's leadership exported its revolutionary model and strategy to other Latin American countries mainly through providing military training and advice and by making available the island's infrastructure as a safe haven and strategic rearguard. The presence of Cuban regular armed forces directly engaged in war situations only materialized in African countries (Szulc, 1986: 637 ff.). In Latin America, Cuban support for the emerging guerrilla movements in the 1960s had been more indirect. Castro's feeble backing of Che Guevara's Bolivian campaign had in fact been limited to dispatching a small contingent of individual Cuban war veterans, including comandantes, who were disguised as Bolivians.

Cuba's support of the Central American *guerrilleros* was, though steadfast and continuous, basically restricted to providing military training and political and military strategic advice. Given the age and the nearly legendary status of Fidel Castro, he assumed something of a fatherly role vis-à-vis the Central American comandantes.

Che Guevara's writings on guerrilla strategy, his personal record in guerrilla combat, and his heroic death after being captured in battle, along with his qualities of will power, courage, self-sacrifice and uncompromising dedication to the revolutionary cause made him something of a civil saint among Latin American revolutionaries. Nearly all the comandantes that I interviewed acknowledged the importance of Fidel and Che as role models. In the 1970s, young recruits of the FSLM solemnly declared their loyalty 'before Fatherland, history and Che Guevara'.

The Salvadoran and Nicaraguan guerrilla movements had their own national heroes: Farabundo Martí and Sandino respectively. They were the men who, as revered heroes of the popular resistance movements in the 1930s, gave their names to guerrilla movements. But Che Guevara had been the role model of eternal youth, the archetypical *guerrillero* whom they remembered reading about during their own youth, whereas the Central American idols were adored leaders of the past who had been dead for many years. Fidel Castro was a living legend, still in power, who had been the victorious strategist of the first successful Latin American socialist revolution. Fatherly Fidel would remain an icon throughout the decades of the Central American wars. The halo of Fidel and Che and of other leaders of the Cuban Revolution also is revealed by the choice of the war pseudonyms of comandantes, guerrilla officers and recruits. Salvadoran member of the *comandancia general* Eduardo Sancho chose 'Fermán Cienfuegos' as his *nom de guerre*. Luis Santa Cruz, who took the name of 'Santiago' in honour of the massacres carried out in the indigenous village of Santiago Atitlán[34] and who later made Santiago his legal name, comments in his memoirs on the evolution of war pseudonyms from the 1970s to the 1990s. These names were at first drawn from Mexican and Cuban guerrilla comandantes like Camilo, Emiliano, Ernesto and Fidel or from biblical figures like Aarón, Abraham, Isaías, Jeremías, Oseas and Tomás, these latter choices reflecting the influence of liberation theology. In the early to mid-1990s, popular adopted names were Antonio Banderas and Mike Tyson, a change he attributes to the recruitment of a new generation of fighters raised in refugee camps, as well as to a loss of deep-rooted conviction at the end of the war.[35] He also stresses the enduring influence of Che Guevara and Fidel Castro on the Guatemalan *comandancia general*. A doctor by profession, Santa Cruz uses the term 'Fidel syndrome':

> Fidel Castro and Ernesto Guevara de la Serna are the revolutionary figures who are an inevitable and fundamental point of reference for all those in Latin America ... I remember that there was a poster that was obligatory in the room of any young person with progressive ideas or who dreamed of a better world. It was that photo of Korda, wasn't it? The photo of Che wearing the beret – I had my poster at home. Well then, after having joined the struggle and gone off to fight, there was no way that I could not listen to all of Fidel's speeches on Radio Havana. In addition, on Radio Havana there was a special programme that was called 'Voices of the Revolution'. And for many years on that programme, the only voice that one could hear was that of Fidel. His voice ended up multiplying and became 'voices' [laughs].
>
> [Che is the] symbol of rebellion, of ideologically driven struggle, of an uncompromising austerity. Then there was Fidel: very intelligent, a very wise man, someone who was knowledgeable about every possible subject and who in addition was an admirable military strategist.... In the daily life of guerrilla warfare, the one who had to be emulated was Che. Because this is what demanded the greatest level of sacrifice. And Fidel you really had to see as more of the total leader, capable of commanding united action, of proposing the needed strategy, and of generating enthusiasm about that action among everyone who followed him.... As far as the concrete reality of the Guatemalan revolution goes, I don't think anyone rose to the level of achieving anything remotely comparable to what Fidel and Che accomplished. It's one thing to want to be like them. It's another thing to realistically be able to do this.[36]

Splinter Parties and Enduring Loyalties

In Santa Cruz de Quiché, capital of the Guatemalan department El Quiché, where there were brutal massacres during the war, there is a sinister military museum in the Plaza Central that commemorates the armed forces' successful counterinsurgency campaigns. Admission is free of charge, and visitors are expected to display an appropriately reverential attitude. On one of the walls there is a world map, on which there are painted gigantic red arrows that are intended to show the various loci of the global communist conspiracy to destroy Guatemala and other countries of Latin America. As depicted on the map, centres of this plot included the Soviet Union, Maoist China, Eastern bloc nations, Vietnam, Albania and, of course, Cuba, all fighting shoulder to shoulder in support of the efforts of Guatemalan guerrilla forces to overthrow the country's democracy, protected by a heroic military dictatorship. This schema of a many-headed world communist hydra poised to crush a lonely outpost of Latin American democracy is a grotesque distortion of reality.

The Central American guerrilla movements, small as they were in the beginning, acted primarily on their own. Cuba was a source of great support, and after 1979 the fledgling Sandinista government also helped the Salvadoran guerrillas. However, the long gestation of each of the insurgent movements transpired without any outside intervention. In Guatemala, as well as in El Salvador and in Nicaragua, the guerrilla movements initially surfaced as minuscule splinter groups with even smaller military wings. A small group of revolutionaries were the founding members of what were initially very small politico-military organizations. In a certain sense, each group was a small fiefdom, each under the authority of strong personalities, the *comandantes-en-jefe*. Isolated from the outer world, these small movements in fact constituted the kind of 'total institutions' so brilliantly described by Goffman (1991). These are social configurations wherein all significant spheres of life depend on, and are controlled by, those in charge of the institution. Examples are asylums, prisons, religious convents, mining towns, garrison cities, military barracks – and guerrilla encampments. The *raison d'être*, the places where one sleeps and lives, the daily routine, food, clothing and uniforms, recreation, every important and trivial aspect of life, are all directly controlled by the comandante. The comandante is transformed into a powerful decision-maker with executive, legislative and judicial power over the very lives of those under his command.

The arbitrary exercise of authority by comandantes was perhaps the darkest aspect of the guerrilla movement. In the Maya highlands the term *señores de horca y cuchillo* (men with pitchforks and knives) is generally reserved for the almighty landowners who until modern times ruled over every sphere of their peons' lives. Victor Ferrigno, a former member of the Guatemalan EGP *dirección nacional*, uses this same term to characterize the absolute power of the comandantes of guerrilla armies.[37] At least during the early years of operation of the Central American guerrilla groups, each comandante functioned as lord and judge as well as a guerrilla commander – he thus held *de facto* civil and military authority over each of his subordinates. In some instances a kind of personality cult developed, as in the case of the Salvadoran FPL. Krauss (1991: 90) compared the group dynamic with that of a messianic religious cult when he visited the villages under control of the FPL, whose comandante was Cayetano Carpio (Marcial), in 1981:

> At least three times a day, in every village behind the lines, guerrillas, militiamen, and supporters lined up in neat rows to dutifully recite the incantation: 'Comandante, Solo Hay Uno, Marcial! Comandante [There Only Is One, Marcial! Comandante]...' They would go for a minute or so, never breaking the repetitious monotone. The rebels treated Marcial as a prophet, not as a human being.

In nearly all guerrilla groups, controversies arose early on about the correct party line, and schisms and disagreements developed regarding strategy and tactics. There were endless debates about the revolutionary potential of workers and *campesinos*, the class consciousness of the indigenous Maya, the relationship between intellectuals and comandantes, and the differences between democratic centralism and social democracy. Strangely enough, there appears to be no record of discussions of the future post-war society or of the merits of socialism.

During the early years of the guerrilla movements internal discipline was maintained, and internal disputes settled, in a variety of different ways. Of the first fifteen members of the Guatemalan EGP, two were executed as deserters and traitors (Payeras, 2002: 68–71, 165–9). Matters were eventually resolved by various disciplinary measures, with expulsions occasionally occurring. There also were instances when executions were ordered by the comandante. Ferrigno, who had escaped an execution attempt by his former EGP comrades-in-arms, comments:

> It was the field commanders who made the decisions. This frequently resulted in recourse to execution in lieu of arguments as a way of settling debates. This is nothing other than summary justice, with no possibility of presenting a defence, and no due process – in a context in which there were numerous informers. So, how does one make an insufficiently trained comandante understand the difference between a spy and a principled political dissenter? It is a complex, complicated issue.[38]

In El Salvador the bizarre trial and execution in May 1975 of Roque Dalton, one of the greatest poets of twentieth-century Central America,[39] who was accused of being a triple-agent of the CIA, the KGB and Cuban intelligence service, caused a split in the constituent parties of the FMLN (Gonzalez, 1994: 116 ff., Sancho, 2003: 100–110).[40] Sancho, one of the five members of the Salvadoran *comandancia general*, characterizes the fragmentation of the revolutionary movements as follows:

> But then there was the historic event of Roque's death. We then split up, in 1975, the ERP split up into the ERP and the RN. This is when the diaspora began – the diaspora of the left. Everything splintered, we lost our strategic vision. The Roque business was in May of 1975. By June, we had already splintered. What I mean is that between 1975 and 1979 the political-unionist movement was completely divided. We were transformed into sects – political sects. And it was worse, because we were Marxists. So we were even more sectarian than before. These were years of division and dispersion.[41]

Humberto Ortega also remembers the sectarian and dogmatic character of the three former factions of the Nicaraguan FSLN. He even explains the mutual distrust that prevailed among the leaders of the different *frentes* when they met after the victory in Managua (1979), describing it as an outgrowth of the sect-like atmosphere within the guerrilla movement during those times.[42] It also was a characteristic of the constituent parts of what later became the Guatemalan URNG. After clandestinely returning from his (first) exile in Mexico, in the early 1970s, Rodrigo Asturias was originally to take command of the south-western FAR forces in Guatemala. He founded ORPA after being confronted with a situation where the thin line between half-organized guerrilla warfare and social banditry had already been crossed by the time he arrived. He recalls the situation as follows:

> We ended up having a disagreement. The disagreement was mainly a result of conceptual problems that in 1972 led to a split. We arrived in two villages near the Bocacosta. We found that the situation there was very complicated. Afterwards, we would come to define it as an area that was in a state of political, ideological and military decomposition. And in that area there was a regional base of the FAR that was called the Regional de Occidente [Western Regional Base] which had been characterized by violence ... they had come to employ terrorist practices on the local population ... Their policy of executions meant that anyone who might become an enemy, whether he was a worker or a landowner, had to be liquidated. So small mobile patrols drove through the villages, determining who would be the following month's victims – these names were written down. I have a document that shows that in one month – in one month – thirty-five persons were shot. There was a total political breakdown. The struggle of the poor against the rich was a pretext for settling a lot of personal problems. If the people made insinuations or thought someone had robbed them, they could kill them. And the other practice ... was to gather together the population of a village and to have them kill two or three cows, and then distribute the different parts of the cow – the large chunks of meat. This was seen as restitution – as a return of what had been robbed before ... I wrote a document titled 'Principles and Objectives' for that first meeting, as the [new] political plan.

> We managed to get out of that ugly situation by just talking it through. 'We can't go on with executions, or else we'll end up like the Mexican Revolution.' They had ended up as outlaws. We had to explain that a revolution meant something else and involved other things ... And the young people in many of the villages that had endured the system of terror began to support us. This later became our main source of support.[43]

Probably the most dramatic episode within any *comandancia general* or *dirección general* occurred in El Salvador with the murder of Comandante Mélida Anaya Montes (Ana Maria), followed by the suicide of the *comandante-en-jefe* of the FPL, Cayetano Carpio (Marcial).[44] His fellow member of the FMLN *comandancia general*, Francisco Jovel, remembers the tragic unfolding of events:

> The first political proposal of the FMLN was the formation of a broad-based government and was made during meetings at a fifteen-day conference [in Havana], held by those of us who were political and military leaders. At that conference, the strongest arguments against the idea that we incorporate a stance in favour of a position of negotiated political settlement were voiced by Cayetano Carpio. It was there, beginning with those debates, that the differences between Cayetano Carpio and Comandante Ana María – or rather Mélida Anaya Montes – first arose. She was someone especially in favour of incorporating a negotiated political solution into our general strategy. Cayetano was opposed to this. His view was that the war ought to be viewed as a long-term war, a popular and prolonged war, and that negotiations would only disfigure the revolutionary nature of any victories that were achieved. Afterwards Ana María went off to Vietnam; she no longer met face-to-face with Cayetano Carpio. And Fidel Castro was one of the people who did the most to try to convince Cayetano Carpio that incorporating the strategy of a negotiated political solution was the right thing to do. At those meetings, some of which were private, with Cayetano, and at others in the presence of the *comandancia general* of the FMLN, I actually personally witnessed the efforts of Fidel Castro to change the point of view – one that I would call very fundamentalist – of Marcial. After Ana María returned from Vietnam, those differences led to Cayetano's stupid act – to the cowardly murder of Ana María. And of course he would later pay the price of that murder with his own suicide.[45]

In Nicaragua, the FSLN was also torn apart by a splintering process in the mid-1970s. A fierce debate about revolutionary strategy and tactics resulted in the development of three different factions around the time of Carlos Fonseca's death. Differences similar to those in El Salvador arose regarding strategy: to opt for a prolonged war scenario and follow the classic *guevarista* formula of rural guerrilla warfare or to place greater emphasis on the organization of the revolutionary masses, the proletariat and the *campesinos.*[46] As already mentioned in the previous chapter, a third Tendencia Tercerista[47] dismissed out of hand the *guevarista* doctrine, declaring that the emphasis on rural guerrilla warfare had been misplaced and advocating instead a concentration of guerrilla forces in cities and the fomenting of popular urban revolts. Largely as a result of Fidel Castro's efforts to bring about reconciliation, the movement was reunited at a March 1979 conference in Panama a couple of months before the final Sandinista triumph. The former factions, however, remained intact. During the liberation of Managua, the peak period of the Sandinista guerrilla campaign in July 1979, the leaders and the subaltern comandantes of the three constituent tendencies entered the city as heads of their own battle groups and guerrilla columns. They did not know who was who and they distrusted one another as well. When in the late 1980s the director of the Instituto de Estudios Sandinistas invited the members of the *dirección nacional* to discuss the former differences and to define the fault lines at the time of the schism, no one could adequately explain what specific issues had been at stake.[48] Eventually the three tendencies would more or less coalesce during the final period of Sandinista rule.

Yet the differences in Nicaragua among the various factions implied personal preferences and bonds of loyalty that endured for many years, and the equilibrium between the former competing tendencies was often a precarious one. The Salvadoran FMLN and the Guatemalan URNG were also umbrella organizations during the war years – marriages of convenience. All internal disputes were for the moment swept under the rug and territorial command arrangements were made. At the level of the *comandancia general*, strategic decisions were discussed and agreed upon. The umbrella confederation of the constituent political and military organizations also served well in diplomacy vis-à-vis third parties, and in fund-raising activities by solidarity groups in Western Europe, the Scandinavian countries and North America. Nevertheless, the various guerrilla groups and their comandantes were regularly at odds with one another and the possibility of ruptures along factional lines was ever present. As will be shown in the following chapters, there were indeed long-term consequences of these differences.

3

Inside the Guerrilla

Military officers are career professionals. Guerrilla comandantes, by contrast, often lack formal military training. Army officers alternate their field periodically with training at special schools and elite academies. Guerrilla leaders generally acquire their training and experience through a combination of ad hoc study and experience by trialling in the field. Irregular warfare is thus a matter of reinvention of strategic principles and tactical manoeuvring. Regular armies are characterized by an elaborate division of labour and a reliance on specialization: high-level strategy, logistical operations, financial planning, transport and communications each represent separate areas of a conventional military force. In guerrilla armies, there is much less reliance on specialized expertise, and it is often the case that highly important missions that, in a regular army, would be put in the hands of specialists with years of training will, in a guerrilla force, be entrusted to talented amateurs with little or no formal training in the matter at hand.

This chapter describes how the three guerrilla movements, through a process that can best be described as trial and error, shaped their war strategy and operational tactics, how they financed their campaigns, and how they secured weapons and carried out logistical planning. Financing the long wars was an arduous enough task for governments like those of Nicaragua in the 1970s and El Salvador in the 1980s, which could rely on supplementary taxation and generous American support. Financing the irregular but equally protracted guerrilla campaigns was infinitely more difficult for guerrilla leaders. Logistics and communications were complicated as well; the regular armed forces clearly had the upper hand in these matters. However, the guerrilla forces enjoyed the enormous advantage of relying on highly motivated volunteer combatants and of receiving generous moral and material support from important sectors of the local population.[1] How did they maintain their morale? How did the leadership meet the day-to-day challenges of feeding and training their fighting men and women? How did guerrilla forces sustain their good relations with the local population and their recruiting bases? In terms of strategy and tactics, logistics and communications, recruitment and morale we will see both striking differences and remarkable similarities among the three guerrilla organizations, as well as their constituent parties and factions.

Guerrilla Strategy in Practice

The basic concept of guerrilla strategy in Guatemala and Nicaragua, the two countries with the longest guerrilla traditions, was initially a rather unstable combination of rural *foquismo* – the Che Guevara-like rural guerrilla operations – combined with attempts at urban insurrection, while the relationship of the insurgent organizations to national civil society, trade unions and popular movements was often unclear. Only in the late 1970s was there a stronger emphasis on the role of the urban population and significant popular support. At that time, the FSLN was preparing for urban uprisings and the Guatemalan guerrillas were launching their major campaigns during the repressive regime of military president Lucas García (1978-82). It is unquestionable that, without the support of the rural population, the incipient guerrilla struggle would have been quickly extinguished. When the Salvadoran leadership prepared for civil war between 1974 and 1981, the five constituent organizations were supported by both rural and urban popular organizations. In the 1970s, the five organizations of the FMLN had always been rooted in both the urban and the rural milieu. Several organizations – the ERP, the RN and the PCTR – had placed a strong emphasis on urban guerrilla warfare from the very beginning. Even though the first offensive on San Salvador in 1981 ultimately failed, it was clear that the insurrectionists enjoyed broad-based support among the general population. The immediate impact of the Salvadoran guerrillas stands in stark contrast with the long-term, and only intermittently successful, implementation of 'rural encapsulation' by the clandestine Guatemalan and Nicaraguan politico-military organizations in the 1960s and most of the 1970s.

In Nicaragua, the possibility of an urban insurrection in the country's capital had never materialized during the sporadic and unsuccessful guerrilla campaigns mounted over a period of twenty years until the final Sandinista victory in 1979. In Cuba the revolution was consolidated in 1959 by the final revolt among the population in Havana after a series of victorious rural and urban guerrilla campaigns that led to the implosion of Batista's dictatorship. Twenty years later, a more or less comparable sequence of rebellions initiated by the guerrilla leadership materialized in Nicaragua. Dictator Somoza was forced to flee, leaving behind him a demoralized National Guard hounded on all sides by both the small victorious guerrilla *frentes* and the popular militias. The *comandancia general* in El Salvador twice launched a campaign to initiate such a popular rebellion in San Salvador: prematurely and unsuccessfully in 1981 and then ending in a military stalemate in 1989. The Salvadoran armed institution was able to absorb the assault, but the atrocities committed by government troops undermined the legitimacy of the army's efforts to continue fighting the war. The Salvadoran guerrilla strategy primarily emphasized rural operations while secondarily developing a capability to eventually seize control of the capital. In Guatemala there was the latent potential for an urban insurrection and a final revolutionary victory in the early 1980s. However, the overwhelmingly brutal and relentless counterinsurgency campaign between 1980 and 1983 forced the URNG into a defensive posture. The leadership continued to resist, holding out hope for ultimate victory: they never regarded themselves as losing the war. It was only after fifteen years that the long war of attrition finally ended following lengthy peace negotiations.

The Nicaraguan urban insurrection

In Nicaragua a radical and conscious break with the *guevarista foquismo* strategy dramatically altered the course of the revolutionary process. For fifteen years the catchword of the FSLN had been: 'We will bury the heart of the enemy in the mountains.' Víctor Tirado, one of the three comandantes who with the two Ortega brothers headed the 'modernist' *insurreccionista* or *tercerista* faction of the FSLN, remarked that what happened instead was that 'The enemy buried us in the mountains.'[2] Carlos Fonseca had previously expressed misgivings about the wisdom of the predominant rural guerrilla strategy; in 1974 he asked Humberto Ortega to present a position paper in Havana about scenarios of urban insurrection. As Ortega recalls:

> While we were in Cuba, Carlos Fonseca created several working groups. I was put in charge of the group that developed our insurrectional theory. ... I learned from the insurrections that took place in Europe after the First World War. I used two important books to develop my theory: one by an Italian named Emilio Lussu and another by the pseudonymous A. Neuberg. [I wrote the text] between 1974 and 1977; it began circulating within the Frente in 1977; it consisted of 28 pages.[3]

This pamphlet gave rise to a fierce debate within ranks of the FSLN and contributed to the forming of the three factions mentioned in the previous chapter. Yet it also led to the emergence of a new urban-oriented strategy and the *tercerista* faction's creation of the *frente interno* [urban *frente*] in Nicaragua's principal cities. Joaquín Cuadra Lacayo, the leader of this new *frente*, remembers:

> [This meant] concentrating forces and human resources in urban centres – so that the guerrilla forces in the mountains cleared out. It was over. No one was left and everyone was sent to the urban centres. The people had to be organized so that they could carry out the insurrection. This wasn't something that could be done by ... the scattered *campesinos*. ... We decided to change course almost immediately – even dissolving our Northern Frente. We were transferred in order to take up commands in the cities – in the Urban Frente. So it wasn't the Southern Frente, which was organized like a regular army ... but the people themselves, you know. For me, this was an important change, very drastic: being one week in the mountains with a full beard, not having bathed for four months, like a typical mountain guerrilla fighter – and then the next week being in Managua, commanding the Urban Frente, disguised as an engineer, driving a pickup truck with the name of a consulting firm, carrying a bunch of blueprints and pencils, wearing an aluminium helmet, etc.[4]

This change in strategy determined the outcome of the war. In the popular neighbourhoods the FSLN leadership began to ambush street patrols of the National Guard and achieved the sympathy and support of the public and the spontaneous recruitment of young militia recruits.

> But who knew how to mount an insurrection? We didn't have a clue. There was no guidebook or manual – no procedure to follow. In one way or another we would fight the National Guard – ambush them in one of the poor city neighbourhoods. And the people would come out and shout in support. But when we wanted to leave we weren't able to, because all of the people were there. So we stayed and did work among the people: organizing, teaching as best we could. Everyone cheered us on, gave us something to eat and drink, etc. The bond between the fighter and the people is something that arises spontaneously in this way.[5]

The final phase, between 1978 and 1979,[6] consisted of a sequence of urban uprisings, organized by the Urban Frente with growing popular support and hundreds, later thousands, of popular militias joining the skeleton staff of the FSLN in cities like Managua, Masaya, Granada, León, Estelí and Chinandega.

> The plan for Managua was the most complex of all. For many different reasons, it was the eastern neighbourhoods of the city that were chosen [as a base for our operations]: they were more combative, had a social consciousness and there were more people there. In addition, these are neighbourhoods that were criss-crossed by streams. So there were bridges here and there. It was easy to block off a bridge and to stay and to take up positions at a point where no vehicles would be able to pass by. This was something that only those looking at a detailed map of Managua would know about [shows map]: at this or that intersection in such and such a neighbourhood there is a stream here or there. One has to construct another barricade and then extend it as much as possible. Three guerrilla men here, a hundred more militia fighters there. This is how we created the plan for Managua.[7]

The original plan called for a quick three-day campaign in Managua. Instead, it turned into seventeen days of heavy combat. Afterwards the Urban Frente retreated to Masaya and Granada, regrouped and then re-entered Managua together with other FSLN units.[8] Meanwhile, the National Guard, demoralized, had left the city, with neighbourhood militias taking over the headquarters of the Somoza regime and the Guard:

> Somoza had fled. So when [our] first organized columns entered Managua the National Guard had already abandoned their barracks, including headquarters – where Somoza's bunker was located. When we arrived, there were hundreds of people, militia fighters who had armed themselves [with the firearms that had been left behind]. There were thousands of uniforms on the ground; people were getting dressed, grabbing food and arms, choosing among dozens of rifles and even machine guns. Ordinary people were stocking up on arms, looking for whatever they could get their hands on [laughs]. So the first thing we did was put up a fence in order to prevent even more people from

> coming and taking what the National Guard had left behind [laughs]. These days were characterized by widespread anarchy. Each neighbourhood organized itself separately, with its own militia leader. Each neighbourhood had a militia commander, along with its own password to determine who could or could not enter the area. From there to the airport you needed to go through twenty different zones – it was impossible. After five days we began the process of disarming the population.[9]

The Nicaraguan guerrilla triumph, the second successfully concluded guerrilla campaign in Latin America following the Cuban experience twenty years before, can be explained as resulting from a particular constellation of factors: the innovative concept of urban guerrilla strategy that broke with the conventional *foquismo* wisdom; the adaptive and dynamic urban guerrilla leadership; a brilliantly crafted and executed two-year guerrilla campaign (1978–79); the massive support of young urban militias; a multiclass alliance with other adversaries of Somoza; extensive popular support; declining international support for the discredited Somoza regime; and substantial assistance from other Central and Latin American governments.

The Salvadoran war zones

The Salvadoran FMLN leadership had the Nicaraguan urban insurrection in mind when, in January 1981, they launched an offensive against San Salvador, an operation that they optimistically termed the 'final offensive'.[10] Instead, it turned out to be merely the first battle in a war that would last for twelve long years:

> The offensive of 1981 involved coming at them with whatever we had – against the army soldiers – in order to cause casualties. We had to stop the massacres. Because the security forces, the army and the military commanders were prepared to draw up a list every night in order to determine who would be killed. But they were not familiar with real-life combat. They were surprised as well – by our boldness, you could say.[11]

The intention of accelerating an instant mass upheaval and final revolution failed. The FMLN succeeded in occupying a couple of secondary cities; there was also a revolt in a military installation in Santa Ana, the nation's second-largest city. The offensive, however, was the result of an overconfident belief in the spontaneous revolutionary enthusiasm of a badly armed population and badly armed guerrilla cadres. A general insurrection did not occur. The FMLN retreated from the larger cities and consolidated 'controlled territories' in the north and east of the country, as well as in the south-eastern region near the capital: Morazán, Chalatenango, Guazapa, Usultán, Cabañas and San Vicente, with *frentes* within a single day's march (Benítez Mataút, 1989: 192–3). The areas along the Salvadoran–Honduran frontier were disputed regions where both Salvadoran and Honduran forces were present. In the other pockets of resistance scattered through this very small country, the army regularly tried to invade, always with limited success. Army assaults generally consisted of search-and-destroy missions that were followed by immediate retreats from the areas of operation. In the FMLN territories, the population heavily supported the guerrillas and the incoming army detachments were always met with ambushes and, later in the war, with mines.

During most of the war, the FMLN relied heavily on rural-based guerrilla forces, operating through surprise attacks, night manoeuvres and ambushes.[12] At times, battalion-size guerrilla formations were deployed to attack urban army garrisons, but when the US financing and training resulted in much better logistics, equipment and air support for the Salvadoran armed institution, the FMLN turned once again to the proven hit-and-run operations by platoon-sized units, ambushing and destroying the infrastructure of the army and the government in 'enemy territory' during the final years of the war. It was in this way that a military stalemate was reached between the armed forces and the guerrilla forces, the latter strongly supported by populations in their rearguard territories that harboured bitter memories of decades-long terror and atrocities on the part of the armed and security institutions. During the war years, the FMLN was always able to count on the sympathy of popular organizations, support which was evident in protest marches, rallies, work stoppages and strikes. The adherence on the part of a critical mass of Salvadorans – in San Salvador and elsewhere – to 'the cause of revolution' from the very start of the guerrilla campaign stood in stark contrast to the situation in both Guatemala and Nicaragua, countries where for a long time there was a heavy reliance on a rural *foquismo* strategy.

During most of the 1980s the FMLN thought that any prominent focus on urban guerrilla warfare would be too dangerous. However, by the end of 1981 the FMLN leadership had initiated the tactical use of Special Forces for rural *and* urban deployment, using a Vietnamese concept of permanent elite guerrilla units.[13] Urban commandos and special units received military training, first in Cuba, later in the controlled territories in El Salvador. Oscar Ortiz, the last comandante of the Special Forces, played a decisive role in the second assault on San Salvador in 1989. He remembers the brutal training regimen and the daily life of the suburban guerrillas:

> It required a lot of organization, a lot of discipline. You had to succeed in dealing with a series of situations that people thought were impossible. Such as swimming one or two kilometres. Like surviving with 200 or 300 men in a city controlled by the enemy. It was a matter of shattering myths. We could not shout, make fires or play music. At times, we could not even touch the leaves. ... The kind of fighter you needed was one who could also fight when he didn't have a gun – and even when he didn't have shoes; one who could go a day or two without any food. The key factor was not fear but rather the stamina needed to endure extreme conditions. The qualities needed in a guerrilla fighter of this sort are twofold: to be able to fight without [adequate] clothing, and to be able to not bathe for six or eight days, or even, as was the case with us in the final offensive, for twenty-five days. At that time we were equal to the task, and we didn't give a thought to whether we would be able to do it or not.[14]

The second and final offensive of November 1989 against the capital city was prepared with detailed planning.[15] The strategic aim was to establish guerrilla attack pockets in the popular neighbourhoods in the northern and eastern parts of San Salvador and to trigger a general revolt. An enormous amount of arms, ammunition, food and medicine was stockpiled to prevent a sudden shortage – as had happened during the final offensive of 1979 in Managua. The army command was surprised, not by the attack (intelligence reports had warned that the offensive was imminent) but by the deployment of such a substantial guerrilla force and by the widespread presence of fighters, even in the elite areas of San Benito and Escalón. Dagoberto Gutíerrez had even established his headquarters in the Sheraton Hotel. But there were some prominent gaps in the strategic plan. Francisco Jovel recounts how Fidel Castro attempted to express politely his own reservations.

> It was thought that with an effort of that magnitude, it was highly probable – almost certain – that the people would launch an uprising. It was then that Fidel Castro let it be known that he did not want to be seen as a pessimist. Still, despite the general enthusiasm and optimism and the fact that we were the ones who could best anticipate the reaction of the people, he thought that we needed to be prepared for the eventuality that our military effort would not lead to victory, but would instead improve the possibility of a negotiated agreement. And he also had other things to say about the guerrillas' specific military plans. For example, he was very insistent about military units needing to be deployed in order to prevent the government troops from mobilizing. And he said he thought that the current plans were deficient in terms of providing adequate control of the roads, something about which – and I say this in the spirit of self-criticism – he was entirely right.[16]

The plan also had underestimated the armed institution's use of air power; anti-aircraft weapons were almost completely absent and the FMLN had not succeeded in destroying the air force bases. The population did not revolt on a massive scale. The military bombarded the FMLN pockets and brought in fresh units near the capital and from outside, leading to heavy casualties among both the guerrilla forces and the general population. Finally, the guerrillas opted for a withdrawal after having established a kind of military impasse. In frustration, the army command ordered the assassination of six Jesuit priests, some of them renowned scholars in the UCA, whom they suspected of being the intellectual mentors of the FMLN.[17] The resulting indignation on the part of the international community led to a certain level of cooperation between the army leadership and the civilian presidency.[18] After the 1989 offensive, the leadership of both the armed institution and the FMLN were convinced that a military deadlock had been reached and that the only alternative was to negotiate the terms of a peace agreement.

The Salvadoran guerrilla campaign ended in a stalemate. A number of factors explain why the Salvadorans were not able achieve the kind of total victory that the Sandinistas had managed in Nicaragua: the immediate and plentiful US financial support of the Salvadoran army, including provision of both sophisticated equipment and training programmes; the absolute ruthlessness of the army command; the repeated collapse of an urban offensive in San Salvador – in 1981 due to poor preparation and in 1989 as a result of the lack of massive popular support. Still other factors help explain the fact that the guerrilla forces were able to hold out for so long in the face of such disadvantageous circumstances: the pragmatic style of leadership of the FMLN, skilfully outmanoeuvring the army; the continuing popular support in the countryside; the highly developed 'diplomacy' of the Frente; and the material and moral support provided by the Sandinista government and the Cuban leadership.

The Guatemalan failure of urban guerrilla operations and protracted defensive warfare

The first decade of the guerrilla campaigns in Guatemala was basically committed to rural campaigns, in the eastern and, to a lesser extent, in the northern regions. Urban guerrilla bases were not completely ignored in the 1960s, but the role of these urban cadres was relegated to that of providing infrastructure like safe houses and provision of logistics and finances (in practice, organizing robberies and kidnappings) in Guatemala City.[19] In August 1968, when Camillo Sánchez, comandante of the FAR, was arrested, the urban guerrillas tried to set up a prisoner exchange by attempting to kidnap US ambassador Gordon Mein, who was killed during the action. The prominence of rural guerrilla operations remained a feature of the 36-year Guatemalan insurgency.

There was a time when the Guatemalan guerrillas seemed to be thinking of forcibly overthrowing the military dictatorship. This was during the years of the brutally repressive government of the García brothers (1978–82), both of whom were army generals – President Romeo Lucas García and Army Chief of Staff Benedicto Lucas García – and then later during the government of Rios Montt (1982–83).[20] It was during these times that the guerrillas, after years of preparations and clandestine organizing activities among the Maya *campesino* organizations and the urban trade unions, launched successful military operations, gaining control of considerable regional infrastructure. EGP, ORPA, the FAR and even the PGT, the small Communist Party, had established their own internal coordination system of guerrilla warfare. ORPA launched its first public operation on 18 September 1979, two months after the FSLN victory in Nicaragua:

> You see, nobody believes that we spent eight years in the preparation stage. There was never any action carried out [during that time]. We met with people, very informally, bringing them medicine. I functioned in the role of physician; in Mexico I had taken a crash course in medicine. There were times when I took medication to a distant village, walking for hours. We explained who we were. 'It's us. We're not the army. We're guerrillas'.... This is how the first generation of officers, commanders and ORPA cadres emerged. After being in the mountains for two years, we began to work in the city. We sent Marcos, the other founder of ORPA, to the capital..... I'm telling you that at that time we had four *frentes*; and of the four, we were able to put two in operation. We must have had 200 armed men in the various *frentes*, right? You see, we even had twenty-five comrades who had participated in the final offensive of Nicaragua. I sent a special artillery force, led by Marcos, to Nicaragua.[21]

The four guerrilla organizations, which for the most part operated independently of one another, tried to consolidate their own politico-military organizations, much like the constituent Salvadoran guerrilla organizations had done until merging to form the FMLN. Around 1980 and 1981, the EGP's guerrilla force numbered 5,000. In addition, there were another 50,000 fighters within the ranks of the EGP's allied militias. According to army intelligence 100,000 civilians were actively supporting the EGP. ORPA had 700 military members and 1,000 civilian members in its sister organization, Resistencia Campesina, providing logistical support. Army intelligence estimated the number of FAR soldiers at 500, with another 1,000 allied militia members.[22]

The most important underground organization in Guatemala, the Comité de Unidad Campesina (CUC), had started in 1974 as a clandestine group and was officially founded in April 1978 as a mass organization of rural workers, landless people and indigenous Maya *campesinos* – in the southern departments some Ladino *campesinos* were also members. Some of the founding members (e.g. Pablo Ceto, Víctor Ferrigno) were affiliated with the EGP. The CUC's organizational stronghold was in departments in the Maya Highland regions – especially in El Quiché, where the repression was extreme – and in the sugar-growing departments of the southern Bocacosta, where ORPA also had a strong presence.[23] After organizing strikes, protest marches and, finally, a mass march on Guatemala City, the CUC was relentlessly persecuted by the military government and its allied death squads. In despair, hundreds, even thousands, of local Maya leaders and *campesinos* sought refuge by joining the EGP. The childhood and family history of Daniel Pascual, the present CUC coordinator (2007), who joined the EGP as a teenager, is representative of many who joined the Ejército Guerrillero de los Pobres at that time:

> My family joined the CUC, but quickly made contact with the EGP. My sister and my brother joined the guerrillas; my father worked with the CUC. Then, at the beginning of 1980, came the secret anti-communist army death squads. They tortured

and murdered seven people. They put a sign in front of our house that read 'These are the first communists'.... I remember that there were brutal massacres at that time. In San Antonio, eighty-seven people died in one day; I saw the men being dragged away and being searched while the children and women were killed.... The smell of corn mixed with the smoke ... shouts were heard ... there was a cloud covering everything. And afterwards we went to see the dead bodies. This spurred my other two brothers to join the guerrillas as well. During that year, my uncle, a deputy in the National Congress, was murdered. During that time, two other uncles of mine were also murdered. At the end of 1982 my sister, the first one who had joined the guerrillas, disappeared. We didn't find her body; we didn't find out what happened; we never found out anything about my sister. Never. She rebelled and joined the guerrillas when she was 14 years old. There was a double blow because, within the next year, my brother died in battle, in Nebaj. And six months after that, my other brother Estéban disappeared. He had been a lieutenant, and then a captain [in the EGP...]. In 1981 the CUC began to disappear. The repression was very harsh: against my father, against my whole family. I went away with my mother; I was the last one left in my family. My mother was left homeless and devastated after the second massacre of San Antonio. It was the civilian patrols, *comisionados militares*[24] and the army [that were responsible for the massacres]. It was a total annihilation. They surrounded us and burned down the forests.... And what hurt the most, I remember, is that several children were with us. They were so small that they weren't able to continue climbing. When their mother left them behind they fell straight into the flames. And the army was right there behind them. There was gunfire and shouting. And by accident my brother went off in the other direction [and disappeared in the flames]. The crops burned, the women were murdered, the children were injured and killed, having walked barefoot amid the flames. I'm telling you: for me there is no other hell [cries]. The pain endured in that place was something out of hell. That was hell; I don't think that there is any other hell on this earth. I'm telling you that it isn't fair that we, the indigenous peoples, were not only massacred and murdered, but that we were also told that there is another place that is called hell. This isn't possible. Is there some other hell? It isn't possible. I've already been through hell over there [cries].[25]

The urban guerrillas, who functioned mostly as a support organization that provided safe houses, clandestine printing offices and magazines, also had armed commando units that attacked military installations, assaulting high-ranking military officers and kidnapping members of the elite for ransom. In retrospect, Payeras (1987, 1991), who was the second-in-command of the EGP in the initial years, characterized the Guatemalan urban guerrilla strategy as incoherent and inadequate in terms of the guerrilla movement's own declared objectives. In 1981–82, they in turn were hunted down and eventually destroyed by government security forces. As part of their counterinsurgency campaign, Guatemalan army intelligence made use of a computer program developed by Israel's Mossad that was designed to detect 'safe houses' through recording significant increases in electricity consumption in urban residences.[26]

> You see, between 1979 and 1981 we had more than 800 urban combatants. We had managed to build up a very large urban network, organized in compartmentalized units in which no more than two people met, and these two would together recruit up to ten people. It was a powerful structure that included an intelligence service. But after the [army's counter-] offensive in 1981, when all of the houses were destroyed, we had almost sixty combat casualties. Nobody surrendered – they fought to the death. ... We lost the entire urban infrastructure. Houses were destroyed within a matter of days, and everything was captured on television. The time of the [army's counteroffensive] in the city, in 1981, was personally the most difficult. It was a desperate time. Within a month I ended up with a head full of white hair.[27]

Around 1984 the urban networks were re-established. ORPA even had informants within the advisory staff of the presidency and in the powerful CACIF;[28] the FAR had reorganized its urban networks as well.[29] But the URNG never completely recovered its strength and would never again attempt to implement a guerrilla strategy with mass support. Instead, a new emphasis was placed on military training and military strategy. The *comandancia general* moved to Mexico City. Logistics was improved and long-distance communication technology was enhanced. In addition, methods of weapons transport were diversified. Nevertheless, while the URNG leadership concentrated on a military strategy and prepared for a long, protracted war that could be sustained for ten, or even twenty years,[30] the guerrillas gradually lost ground. During the war's final years, both the direct relationship and formal contacts with the old and new popular organizations seemed gradually to erode. By the late 1980s and early 1990s, the UNRG's fighting spirit itself seemed to be on the wane, as it engaged in campaigns of ad hoc assaults and hit-and-run ambushes. After the atrocious counterinsurgency campaigns during the governments of Lucas García and Rios Montt, the UNRG was always on the defensive.

Eventually, the Guatemalan guerrilla forces lost the war. The situation deteriorated slowly due to a number of different factors: the extremely brutal nature of the counterinsurgency campaigns of the armed forces; the massive use of paramilitary forces, whose wanton violence devastated the support of the Maya communities; the reliance on guerrilla operations in the countryside after the loss of the urban guerrilla infrastructure; the emphasis on the purely military aspects of the guerrilla campaigns while disregarding the importance of building relationships with the Maya communities and the popular organizations; the lack of organizational unity of the URNG until the late 1980s; and the half-hearted support of the Cuban and Nicaraguan allies. Each of these factors will be addressed in the following section.

Arms, Financing and Logistics

While fighting the guerrilla campaigns in the 1970s, the Nicaraguan FSLN was always short of both money and weapons. Some arms were obtained on the national and international black market. Another source of arms acquisition was those weapons that had been captured from the National Guard. Individual and collective contributions from overseas were a third source of both arms and money. In addition, the FSLN obtained funds by carrying out bank robberies. Humberto Ortega was among the prisoners detained for robbing a bank in Costa Rica. Yet another source of aid were periodic small gifts from local sympathizers – in the form of cash, food, clothing or housing – and a series of spectacular raids: on the town house of 'Chema' Castillo in 1974 and on the National Congress in 1978, where sufficient hostages were seized to obtain a ransom of several million dollars. In 1978 Resistencia Nacional, one of the five factions of the future FMLN, having amassed a considerable war chest, contributed $5 million to the FSLN on behalf of the Salvadoran guerrilla movement.[31] In fact, it was only in 1978 and 1979, when the FSLN had made an alliance with prominent members of Nicaragua's civil society, and the prestige of the Grupo de los Doce helped win the support of Costa Rica, Cuba, Panamá and Venezuela, that a sufficiently regular flow of arms and money reached the Sandinista Frente in Nicaragua. These weapons were used to equip a more or less regular guerrilla army of 1,000 officers and troops – the Southern Frente – and to set up a national radio station.

After their victory in 1979, the Sandinista government created a formidable army with Cuban technical assistance and military aid from the Soviet Union and the Soviet bloc. General Humberto Ortega had signed an agreement with Soviet Marshall Dmitri Ustinov.[32] Nicaragua then became both the strategic rearguard and an important source of arms and equipment provision to the Salvadoran FMLN. The Guatemalan URNG was excluded from this revolutionary coalition. After secret negotiations among the Sandinistas, the United States and the Guatemalan government, the *comandancia general* of the URNG had inferred that any Sandinista transfer of arms to Guatemala would be understood by the other two parties as a *casus belli*. The URNG resented this exclusion, but was forced to live with it.[33] On the other hand, strong bonds were forged between the FMLN and the FSLN leadership during the 1980s.[34] Tomás Borge, the powerful FSLN interior minister, was a friend of the FMLN comandantes Cayetano Carpio, his successor Sanchez Cerén, and of Schafik Handal. The two military leaders of Nicaragua, Humberto Ortega and Cuadra Lacayo, developed a personal friendship with FMLN comandante Joaquín Villalobos, which resulted in a privileged access to arms for their Salvadoran *compañeros* guerrilla fighters.[35]

During the years before the guerrilla upsurge, the factions of the FMLN had built up a substantial war chest, mostly through robberies and kidnappings of family members of the Salvadoran oligarchy. Roberto Cañas describes these operations:

> The typical guerrilla fighter who joined an armed struggle during the early 1970s began to [conduct operations in which he could] capture weapons. So night watchmen would come – we call them *serenos* here. We would make sure that they had weapons, and we would carry out an operation – to capture the gun[s]. There were also pawnshops.... They sell weapons. This is because in El Salvador, in the country, people buy weapons. We began to familiarize ourselves with the weapons, to conduct armed propaganda – a Vietnamese concept of [armed] struggle. But the guerrillas in El Salvador began to carry out kidnappings and there were deaths within the most distinguished families of this country. Because the first money that financed the armed struggle in this country was money received through kidnappings. In the organization that I was involved in, we eventually accumulated $35 million. In order to carry out a struggle, you have to have funds. There was a lot of money here, a result of the fact that we were specialists when it came to kidnapping and robbing banks. Well, during the early years the most distinguished members of powerful families were kidnapped. Ernesto Regalado was kidnapped. He died. The Pomas, the De Solas: the most prestigious families of this country had members who were kidnapped. Millions of dollars [were paid as ransom]. And Swedish, Dutch and Japanese businessmen were in our jails. A lot of money [was extorted in] these kidnappings.[36]

During the war years, in the 1980s, the FMLN was generally well-equipped. In the early 1980s the war was mostly financed by local networks of sympathizers and 'war taxes' (crops, goods or money) collected from the more uncooperative sectors of the population.[37] Then Nicaraguan and some Cuban and Vietnamese arms poured in.[38] Cuba also offered technical assistance with communications and radio equipment. Radio Venceremos, a clandestine radio station that started in 1981, contributed much to solidify the internal cohesion of the Frente and to broadcast FMLN news bulletins to the outside world.[39] International solidarity organizations also contributed money. The FMLN had an excellent network of politico-diplomatic relations. This network generated international political support (most remarkably, French and Mexican recognition of the FMLN) and financial assistance. Guardado estimates that around 80 per cent of the war budget between 1981 and 1991 was acquired via Western solidarity committees:

> Financing was made possible during the initial years – until 1981 – as a result of kidnappings. From 1981 until the end of the war, financing was for the most part obtained from organizations – from allied groups all over the world. In Finland, the Netherlands, Sweden, Denmark, France, Germany, the USA – primarily Europe and the USA. This was where we got the money to finance, without exaggerating, at least 80 per cent of the war, from 1981 to 1991. That one German newspaper alone that was called *Weapons for El Salvador* delivered $3 million to us. That's why I told you: the political dimension during the entire war also allowed us to receive a certain amount of support that was never in danger of being cut off.[40]

The logistics of arms provision was always a top priority. The quality of arms and equipment improved considerably during the war. In 1980 and 1981 only 40 per cent of a typical guerrilla column of 100 men could be armed:

> Where did the weapons come from? There was a first batch that we bought from smugglers. But afterwards, they came from Ethiopia, Vietnam, Bulgaria and Czechoslovakia. Not from Russia. Russia bought all of our flights on Aeroflot. In a symbolic gesture, the Vietnamese delivered a boatload of American weapons. And afterwards, North Korea and East Germany gave us weapons. We brought back Russian rifles from these countries. And Nicaragua gave us a lot of weapons. There was the Belgian Light Automatic Rifle. And the Cubans gave us weapons as well.[41]

Later on, a typical Salvadoran column would have mortars, heavy machine guns and recoilless rifles at its disposal. Moroni

Bracamonte and Spencer (1995: 54–6) show photos depicting the development of weapons utilized by the main guerrilla forces in 1982, 1985 and 1990, with a notable improvement over time. Guardado points out that, in 1983 and 1985, considerable equipment was requisitioned after two successful raids on army depots. In the late 1980s armaments captured from paramilitary forces or police detachments by the guerrillas were destroyed; their combat quality was below the standards used by the FMLN. In 1988 arms were obtained on a regular basis from North Korea and East Germany. Ammunition was steadily acquired from Cuba and in later years in the United States as well. And during the last two years of the war, between 1990 and 1992, the political chaos and turmoil in Nicaragua after the electoral defeat of the Sandinista government made it easy to make a purchase or get a gift of large quantities of Soviet and Eastern bloc armaments.[42] During the offensive of 1989, the FMLN had painfully felt their lack of surface-to-air missiles:

> We thought that the main weakness of the guerrilla forces during the offensive of 1989 was not having enough missiles and bases to shoot down the helicopters of the government's army. [We] had suffered more than 400 casualties. Since the Sandinistas lost the elections [in 1990], the ranks of their army were in complete disarray. So then, even though we knew that it would create a major political and diplomatic problem but knowing that there would be no military intervention in Nicaragua, we went about acquiring, through various means, a variety of surface-to-air missiles from our numerous friends in the Sandinista army.... And the Americans began to threaten to remove the Sandinista army commanders.[43] That is why the Sandinistas began to force us to return the missiles to them. And we had to return a lot of them.... There were a lot that we did not turn over for the simple reason that we knew that they had lost track of exactly how many we had, and how many they themselves had. But for us, having these missiles was of inestimable strategic value during the [peace] negotiations.[44]

In Guatemala, the URNG was financed by comparable sources: 'war taxes' imposed on the proprietors and managers of the landed estates and the agro-industrial sugar complexes, a couple of small bank raids in the early years and then, increasingly, international solidarity funds. Rodrigo Asturias explains:

> To be honest, we began to finance our operations with small-scale robbery. The booty of the first hold-up was 10,000 quetzales. Later, we received donations of support. From overseas, we would at times get contributions of up to $50,000. With these donations, we began to create an urban infrastructure: in Guatemala, in Chiapas, in Mexico City. [The money was used for] safe houses, medical care, walkie-talkies, radio – later on for cellular phones. We even set up a radio station. International solidarity helped finance 'non-combatant operations'. And we charged 'war taxes', a political means of resolving part of the problem. I would guess that we managed funds in the amount of $20 million during that entire time.[45]

Faced with a lukewarm Cuban connection and a reluctant, even uncooperative, Sandinista government, the URNG factions turned to the Central American and North American black markets and, after the electoral defeat of the Sandinistas in 1990, to the demobilized Contras, who were very eager to sell their arms.

> After the Sandinista victory in 1979, we had tried to buy weapons from them. They refused [to sell]. It was then that we began to purchase weapons in the United States. We bought weapons on the open market, through intermediaries who were able to prove that they were [American] citizens. Those who did the buying were not suspicious characters; they were generally *internacionalistas* and American citizens. They had strong moral convictions and we owe a great deal to their efforts. First we warehoused the weapons in the USA. Then we transported them to Mexico and Costa Rica – by car and sometimes via mobile homes that had American licence plates. After travelling through Mexico, these vehicles could unload a cargo of 150 long rifles with 500,000 rounds of ammunition in El Quiché. ... After the Sandinistas were defeated, we again made a plea for solidarity. They said nothing – they rejected us yet again. Given the huge quantities of weapons on the black market, we decided to conspire against our reluctant Sandinista comrades. We also bought from the Contras. There was an opportunity to stockpile huge quantities. Each weapon was going for $50; at no time

> was the merchandise so cheap and so good. We were able to acquire AK-47 rifles, the weapon of choice in Central America. We transported on a large scale and moved huge quantities.... When we demobilized, the [Guatemalan] army was surprised. We had everything: huge quantities. ORPA also supplied the other elements of the URNG. We stored the reserve supplies in five secret locations in Mexico. I would guess that, by the time that the peace treaty was signed, we had enough weapons for two more years of fighting. We had everything: machine guns, rocket launchers, 3 million cartridges. We handed everything over to the Mexican army; we conducted negotiations at the level of the military high command. In this way we showed how serious we were. We did not engage in arms trafficking, although we could have made a lot of money by secretly selling off our reserve weapons.[46]

ORPA's and URNG's smooth logistics would have been impossible without the loyalty and continuous risk-taking of the anonymous *internacionalistas*, who consisted for the most part of US and Western European volunteers, some of them inspired by liberation theology, others highly indignant about the sins of commission or omission of their own governments.[47] They remained, even after the war, absolutely anonymous, as did the urban guerrilla members of the URNG, most of whom were recruited from the urban middle classes, and who were for the most part either professionals or government officials. These persons would have lost their reputation and almost surely in all likelihood their jobs had their identities been disclosed. Villagrán, who set up a new FAR urban guerrilla network starting from scratch 'with one man and one pistol' after the disastrous period of repression between 1980 and 1983, sometimes meets some of his former comrades-in-arms in the streets of Guatemala City. They wink at one another or exchange knowing glances.[48]

Daily Life and Relations with the Local Population

At age 78, former guerrilla fighter 'Uncle' Cros, whose residence served as the first ORPA headquarters in 1971, recalls an old saying: 'The best home for the poor man is in the mountains; the guerrilla's best home, where he can hide from the enemy, is in the mountains.'[49] In 'the mountains' there were generally temporary encampments or a more stable base camp, connected by concealed routes with faraway rural communities, and sometimes with suburban settlements. The temporary sites – at least in El Salvador and in Guatemala – were changed every couple of weeks or months; outside these bivouacs food, ammunition and weapons (sometimes also clothing and medicine) were stored in camouflaged caches.[50] In El Salvador, provisional field hospitals and schools were established as well. Sometimes, Western European religious foundations funded 'opposition-friendly NGOs' in the controlled territories.[51] In Guatemala, many recruits of the participating guerrilla movements of the URNG received literacy training and the equivalent of primary education in the base camps. ORPA developed an educational and cultural training programme, which even included poetry, history and the Maya calendar, with booklets and brochures personally written or edited by Rodrigo Asturias.[52]

In all politico-military organizations of the three umbrella guerrilla consortia – FSLN, FMLN and URNG – the courage and sacrifices of guerrilla icons of the past – such as Che Guevara and other 'heroes and martyrs', the guerrilla movement's civil saints – were from time to time commemorated in public events. For many of the fighters, it was the personal example of their own comandante that served to sustain their morale, especially during difficult times. In El Salvador, Guatemala and Nicaragua, field officers were explicitly reminded of their role as exemplars for the men and women under their command. Here are two examples of the preferred style of leadership within the FSLN in the 1970s and the FMLN in the 1980s:

> Everyone learned from the leader since, in our case, the leader not only gave orders, but gave orders on the front lines, demonstrating himself what it was that we needed to do. He always led by example. On the Frente, it was never acceptable for someone to give orders by simply saying, 'OK, do it'. This was something that was inconceivable.[53]

The personal example set by the field commander or the *responsable*, the guerrilla officer who served as the commander of a specific mission, also had a catalytic effect upon both the morale and the combat-readiness of the troops. This was especially true in the case of the elite guerrilla units, the 'special units' that carried out those tasks involving the highest risk. The last commander of the FMLN elite troops, Oscar Ortiz, reflects on the ethos of the men and women whom he sent away on 'semi-suicide missions':

> Since nobody was being paid – since nobody was involved for money but rather because of their ideals – you always had to be ready with moral arguments and persuasion. [In this kind of situation] you could ask people to do the impossible. So the fighter would always carry with him the question: 'My comandante is demanding that I do things that will in all likelihood get me killed. The issue is whether he is able to do the same thing.' So you needed to show everyone that this nearly impossible thing that you were asking was something that you yourself were able to do as well.[54]

Religious services were officially neither encouraged nor prohibited. All of the *frentes* included at least one guerrilla fighter who was also a Catholic priest. Church-based relief NGOs provided support to the non-war activities of the umbrella organizations. Given the pervasive influence of liberation theology, most politico-military organizations were characterized by an undercurrent of sympathy for religious issues. The majority of the Guatemalan fighters had a Maya background; a few times a Maya priest was present and performed the ritual ceremonies. In Guatemala, the ethnic divide between Ladinos (whites and mestizos) and Mayas was always a matter of some sensitivity. Formally there was no distinction between Ladino and Maya participants. Notwithstanding the day-to-day camaraderie between the regular combatants, Santiago Santa Cruz acknowledged latent ethnic friction, even reverse discrimination on the part of the (many) Mayas against the (fewer) Ladinos in his *frente*. The norm for Ladino officers was an ethnically neutral appearance and looks:

> One of the first rules in ORPA was that beards and moustaches [the grooming fashions of the Ladino landowners] were prohibited. Because these were things that reminded the indigenous peoples of the image of the conquistador. This was an internal rule in ORPA – beards and moustaches were forbidden. And I remember that when I joined [ORPA] as a doctor, they told me, 'In your case, we'll have to reconsider since you're a civilian. You're a doctor, so maybe we'll let you keep your moustache.'[55]

Two authors who wrote about gender relations within the Central American guerrilla movements, Kampwirth (2002) and Luciak (2001), quote extensively from the official guerrilla statements about the equality between men and women. Indeed, in the FSLN, the FMLN and the URNG some prominent women guerrilla comandantes emerged, like Mélida Anaya Montes (second-in-command of the FPL), Ana Guadalupe Martínez (ERP) and María Marta Valladares (Nidia Díaz, a member of both the Salvadoran PRCT and the Guatemalan EGP) in El Salvador, Dora María Tellez and Mónica Baltodano in Nicaragua, and Alba Estela Maldonado (Lola, EGP) in Guatemala. The percentage of women fighters in the two *frentes* and the URNG varied: from 10 to 20 per cent in the FMLN, increasing to 40 per cent within the urban commandos (Kampwirth, 2002: 149, 153), 10 per cent in the URNG (see below) and 30 to 40 per cent in the FSLN (Luciak, 2001: 351). In the Ejército Sandinista Popular (EPS), the regular army that succeeded the FSLN guerrilla forces, 30 per cent of the fighters were women. Luciak, who analysed in detail the division of labour between men and women in the FMLN, found that 30 per cent of the female members were assigned kitchen tasks, 15 per cent in health services, 11 per cent in support tasks and 40 per cent in other functions. As long as the guerrilla campaigns lasted, men and women alike were considered intellectual and physical equals. However, Mónica Baltodano, FSLN *comandante guerrillero* who in 1979 took the National Guard fortress in Grenada, remembers the gender bias that arose when it came to appointing members of the new Army Staff of the Sandinista Popular Army a couple of months after that historic victory:

I really wanted to stay in the army. And the reason that I didn't stay in the army had to do with the Cuban advisers. They were really sexist ('machista'). The Cubans really didn't have the concept of a woman holding a position of command. I was a *comandante guerrillero*. If I had stayed, they wouldn't have gotten away with putting me in charge of a unit. They would have had to make me one of the leading commanders in the Army Staff. But what I actually got instead was political work. At first, I was somewhat resistant. But afterwards, I accepted it.[56]

In matters of sexual intimacy, an official standard of revolutionary puritanism was the norm. The usual punishment imposed in the case of sexual assault was death by firing squad. In most politico-military organizations, a love relationship had to be transformed into a 'revolutionary' (i.e. common law) marriage. 'I am with my compa' was the standard term for the Salvadoran guerrilla marriage. The secular ORPA of Guatemala promoted a less ascetic lifestyle:

The proportion [of men to women] was 10 to 1. [You really can't deny young people the chance] to fall in love, discover sex – sex without love, sex with love, love with sex. You had something of everything. And we didn't want to be moralistic or hypocritical, demanding absolute respect, making them go through an official ceremony of comrade spouses uniting in revolutionary matrimony. I know that this is something that was done in other organizations. [With us] a fighter would come to me and say, 'Hey, comandante, I'm going out with my compa.' [I would say] 'Great. Be careful that you don't get her pregnant.' We ordered them to use condoms, or we would give birth control pills to the woman so that she wouldn't get pregnant. But so far as everything else that was going on, there was everything that you could possibly imagine in a chaotic encampment where there was really no place for romantic relationships.[57]

Day-to-day life always had to follow a prescribed regimen. It is interesting to note how similar the daily rhythm of the Guatemalan and the Salvadoran guerrilla soldiers were. Dagoberto Gutiérrez and Santiago Santa Cruz described an average day in the life of a combatant. One frequently used tactic to bolster morale and fighting spirit was always to keep the combatants busy by maintaining structure and routine. This was often done by providing study assignments, training exercises and drills, and by assigning fighters support tasks in hospitals, kitchens and schools, and so on. In the words of Dagoberto Gutiérrez:

> The fighter is a *campesino*, a student, a professional: but he must fight. The day he doesn't fight, things get very dangerous. Because this sort of attitude affects everything. There is no such thing as an idle guerrilla fighter.... He also studies. He has to learn how to read. Whoever didn't know how to read was taught how, in school. Specific problems were dealt with. All of this had to do with what was called morality, spirituality, moral force. We were not cultivating supermen. It was a matter of each fighter being spurred on by the efforts of his or her comrades.[58]

Santiago Santa Cruz notes:

> We all had our order of the day. This is something that is part of the military code. One has to know what to do from dawn until dusk. The order of the day that followed was generally read the preceding night. So: reveille at 05:00; review of troops and inspection of camp at 05:30; thirty or forty-five minutes of exercise at 06:30; breakfast at 08:00; group study for fighters and officers from 09:00 until 12:00. Lunch from 12:00 until 14:00, and military training afterwards. Then a break, dinner, reading and sleep. This was more or less a routine day in a large guerrilla encampment in the mountains. Along with all of this there were other complementary activities. Patrols would go out in search of food, or to make contact with the populations. Or fighters would be sent out to get weapons or to hide weapons. So there was a lot going on when there wasn't any actual fighting.[59]

Relations with the local population were of crucial importance. Early on, Wickham-Crowley (1987, 1990) emphasized the cooperation between guerrilla combatants and the civilian population with respect to both military support operations (intelligence providing, safe houses and rearguard resources, food and supplies, and fresh recruits) and the formation of associated militias. In the case of the three Central American guerrilla organizations, the FMLN, the FSLN and the URNG depended on the local population both as a vital source of material and moral support and as a reservoir of popular militias that served as allies of the guerrilla cause.

In El Salvador, the FMLN organized separate urban and rural popular organizations from the very beginning, and at the outbreak of the civil war the guerrilla organization had a strong presence among a very considerable segment of the population. Recruitment and militia formation were continuously nurtured by the population of the controlled territories within El Salvador and in the refugee settlements in Honduras.[60] Moreover, in the densely populated guerrilla areas, family members generally cooked and washed for their fighting sons and daughters as part of their daily routine; in the semi-permanent guerrilla settlement at Guazapa, mothers or younger sisters brought prepared lunches to their sons or brothers.[61] The flip side of this combatant-family symbiosis was that the FMLN also had to provide for the nuclear family of its members:

> The fighter would say, 'Look, I have a baby daughter, and I have nothing to give my wife. What should I do?' You should at least give enough to her so that she can buy clothes and medicine. The fighter isn't the only one who needs things – so does his immediate family. They expected that, in some way, their son who was fighting would do something to help them out.[62]

In Nicaragua the guerrilla movement's relationship with the local population was, until the mid-1970s, mostly limited to provision of food and shelter, and to obtaining local intelligence. The development and utilization of larger territorial networks formed by the members of an extended family and headed by a man whose relatives had fought in the army of General Sandino was not uncommon. One such clan chieftain was Gonzáles Quiñónez, whose uncle had been a colonel in Sandino's army. His and his wife's extended family formed a network of persons who provided intelligence about the movements of the National Guard in most of the area encompassing Regions I and II in the northern part of Nicaragua. This same network provided food and clothing, as well as information, to the FSLN on a regular basis:

> The network consisted mainly of two different families: my family was González Quiñónez, and there was the Rodríguez family [of my wife]. Out in Limay there's the Rodríguez family again. And then there are those from the Ramírez family. This is how bonds of trust were formed ... 'You,' they told me, 'we are going to put you in charge of the information network.' And they named me head of the [local] information network in 1970. And I managed my people. Some served as couriers, taking papers from one encampment to another. Others collaborated with me by providing food, by providing water, leaving it in the guerrilla encampments. Beginning at 19:00 hours [the guerrillas] began arriving from the ravine; they came to get food and drink their coffee.... Their encampment was never discovered, and it was right there, so close. Just over there in a little ravine, about 50 yards from here. There were eighty-eight men there. They had a cave where they kept their medicine for their injured fighters, to stop the bleeding. One of my sons made their uniforms. He had a workshop with five machines at that time.[63]

Massive popular support for the FSLN was something that emerged only late during the guerrilla struggle in Nicaragua – no earlier than 1977. By this time, young boys and girls in the cities were joining FSLN forces under the spontaneous leadership of neighbourhood 'commanders'. After the military victory in 1979, many of these local militia members were incorporated into the Sandinista Popular Army and the Sandinista Police.

In Guatemala, the URNG also depended on the local population for support and auxiliary forces, which were called the Fuerzas Irregulares Locales or FIL. Indigenous *campesinos* generally associated with the CUC as a result of the counterinsurgency campaigns by the military and paramilitary forces in the Maya regions. New recruits of the EGP, the ORPA and the FAR came during the last ten years of the war (from the mid-1980s to 1996) mainly from the refugee settlements in Chiapas (Mexico) and from *campesino* hamlets all over the northern and western departments of Guatemala.[64] Brutal repression on the part of the military between 1980 and 1983 – decreasing slowly in intensity and number of victims until the end of the military regimes in 1985 – resulted in a rupture between the guerrilla forces and the popular organizations. In the words of Alba Estela Maldonado (Lola), the URNG's sole representative in Congress in December 2006:

> Large organizations sprang up in Guatemala. This could be seen, for example, during the miners' march in 1979, as well as in the mass march of the sugar cane workers in 1980, when 80,000 *campesinos* mobilized and successfully demanded a minimum salary – the same one that is in effect today, isn't it? These organizations have from the beginning had very close ties with revolutionary organizations ... But you could see a gap there between the two forms of struggle. Because we had a very broad-based popular struggle that was highly political in nature along with a military development that was still very precarious. So it was this more than anything else that led to repression at the highest levels. We were caught in the net of repression because we were a mass revolutionary organization without the military capacity to respond properly [to what was being done to us]. Afterwards, beginning in 1983, a process of refinement began with respect to our military development. There was a great deal of development: with respect to both military activity and political activity abroad – the whole diplomatic aspect. But we were lacking when it came to mass organization. We were beaten down, destroyed, deprived of our leadership, our urban infrastructure [dismantled], all as a result of repression. And the guerrilla forces were actually pushed out towards the mountainous, rural regions of the country. We never again were able to attain a balance between our military development and our political organization of the masses. We always knew this was an issue, but we were never able to modify either our urban structures or our mass political organization.[65]

The wave of brutal repression between 1980 and 1983 decapitated nearly the entire leadership of popular organizations like the CUC and other trade unions. As a consequence, the *comandancia general* of the URNG decided to 'militarize' the guerrilla forces.[66]

After 1985 the URNG lost contact with the younger generation of Maya leaders. During the presidency of Cerezo (1986–90), when the military formally had ceded political power to a democratically elected government, a new political movement, Xeljú, was formed, a municipal coalition with strong indigenous representation in Quetzaltenango, Guatemala's second largest city and the urban capital of the Maya region. The URNG discreetly invited the Xelјú members of the municipal council to meet in order to explore a possible alliance between the two political movements. The meeting was a resounding failure: all Ladino (white and mestizo) guerrilla comandantes were seated; the Maya officials present were standing upright behind their commanders. The Maya politicians – the future mayor and some future aldermen – decided that 'the revolution of the URNG was alien to the Maya movement'.[67] It was a bad omen.

From the mid-1980s on, the URNG leadership devoted most of its energies to military affairs. ORPA even suspended its formal linkages with the popular movements, in order to diminish the risks of retaliatory action on the part of the (para)military towards the local and indigenous population. Opting for a military solution to the war, rather than bringing the conflict to a rapid conclusion, resulted in ten years of fighting between the two sides. Rodrigo Asturias explains the convoluted nature of the URNG leaders' reasoning:

> It was, strangely, a vicious circle. What I mean is that there was no more growth [in the URNG], and this resulted in the war being prolonged. But the prolongation of the war itself prevented further growth.[68]

The three guerrilla movements in El Salvador, Guatemala and Nicaragua followed different trajectories, utilized different strategies and carried out different tactical manoeuvres. In the case of Nicaragua, the strategy of urban revolt eventually proved to be successful in 1979. By contrast, the strategy followed by the Salvadoran guerrillas led to a military stalemate after a long and brutal decade of civil war in the 1980s. In El Salvador, where the guerrilla movements came to administer larger territories, and in Nicaragua, where the FSLN governed the country for more than ten years, the guerrillas succeeded in forging strong and enduring bonds of solidarity with the population. In Guatemala, guerrillas fought a war that lasted thirty-six years, most of the time operating in relative isolation and in remote areas. Gradually they lost their popular support bases: the local Maya communities and the popular associations. The consequences for the post-war configuration of political parties was considerable, as will be shown in Chapter 5.

The conflicts and disruptions within the Nicaraguan economy and society during the decade of the Sandinista government in the 1980s is the theme of the next chapter. After the guerrilla triumph in 1989, a revolutionary government was formed amid the buoyant enthusiasm and surging hopes of a long-oppressed nation. Ten years later, the Sandinista experiment ended amid widespread bitterness and disillusionment, and only after another civil war and an economic crisis.

4

Utopia and Dystopia, Nicaragua

Up until the time of his death, Marx was convinced that the first socialist revolutions would take place in circumstances similar to those that had obtained at the time of the Paris Commune. Olivier (1939) evoked the unbounded happiness of that time, even in the midst of the privations that accompanied a war that had been lost and the anguish of a city under siege. The prevailing sense was of the dawn of a new age – of a world that was better and more united, and that would give rise to a New Man liberated from the chains that had enslaved him. These were the same sentiments that Orwell (1977) later perceived as an eyewitness to the anarchist uprising during the Barcelona Commune of 1936. Orwell's euphoric outburst occurred in the middle of the bloody Spanish Civil War. These two communes, separated in time by sixty-five years, were both characterized by intense expressions of generosity, profound solidarity and collective enthusiasm. The heretofore unknown solidarity displayed among the Spanish Republicans, both at the time of the Barcelona Commune and throughout the three years of their ultimately failed struggle, would later be remembered nostalgically during the long years of the Franco dictatorship.

Something similar happened in Nicaragua after first León and then Managua fell to the Sandinistas in 1979. Dora María Téllez commanded the military forces that captured León. The person in charge of civilian organization and agrarian reform in the liberated territories was Orlando Núñez, who has vivid recollections of that historic event:

> After [the liberation], I was the one in charge of everything to do with the civilian organization of the city and the countryside. The economy was on a war footing. ... There was no state. There was no family. There was no market. There was no money. Everything was a commune – a total commune. Everyone wanted to be assigned a task, to have something to do. There was always a sea of hands: 'I'll do it! I'll do it!' It was easy. We put someone in charge of everything: a doctor, an agronomist. It was at that time that the agricultural and urban communes were formed. ... There was no place for a hierarchy. Everything was administered collectively. Everyone thought that this was the way things should be done in a revolution. It was thus very easy to say to them: 'This is yours. Manage it, without salary and without set working hours.' It was a real-life utopia. I thought: 'This is what "Liberty, Equality and Fraternity" is all about – from the French Revolution to the Sandinista Revolution.' ... There was no division of labour. All men and women were brothers and sisters. It was like an extended family. There was a competition to see who could be the most generous, of who could love his or her neighbour the most, of who could sacrifice the most. There were no police, because there was nobody to guard. Everyone watched over everything at the same time that they did whatever they were doing, and the enthusiasm was pervasive. It was absolute happiness, a wonderful party. There was enthusiasm, focused energy, solidarity and self-discipline in great abundance. This explains why there was a certain disappointment when we formally took control of the government of Nicaragua; everyone wanted things to go on just as they had begun.[1]

Spirits were also very high after the fall of Managua, and examples of altruism, kindness and solidarity were everywhere to be seen. There was no crime; no one stole anything. There still were no police. Instead, teenage members of the militia as young as 14 years old served as guardians of the public order in August 1979.

The general opinion that emerged from interviews with eyewitnesses of these events was that the atmosphere during the weeks and months following the Sandinista victory was one of a honeymoon period. Nearly everyone, including the foreign sympathizers who began pouring into the city by the thousands, fondly remembers the prevailing happiness: one neighbourhood after another organized parties throughout the months following the takeover of the city. Houses kept their doors open twenty-four hours a day, with unknown passers-by invited in for lunch or a drink.[2] This period of euphoria remains present in the collective memory of the Sandinistas more than twenty-five years later. Even those who later opposed the FSLN often remember sharing in the joy and hope that prevailed in the aftermath of the Sandinistas' final triumph.

The FSLN enjoyed widespread popular support. While the Sandinista Frente took over responsibility for public safety and placed party members in key government posts, their sympathizers were convinced that the comandantes and their advisers – many of whom were *internationalistas* – were constructing the New Society, forged by the New Man whose creation had been heralded in the previous decade by Che Guevara. There was a cultural boom. A 'poetry marathon' was organized in Ciudad Darío which was attended by 200 poets in front of an audience of poor citizens. The new Ministry of Culture, led by the poet-priest Ernesto Cardenal,[3] organized cultural centres, poetry workshops, popular theatre troupes and revolutionary publishing enterprises.[4]

A nationwide literacy campaign, the National Literacy Crusade, headed by his brother Fernando Cardenal, was held between March and August of 1980. Tens of thousands of urban youth volunteered as 'brigadiers', organized in *frentes*, brigades and squadrons and donning red berets; these volunteers worked to teach basic literacy skills to half a million of their rural countrymen.[5] The new government proudly announced that, within a few months, it had succeeded in reducing the nation's rate of illiteracy from 52 per cent to 12 per cent and UNESCO called the campaign a cultural triumph.[6] One consequence of this was that the FSLN enhanced its status as a revolutionary, patriotic and social welfare organization, winning over not only a generation of youth who had grown up amid desperate poverty in the countryside, but a large proportion of the *campesinos* as well. The FSLN named these brigadiers members of the Sandinista Youth, one of the new social organizations in which the Frente was enrolling the national population. There were even more volunteers who took part in the cotton harvest. And in 1983, 73,000 youth joined the ranks of the Popular Health Brigades for a day-long nationwide anti-dengue and anti-malaria campaign (Núñez Soto, 1998: 238).

The FSLN organized a majority of government employees along with other segments of the population – small business owners, industrial workers, rural labourers, women and young people – into government-sponsored associations. Members of these organizations, 'liberated from their selfish impulses' and guided solely by the ethics and mystique of the Revolution, were convinced to volunteer their free time on Saturdays – in emulation of the model of the Sandinista 'New Man' that was constantly held up as an ideal in government propaganda. The phenomenon of voluntary work on 'red and black Saturdays' (named for the colours of the FSLN) would endure throughout the 1980s, although with increasingly less willingness on the part of the workers.

Collective euphoria characterized the first years of the Revolution. But uniting the population in revolutionary organizations was accompanied by a gradual exclusion of certain social classes, categories of persons, and institutions. In order to appreciate the complexity of this process, which led to the rise of the Contras, the following section contains a summary of the changes introduced by the FSLN in its economic, social and administrative policies.

A theme of this chapter is the role and development of the FSLN, the revolutionary party that carried out the Sandinista revolution. Throughout this chapter I will analyse the relationship between the party, state and government, focusing particularly on the character of the revolutionary leadership, the exercise of governing power, and the leadership of the new army and the new police – both of these organizations being direct heirs of the FSLN guerrilla forces. The truth that emerges is that the party elite – and especially the *dirección national* of the nine Comandantes de la Revolución – obtained and maintained decisive control over state and government. Even the most important appointments of the senior ministers and the leadership of the army and the police reflect the dominance of the revolutionary aristocracy over both the government and the state apparatus. The same process can be shown with respect to the new mass organizations: it is impossible to deny the subordination of the popular organizations to the state and, by extension, to the controlling FSLN elite. Equally interesting is the relationship between the army and the general party leadership. A year after the Sandinista triumph the first adumbrations of armed rebellion and civil war are dimly yet unmistakably visible, at least in retrospect. The slowly emerging discontent and alienation of significant institutions and population segments will be analysed in this chapter. In the early 1980s an armed resistance surfaced, geographically localized in the northern rural region, along the border with Honduras and on the Atlantic coast, heavily financed and trained by the United States. The more serious the war became, the more autonomy the army leadership obtained vis-à-vis the party; eventually they not only conducted military operations but also devised and implemented the war economy. The labyrinthine management of the national economy is another theme that will be followed throughout the chapter. It will be seen how the collapsing economy and the pyrrhic victory over the Contras directly led to the FSLN electoral defeat in 1990 – a defeat that sealed the fate of the Sandinista Revolution.

Managing the Revolution

Government and national leadership

Prior to the fall of the Somoza regime, the FSLN and the Grupo de los Doce had previously reached agreement regarding the composition of the Junta of the National Government of Reconstruction and the distribution of ministerial portfolios. On 19 July 1979 the FSLN marched victoriously into Managua. The following day, the ruling junta arrived, escorted by guerrilla columns. The junta was led by Daniel Ortega and included four additional members: the intellectual and novelist Sergio Ramírez, the politician Moisés Hassán (both sympathetic to the FSLN), Violeta Barrios de Chamorro (widow of the murdered opposition leader Pedro Joaquín Chamorro) and the businessman Alfonso Robelo. Various members of the Group of Twelve assumed their ministerial portfolios: for example, Joaquín Cuadra Sr as finance minister and Father Miguel d'Escoto as foreign minister. A new State Council, presided over by Comandante Carlos Nuñez and comprising thirty-three members representing the 'vital forces of the nation', functioned as a legislative institution within which the FSLN had the majority of representatives.

However, the relationship between the junta, the cabinet and the *dirección nacional* of the FSLN was a delicate one. Since Daniel Ortega led the junta, it only seemed natural that he would also be placed at the helm of the *dirección nacional.* The nine comandantes that comprised this latter body had been those who had been the real power brokers within the FSLN.[7] Without the matter being openly discussed, they assumed that they would continue as leaders of the FSLN after its triumph. Power had been achieved through force of arms, and those who had been in command during the war decided to assume positions of leadership in the government. Humberto Ortega declares bluntly: 'We established the rules; our appointments reflected the real power balance.'[8] Dora María Téllez concludes: 'The *dirección nacional*, which controlled the party and which had a fair measure of power within the state itself, basically decided what would happen.'[9]

The most important decisions were taken in the *dirección nacional*, generally following discussions airing diverse opinions that could go on for many hours and that covered a wide range of topics:[10] the new army and the police force, state security, changes in the economy, the formation of popular organizations, the advice being provided by Cuba, and relations with the USA and the Soviet bloc, among other matters. There were many instances of power struggles within the *dirección nacional*.[11]

Revolutionary aristocracy

In the beginning there were very few members of the FSLN, although their numbers soon grew exponentially: from 1,500 in 1981 to 16,000 in 1985 to 50,000 in 1990.[12] The guerrilla aristocracy, which grew out of the first meetings of the FSLN in May and September 1980, had four 'categories of honour': *comandante de la revolución* (the nine members of the *dirección nacional*), *comandante guerrillero* (some thirty persons, three of whom were women[13]), the *primera promoción de militantes* (first tier of party cadres, a total of 130) and the *segunda promoción de militantes* (second tier of party cadres, about 170 persons).[14] The *comandantes de la revolución* were being named to key posts: Humberto Ortega as minister of defence, Tomás Borge as minister of the interior, Henry Ruiz as minister of planning, and Jaime Wheelock as minister of agriculture and agrarian reform. In addition, Bayardo Arce and Victor Tirado[15] held prominent positions in the party leadership and popular organizations respectively. Some *comandantes guerrilleros* held key posts on the general staff and in the intelligence and security branches of the nation's new army and police force. Others held cabinet portfolios or were appointed vice-ministers. Members of the *primera promoción* and *segunda promoción* generally obtained management positions in either national or municipal government, or leadership posts in the popular organizations.[16]

Popular organizations

From the very beginning, the FSLN sought to 'integrate the masses' into the revolutionary process by forming organizations of urban and rural workers, and of the middle-class farmers and smallholders of the nation's Pacific coast. The government also unionized other key sectors of the workforce. According to records of the labour ministry, there were 133 labour unions in 1979 with a total of 27,000 members. By 1982, the number of unionized workers had reached 150,000 (Núñez Soto, 1998: 238). Of all the organizations that were created, those that could be said to have formed the popular backbone of the Sandinista Revolution were the Comités de Defensa Sandinista – CDS. The CDS groups grew out of the community defence committees that had arisen during the uprisings of 1978 and 1979 and these were now organized by the FSLN (led by Comandante Ómar Cabezas) along the lines of the Cuban Comités de Defensa de la Revolución. These were essentially community watchdog organizations that functioned as 'the eyes and the ears of the Revolution', in the words of the party newspaper *Barricada* in its edition of 23 September 1979.

Between 1980 and 1990 the FSLN organized the population along revolutionary lines, as indicated in Table 4.1. Núñez Soto (1989: 238) reached the conclusion that 'democracy came to naturally acquire the adjective "participatory" in Nicaragua'. But it should be borne in mind that the relationship between the FSLN and its affiliate organizations was not one of equals; that is, it did not imply organizational autonomy. On the contrary, Tomás Borge, looking back on those early days, characterizes the popular organizations as 'highly subordinate, exercising very little initiative – subordinate to the Party'.[17] This view is shared by Dora María Téllez:

> The popular organizations [were] in fact placed in the service of political action. The action of the masses was subordinated to the needs of the state to carry out the transformations that it deemed necessary. This was the logic that prevailed for many years.[18]

Defence and public safety

Immediately after 19 July 1979, there were deliberations regarding the composition and leadership of the new army. Tomás Borge, a veteran revolutionary, tried to secure the position of defence minister for either himself or his companion-in-arms, Henry Ruiz.

Table 4.1 Organizations affiliated with the FSLN, 1980–90[19]

Name	Year	Member profile	No. of members
1. ATC	1985	rural workers	40,000*
2. ANE	1990	teachers	-
3. ASTC		fine arts and cultural performers	-
4. CST	1985	urban workers	-
5. FETSALUD	1985	health workers	-
6. UNE	1990	civil servants	-
Total 2–6	1990		200,000
AMLAE	1988	women	60,000
CDS	1988	neighbourhood residents	600,000
BPS	1983	health-care volunteers	73,000
Agricultural co-ops	1983	co-op members	60,000†
JS19J	1983	youth	30,000
EPA	1980	youth literacy workers	52,000
UNAG	1990	*campesinos*	125,000
MPS	1983	voluntary militia	300,000
UPN	1990	journalists	800

Notes: * 40,000 full-time. † 60,000 families.
Source: Martí, 1994: 44, 1997: 85; Nuñez Soto, 1998: 237–8.

But the three comandantes of the Tendencia Tercerista – the Ortega brothers, Victor Tirado as well as Joaquín Cuadra Lacayo, head of the Urban Frente that had liberated the cities, felt that only they should control the nucleus of the nation's armed forces: the Ministry of Defence and the new Sandinista Popular Army (EPS). Humberto Ortega, who had been the chief Sandinista negotiator during the final month preceding the downfall of the Somoza regime, was minister of defence and commander-in-chief of the army. Joaquín Cuadra organized the general staff:

> I began to restructure the guerrilla formations, allotting bases to each of them in Managua in order to help establish the regime, attempting to control the huge number of militiamen who had spontaneously formed units. ... I called upon the principal leaders of the guerrilla columns to help in this effort. These guerrilla columns were the true beginnings of the army. ... The military ranks were established according to time served as guerrilla fighters. We established various parameters in terms of years of service for captain, for lieutenant. If you fell below a certain level then you would be a second lieutenant. If you had three years in you would be a lieutenant colonel, you know. And there were only two of us who were generals – Humberto Ortega and me. After that, everyone was a colonel. ... Very quickly, before the end of the first year, the first Cuban military mission arrived. We then proceeded to work with them to organize the army. The Cubans did not get directly involved [in military matters] – they were just advisers. We formed brigades, ... divided territories for military, political and administrative purposes, and so on. ... At the first signs of the counter-revolution, we began fighting. We speeded up the training of officers. At that point, the Cubans began arriving here en masse. We sent hundreds of officers to Cuba for training – for quick courses, you know. We didn't need doctors. We needed people with combat experience; they would get a quick theoretical orientation, then a more conventional training, if you want to put it that way. And, in the end, each of us took a number of different courses. Including the whole general staff here in Managua.[20]

Humberto Ortega chose to develop the armed institution under the banner of a single organization, with the army, navy and air force all under the command of one general staff, like in other Central American countries. The EPS was both an armed institution of the state and a party organization. From 1982 onwards, there was a directorate of political affairs organized along the lines of the Cuban model under the leadership of Hugo Torres.[21] With regard to arms, military training and military relations with Cuba, the Soviet Union and other socialist countries, it was the ministers and vice-ministers of defence who negotiated and signed contracts, bypassing the Ministry of Foreign Affairs and the Ministry of External Cooperation. In the case of the Ministry of the Interior, this same process applied.[22]

The Ministry of the Interior, headed by Tomás Borge, would comprise the police force, State Security, the migration service, the prison system, and the nation's firefighters. At the beginning of the Contra War, in 1981, Borge was called upon to form the so-called Special Forces, trained for counterinsurgency warfare by means of guerrilla combat methods. Comandante Lenin Cerna was named director general of State Security; from 1981 onwards, he 'dismantled [the] armed bands that formed the front lines of the Contras'.[23] Borge said that Cerna was so effective that 'not only the KGB, but the CIA and the security services of [East] Germany were envious of what they considered one of the most efficient [intelligence] services in the world.'[24] Nicaragua's State Security apparatus, although feared, never was that invasive or as repressive as the Russian KGB or the East German STASI. Other civilian branches of the Ministry of the Interior also came to acquire an excellent reputation. The prison system created a network of 'open farms', where the inmates remained unsupervised, without cells, iron bars or guards. They received literacy classes and there were volunteer workshops. The new Sandinista Police Force (which was, like the EPS, both a state and a party institution) had the reputation of being incorruptible and enjoyed widespread public trust:

> We had no idea what a police force was, and at first we implemented a military organization, with battalions and companies: an inheritance of guerrilla warfare. A civilian police force is really something else altogether. ... We had Panamanian and Costa Rican advisers: Torrijos was the first to provide us advisers. And afterwards there was the aid from the socialist countries: Cuba, the USSR, Bulgaria and East Germany. We trained thousands of officers in Cuba – thousands – in every specialized branch: criminology, transportation [for example]. We sent hundreds to the Soviet Union and Bulgaria for training.
>
> ... I remember the year 1983, 1984, I think, when we only had 8,000 crimes in the entire nation. There was hardly any crime in those days. In one year, 8,000 crimes – a total now reached in

> fifteen days.... You could walk alone in the streets at 1.00 a.m. There was a high degree of public safety.[25]

Property reforms

One of the first measures enacted by the Junta of National Reconstruction was the expropriation of property belonging to Somoza and his closest collaborators.[26] Violeta de Chamorro, member of the junta, signed the decree that set this process in motion.[27] Houses and farms that were expropriated were distributed among those who had distinguished themselves in battle. A large majority of the goods and businesses were transferred to the newly emerging sectors of the 'mixed economy',[28] to the Área de la Propiedad del Pueblo (People's Property Zone) and to the agricultural co-operatives sector. An agrarian reform was undertaken by Jaime Wheelock, between 1979 and 1990. Wheelock served as a kind of 'superminister' who had oversight of agropecuarian affairs, agrarian reform, and provision of credit in rural areas. Both redistribution and agrarian reform enjoyed widespread popular support. Within a few years, 'all of the large idle estates that were greater than 500 manzanas[29] in the case of the Pacific region and greater than 1,000 manzanas in the rest of the country were expropriated.'[30] In 1978, land ownership was 100 per cent private (with 41 per cent comprising estates larger than 350 hectares). In 1983, the proportion of estates this large was reduced to 19 per cent (Núñez Soto, 1987: 98). Co-operativization accelerated rapidly: in 1982, the number of co-operatives was 2,800 and comprised a total of 65,000 individual members (Fitzgerald and Chamorro, 1987: 32). In 1988, the 'reformed sector' comprised 40 per cent of the nation's rural area. By 1989, a total of 112,000 families jointly held title to land (Wheelock, 1990: 115, 117).[31]

Managing the economy

The nation's economic policy was shaped between 1979 and 1990 by Sergio Ramírez, a distinguished intellectual who had no real background in economics. Ramírez filled this role in addition to carrying out his duties first as a member of the governing junta

(1979–84) and then as vice-president (1984–90).[32] In daily practice a group of ministers – of finance, agriculture, economics, commerce and industry, and planning – each carried out their own policies, while the management of the Central Bank also acted more or less autonomously. The inevitable result was a labyrinthine decision-making process in which each minister tried to impose his own ideas, policies and way of looking at things. The Planning Ministry, which until 1985 was under the leadership of Henry Ruiz, attempted to bring order to this chaotic situation. In Ruiz's own words:

> This is what gave us the idea that a plan was necessary – and, most importantly of all, an economic plan. For example, the first [plan] that I signed was called 'Economic Reactivation'. But the second one was already being called 'Efficient Economic Austerity'. Because there were no resources ... And among the tasks at a national level was that of the military defence of the Revolution. And this involved economic and financial expenditures.... Cuba was ready to help us, but Cuba could not run a country of three and a half million people. That was impossible. But we were going to coordinate the help of the socialist countries – by means of monetary compensation. That's how it was.... When did we reach the point of no return? When the costs of war did not allow us to even minimally repair the costs of our ruined economy; when we could no longer import food, medicine. When we could not meet the basic dietary needs of the population. And the war went on and on with no end in sight.[33]

In 1985 Henry Ruiz was put in charge of the newly created Ministry of External Cooperation, with Dionisio Marenco, who did not carry the authority of being a member of the *dirección nacional*, replacing him as head of the Planning Ministry. Néstor Avendaño, an econometrist who held a Ph.D. from Yale and who, beginning in 1980, served for twenty years as a vice-minister or ministerial adviser in three consecutive governments, recalls with bitter irony the economic management of the Revolution:

> I found myself in a ministry that was filled with the so-called *internationalistas* – Chileans, Argentines, Uruguayans, [people] from the former East Germany – who didn't have a clue about

> the market economy. It was pleasant enough, I learned a lot. I had never studied political economy. But I did know about economic policy, which is something different. The minister of planning at the time, Comandante Henry Ruiz, had a great deal of personal and professional confidence in me and named me his vice-minister. Because I corrected all of these advisers in front of the minister. Because when politics and professionalism are mixed together, the latter suffers. And I made clear that things could not go on like that. But the leaders were also very romantic – including the literati who ran the economy. I'm referring especially to Dr Sergio Ramírez Mercado, coordinator of the economic cabinet, who in the face of these observations responded that we were the rulers of a free and sovereign nation, [and] that we could do as we pleased.... I went as far as to say to the president of the republic: 'Please learn how to say *no* to your ministers. They come here to request increased budgets and you say, "sure, sure, sure".' I told the finance minister, Dr Joaquin Cuadra, father of the army chief of staff, 'I don't know why you don't advise that these expenditures be discontinued – expenditures that serve no purpose.' Doing this cost me my position as vice-minister of planning, because I said this to him in front of the entire cabinet.[34]

Throughout the 1980s there was a rapidly increasing external and internal debt for a number of different reasons: first, because of the expense of war material; second, because of the financing, with credits from socialist countries, of a series of megaprojects – like a sophisticated milk production scheme with Canadian cows, massive Cuban-style sugar plantations, a mammoth Bulgarian horticulture project that featured centralized computer supervision, voluminous studies for never-implemented hydroelectric power stations, and state land cultivation of vast tracts of uncultivated land that involved irrigation on a massive scale – that either turned out to be white elephants or that were simply never carried out;[35] third, because of local co-financing, at a level of about 50 per cent, of development projects on the part of socialist countries; fourth, because of the practice of forgiving debts in each agricultural cycle as a result of favoured treatment of the co-operatives; fifth, because of currency exchange rates. Nicaragua had about 200 different exchange rates between 1985 and 1990. The highest annual exchange loss, in 1986, was of 42,000 million córdobas. This was the equivalent of 10 per cent of GDP. Exchange loss ranged from 5 per cent to 27 per cent of GDP between 1982 and 1988. The budget deficit eventually reached 30 per cent of GDP.[36]

Foreign policy

Sandinista foreign policy was without question fuelled by profound anti-imperialist sentiment – a feeling that prevailed not only among the comandantes but among a large number of their civilian compatriots in the government. In 1979, Carter invited the Junta of National Reconstruction to the White House and offered US$15 million for Nicaragua's post-war reconstruction, while Congress offered another US$75 million. But when Reagan took office, in January 1981, there was a dramatic change in American policy. The new administration assumed that Nicaragua was a serious threat to the most important military power in the world and rapidly devised plans for low-intensity warfare – the Contra War, as it came to be known. In addition, the Reagan administration fomented economic destabilization, support of civilian dissenting elements, financing and operational support of the armed opposition, and undercover paramilitary operations. Comandantes and government ministers alike seemed to be justified in their suspicions of 'the Empire', as the USA was referred to in official government language. Father d'Escoto, minister of foreign affairs, described the prevailing attitude as follows:

> I know the USA very well: I was born there, was educated there, and am a Maryknoll priest. But I am not an American. Our Lord was born in a stable and he wasn't a horse.... We were never against the USA. We were against abuse, against its interventionism ..., against the monstrous new ideas. Our foreign policy became a matter of – knowing full well what was in store for us – 'outfoxing the USA', of being smarter than they were.[37]

The foreign policy of Nicaragua was, from that point on, defined within the following frame of reference: confrontation with the

USA, trying to maintain the sympathy of international public opinion and the support of other Western and Latin American countries, and seeking allies among the socialist countries. Economic and moral support was sought and found in Cuba, the Soviet Union and Eastern European countries. Victor Hugo Tinoco, vice-minister of foreign affairs, describes the evolution of Sandinista foreign policy:

> The Republican administration thought that it would be possible to militarily overthrow the Sandinista Revolution without too much trouble – say by just supplying arms to counter-revolutionaries. And they began working to expand the extent of military operations. While this was going on, in 1981, we were making efforts to seek military support in Europe. I myself went to Paris with Daniel Ortega in search of military resources. The truth of the matter is that the response in Europe, and especially France, was very anaemic. And the war continued to increase in scope. This is what made our approach to the Soviet bloc inevitable, as we sought both military support and political backing in the conflict. This is what sharpened the divide in the conflict, and defined it in terms of East against West. All this happened despite the fact that the Revolution was in principle of an essentially nationalist and mildly leftist character – socialist, but with a strong nationalist flavour.[38]

In 1985, when the costs of war had begun to grow alarmingly high, the new Ministry of External Cooperation was charged with seeking technical and financial assistance wherever it could be found. Nicaragua had become highly dependent, at least in terms of financing and armaments, on the East European countries as well as Cuba, which was the most generous of all the countries providing aid to Nicaragua.[39] Without Soviet and Eastern European credits, oil, machinery and edible goods, Nicaragua would probably not have been able to survive. Relations with multinational banks – the World Bank, the Inter-American Development Bank and the Central American Bank of Economic Integration – also grew difficult, in large part due to US actions. The governments of Great Britain, France, Germany, Spain and Italy, however, generally followed Washington's anti-Sandinista lead. On the other hand, the Scandinavian countries, especially Sweden, as well as the Netherlands, maintained cooperative bilateral relations with Nicaragua throughout the years of the Sandinista government. There was also the help extended by non-governmental groups who supported the regime as well as the cooperation of private individuals. The Fiat magnate Giovanni Agnelli, for example, offered a large quantity of replacement parts for the Russian Lada cars, which were based on an Italian model.[40]

In the first years of the Sandinista government, the FSLN leadership quickly consolidated its position of command over economy, society and the political order. The most important positions in the cabinet and the key posts within both the new Sandinista army and the Sandinista police were all occupied by the leading comandantes of the 1978–79 guerrilla campaign. Although an impressive array of popular organizations, neighbourhood committees and trade unions were created, they were subordinate to party – and thus state – initiative. Important property reforms were carried out, benefiting the poorer segments of the population. Meanwhile, the management of the economy had become disorganized. Moreover, the FSLN appeared to be slowly transforming the national political order into a *de facto* one-party system. Eventually the Contras and their American patrons reaped the rich harvest of general discontent that resulted from the implementation of the FSLN reform programme. The gradual process of alienation and opposition, and the Contra War that eventually followed, require a more detailed analysis, and will be examined in the next two sections.

Alienation, Exclusion and Opposition

While analysing the gradual breakdown of commonality among the general population and its growing alienation, exclusion and eventual resistance, it must be kept in mind that, at the outset of the Revolution, the Sandinistas enjoyed overwhelming support and a large proportion of the population continued to identify with the regime. In the 1984 elections – in which several opposition parties declined to participate – the FSLN presidential ticket (Daniel Ortega and Sergio Ramírez) obtained 67 per cent of the vote and the party captured 61 of the 96 seats in parliament. There are no reliable data regarding the popularity of the government in the years that followed, but it can be estimated with a fair degree of confidence that the percentage of Sandinista supporters always remained above or around 50 per cent of the population throughout the final years of the regime.

On the other hand, opposition elements had already begun to crystallize shortly after the Sandinistas took power. The first major expression of discontent occurred when the non-Sandinista members of the junta resigned in April 1980. During the first three months of 1980, the FSLN had named more and more members of the revolutionary elite to head ministries and to fill important positions in the public sector. When the *dirección nacional* unilaterally decided to expand the number of members of the State Council, first Alfonso Robelo and then Violeta de Chamorro resigned as members of the junta. And in November 1980, when the revolutionary government announced the postponement of national elections until 1984, the first fissures began to emerge among the different political groupings that had initially supported the revolution (Martí, 1997: 64 ff.). Edén Pastora and José Valdivia Hidalgo, another vice-minister of the interior, resigned from office, protesting against the course that the revolution was taking and, especially, the growing influence of Cuba and the Soviet Union.[41] Pastora's resignation was full of melodrama, with allusions to Che Guevara and his announcement that he was leaving to 'follow the scent of gunpowder'. But Pastora was cut from a different cloth than Che. Unlike Che Guevara, who died as a revolutionary hero, Pastora assumed the leadership of a counterinsurgency force, financed by US and other anti-Sandinista sources. Shortly afterwards, he left for the south of Nicaragua and then Costa Rica, assuming leadership of the Contra forces there.

There was also dissent within the private sector, and COSEP,[42] the national association of entrepreneurs, gradually became one of the focal points of opposition to the government. COSEP, which from the beginning was opposed to land reform and expropriations, attracted other opposition elements to its ranks. The policy of expropriations affected not only those who had supported the Somoza regime, but all those who, for whatever reason, opposed the FSLN, including those who were initially allies but who afterwards broke ranks. In 1982, for example, the property of former junta member Alfonso Robelo was transferred to the state.[43] The democratic right joined COSEP in opposing the regime. Some political parties simply withdrew from open and public activity, but would later become part of the clandestine opposition which formed the nucleus of political support for the Contras' military activities.

Opposition also arose among the conservative hierarchy of the Catholic Church, a factor that carried considerable weight in an overwhelmingly Catholic country. This Church hierarchy was fiercely opposed to the followers of liberation theology. The pace of the Revolution and the direction it was taking, the emphasis on the 'Church of the poor' in the official press, the Base Communities of progressive priests – who came to be called 'Christian revolutionaries' and the presence of four priests in key cabinet posts[44] increasingly angered the Nicaraguan Church hierarchy, headed by the Archbishop of Managua and future cardinal, Miguel Obando y Bravo.[45] In 1980 the image of the Virgin Mary of Cuapa began to 'sweat' drops of moisture. *La Prensa*, at that time an opposition newspaper, explained that the Virgin was suffering because of the materialism and atheism of the Sandinistas. Beginning in December 1981, the Holy Virgin began to 'cry' instead of sweat, according to the same source. This 'miracle' was mentioned from time to time by the bishops, who were constantly on the attack against the policies of the FSLN. In 1981, the *dirección nacional* released an 'Official Statement on Religion', which emphasized that

> [a] large number of militants and fighters of the FSLN found, in their interpretation of their faith, reasons for joining the revolutionary struggle and therefore also the FSLN. ... Constructing the future of Nicaragua is a historic challenge that transcends

> our borders and that is an inspiration to other peoples in their own struggles for liberation and in bringing about the complete transformation of the New Man.[46]

Relations between the Contras and the Church grew more and more distant, with the visit of Pope John Paul II to Nicaragua in 1983 further widening the chasm. The Catholic hierarchy organized a meeting to coincide with the pope's visit and the FSLN ordered that a counter-demonstration be held at the same time. Thus a strong divergence emerged in the country with respect to religion. The two points of view were mutually exclusive and, although the Sandinistas officially adopted a triumphalist posture, within the rank and file of the party, the schism between the government and the Church was widely lamented.

As if this ideological clash were not serious enough, an even more troubling conflict arose with regard to the rural population, especially a large proportion of farmers and cattle ranchers, in addition to small landowners and *campesinos*. In the case of the indigenous peoples of the Atlantic coast, this opposition was slowly transformed into open hostility. The FSLN, as the party holding power, began to transform the government of the country into a model of one-party democracy, which enjoyed widespread support in the cities and in the country's Pacific region. But as the FSLN slowly consolidated its standing among the general population of the country, it began to come up against other viewpoints that were foreign to their own fundamentally urban outlook. This phenomenon occurred especially in the northern regions. The party also underestimated the important role of the ethnic, religious and linguistic identities of the peoples of the Atlantic regions, especially the Miskitos, Sumos and Ramas. The 'arrogance' and 'intransigence'[47] with which the FSLN applied their programme of incorporation, integration and forced assimilation to Sandinista ways of thinking, and to the party's social policies, especially its agrarian reform measures, created among a large segment of the rural population such a deep sense of alienation that many of them ended up joining the Contras:

> Those in the indigenous population were not interested in land, because they were fishermen [or] they farmed their owned small parcels of family land. They didn't have any problem with regard to land; they had enough land. The problem was that they became suspicious of their religious and political leaders. The USA also played a very important role in this. And in the case of the north of the country, it can be said that the agrarian problem was not something that had to do with land. There is [in that region] a very important *campesino* population.... There was a great deal of [negative] reaction on the part of *campesinos* with medium-sized agricultural holdings – on the part of people working the land even if they did not hold title to it. We had a programme that would enable them to obtain title to the land. We did not want to make changes as to who would occupy the land; we wanted to legalize [the *de facto* situation that currently existed]. But they were highly suspicious, because they believed the US and Contra propaganda that we had come to take away their lands, their property – that we would go so far as to confiscate their families, their children and even their wives. That we wanted to organize them into CDS groups, into communes, and that we were going to force the women into AMLAE[48] groups. There was a cultural problem involved here, a clash between a modernizing, innovative and, in some ways, extremist, culture as against a culture that was traditional, patriarchal, cautious, very family-oriented and very rural – a culture that sensed its own world falling apart. It was an anthropological clash.... Where we saw a utopia, they saw a hell on earth.[49]

The Contra War

Despite the fact that the Contra War was a civil war, with at least 20,000, maybe 30,000, combatants on the side of the Contra forces fighting against something like 300,000 troops on the side of the Sandinista government,[50] there is little doubt that outside actors instigated hostilities, provided advice and sought to expand the scope of the conflict. The first country that provided military aid to the Contras was Argentina, a country then governed by one of the most oppressive military dictatorships of the continent and whose army and intelligence officers arrived with the mindset of 'conducting a crusade against communism and who helped inject the element of a highly criminal and fascist mentality into the training of the contra forces'.[51] General Álvarez Martínez, commander-in-chief of the Honduran armed forces, was a student at the Argentine Military Academy and an admirer of the Galtieri regime. He welcomed with open arms the Argentine advisers who came to help reorganize the remnants of Somoza's Nicaraguan National Guard, who had taken refuge in Honduras. Afterwards, CIA experts arrived and the Argentines, annoyed at having been shoved aside, left open field for the Americans. In February 1982 the CIA reported to Congress that it had at its disposal an army of 1,000 men, along with another 1,000 Miskito indigenous troops and 1,000 fighters trained by the Argentines. In December 1982 the size of the army had increased to a total of 4,000 troops.[52] Those participating in the Literacy Crusade in 1980 had already felt threatened by Contra forces. There had even been a couple of deaths among the ranks of the Crusade brigadiers. The Contras periodically conducted raids against settlements in 1981 and, during the following two years, considerably stepped up their acts of sabotage. But from 1981 on, they began systematically to terrorize the population, as Marta Isabel Cranshaw explains:

> In San Francisco del Norte, in Chinandega, there was a Contra raid, the first such raid carried out by the Contras. At that time, the small village was home to 600 persons; some 13 or 15 youth died. [The Contras] behaved very cruelly. For example, they dragged the mayor, who was in charge of the [FSLN] militias, through the stone-paved streets. They then tied him up to a horse and the horse ran through the entire village, and the guy was still alive. He ended up dying. His brains were splattered all over the village. A boy who belonged to the Sandinista Youth was fighting and had been disarmed. In retaliation, both of his hands were amputated. He survived, but with both of his hands gone. The political secretary of the FSLN was hanged and castrated. The blood of the wounded and murdered was used to write a message on the wall in large letters: 'Death to Communism'.[53]

With the moral support of COSEP and of the Catholic hierarchy, the CIA consolidated an anti-Sandinista political platform, the FDN (1982), which was renamed the UNO[54] in 1985, with businessman Adolfo Calero named as its president. The CIA also provided advisers as well as technical and financial assistance to the various groups that together received the name of Contras:[55] the MILPAS (*campesino* militias), operating out of bases in Honduras; ARDE (Alianza Revolucionaria Democrática), led by Edén Pastora and deployed on the 'Southern Frente' near Costa Rica; and MISURASATA, a force that comprised the indigenous Miskito, Sumo and Rama peoples of the Atlantic coast, all of whom were opposed to the Sandinista regime because of what they came to see as its 'genocidal intentions'. The Contra forces grew in number from 4,000 in December 1982 to 15,000 in September 1983. In 1984, the FDN alone numbered 16,000 troops (Núñez Soto, 1998: 316). 'In the face of the threat of the Nicaraguans wanting to share their joyous revolution with the rest of Central America, including us',[56] the government of Costa Rica allowed Pastora's Contras to operate freely along its frontier with Nicaragua. Pastora himself describes the situation:

> In the Rivas region, and in the entire southern part of the lake, there was Comandante Emiliano Torres along with another comandante, Domingo, who [between them] had 500 fighters under their command. The entire eastern coast of this lake, from El Almendro to San Miguelito Morillo, was [patrolled by] Comandante Leonel and his 700 fighters. In the entire south of Nueva Guinea, Polaina, La Fonseca and Rama there was Navegante with his 800 men. From the basin of the Punta Gorda river all the way to the coast there was Franklyn, with 600 to 900 men. And in Rama and along the Plátano river – all around there – along the Escondido river, there was Comandante Pedro Lara. I was in the southernmost region. Between the people of Coyote, Indio Ramaquí and my own men there were a total of 7,500 men in Nicaragua, and we were constantly at war.[57]

The USA imposed a commercial embargo on 1 May 1984, enforced by the navy and Marines, who patrolled the Pacific and Atlantic coasts. US-related operatives destroyed the installations of Corinto, the nation's most important port. But the military situation within the country had also grown worse. In the final months of 1983 and the first months of 1984, the Contras had succeeded in acquiring a military superiority in the interior of the country. With regard to training, arming, provisions, logistics, organization, communication and technological capabilities, the Contra forces had the upper hand on the Sandinista army (EPS), which comprised hastily assembled volunteers. As Sandinista General Hugo Torres recalls:

> we faced the Contra forces with reserve units that required a great deal of effort to mobilize. We were in the process of training officers who immediately were placed in command of reserve units. These reserve battalions comprised citizens of all ages. Battle-hardened though they were, we could not expect them to make the best soldiers. On top of this, they were volunteers. They mobilized and demobilized as they pleased. After being mobilized for three months, they said they had to leave in order to feed their families. 'I have to go home; I'll mobilize again another time.' This meant that we were only able to prepare a few substantial units that were properly equipped to do battle with Contra forces that for their part were organized with US support – with a great deal of American logistical and intelligence support. And they were permanent, full-time soldiers.[58]

There were bitter disagreements between the military leaders of the EPS and the members of the *dirección nacional*. In particular, there were prolonged debates between the members of the *dirección nacional* and the members of the general staff:

> By the end of 1983, we were in bad shape ... The Contras were winning the war. The Contras had major logistical support and superior training – they were training lots of people in Honduras – *campesinos*. And, meanwhile, we were fighting with a volunteer army. They were the reserve infantry battalions – all volunteers. People from the city: workers, cab drivers, people from the poor neighbourhoods – pot-bellied men, you know. A battalion was organized and was sent to the mountains. And when they got to the mountains, they thought that all the *campesinos* were Contras. The treatment of the *campesinos* was terrible. On top of this, they were fighting on terrain that was unfamiliar to them – the mountains. The *campesinos*, on the

> other hand, were familiar with the terrain. And this is why they had the upper hand on the heights, in the valleys, and on all sides. We had no troops to fight them with.[59]

Joaquín Cuadra, chief of staff, requested a meeting with the Ortega brothers and Jaime Wheelock, the political commissar for the northern zone, which was the principal theatre of war. He asked for this meeting with a view towards reaching final decisions. His message was that the EPS was losing the war and that, without drastic changes in strategy, the Contras would be in Managua within a couple of months. Cuadra insisted on a fundamental change in recruiting tactics. Instead of training an all-volunteer army, he proposed the creation of an army of soldiers drafted from among young citizens for an obligatory two years of military service. A discussion ensued as to which was better: to lose the elections or lose the country. Once compulsory military service was approved, Humberto Ortega and Cuadra also demanded a change in the political and military management of the war:

> All authority must be subordinated to the War Plan. In the provinces, everyone is doing as he pleases. [Those working on] Agrarian Reform are doing as they please. The Health Ministry has its own plan. The party has its own plan. The police and the Ministry of the Interior each have their own plans. A Military Plan must be created and everything needs to be coordinated with that Military Plan.[60]

From that time onward, there began a gradual process by which the EPS began functioning as an autonomous entity, thus avoiding any direct control by the *dirección nacional* of the FSLN.[61] There was also a change in the way that the war was conducted – a change that had long-term consequences for both the course of the war (the EPS would end up winning the war against the Contras) and the party (the FSLN would end up losing the elections of 1990). Joaquín Cuadra describes the military strategy:

> We introduced two types of military service. The first was *national* military service, for those on the Pacific coast as well as in the universities, secondary schools, etc. [We created] mobile

> battalions that could deploy anywhere in the country and move in any direction. Three or four battalions were deployed in a coordinated fashion; these would then be demobilized while others took their place. [The other type of service was] *territorial* military service. Those who were recruited operated within their own territory, within their own towns [and villages]. We organized everything, all in the service of the Military Plan ... 'Gentlemen, here is the Plan for the following six months. Here are the Contras, here is the zone that we control, and here is where I want there to be agrarian reform. Agree as to the specific day that you deliver the [land] to *campesinos*; and along with the deed, we'll give him a rifle. We're going to train this newly armed man in 15 days. That man then immediately became an enemy of the Contras.' In this way agrarian reform was carried out as a function of the war, and not as [an independent] economic concept. And that's why it was never successful over there. Recruits, combatants in the permanent territorial companies, operated in their own towns. We thus attained two strategic objectives of the war: territory and the struggle for territory along the lines that I've described to you, on the one hand, and, on the other, elite forces, mobile forces, in the Pacific, organized in five or six separate battalions. And, finally, we carried out an operation in Honduras in order to keep them [i.e. the Contras] in Honduras. We brought together all of our battalions and crossed into Honduras. ... We penetrated 18 kilometres inside Honduran territory in order to crush the Contras on their own turf: they were materially and morally defeated.[62]

The first battalions comprised members of the Sandinista Youth. Between 1983 and 1988, the number of combatants in the regular army doubled from 40,000 to 80,000 (Núñez Soto, 1998: 448). To appreciate the significance of these numbers, it should be borne in mind that the total number of Nicaraguan public servants[63] was 75,000 in 1980 and 95,500 in 1989. Defence expenditures skyrocketed: in 1980, these accounted for about 20 per cent of the national budget, while in 1987 they grew to 46 per cent.[64] In the following years, the defence budget would come to exceed 50 per cent of the national budget (Núñez Soto, 1998: 448). It was not only the burden of fighting the Contras that accounted for an increase in the military budget. In 1984, the CIA had recommended extending the scope of the war and carrying out strategic bombing.[65] In the face of the perceived threat of an invasion of US forces, the Nicaraguan military leadership organized two separate general staffs: one to lead the war against the Contras and another to respond to a US-led invasion. During the war against the Contras, part of the EPS was being trained to rebuff a possible invasion, as Joaquín Cuadra recalls:

> All efforts were aimed at carrying out a war of resistance. If there was going to be an invasion, all notion of borders would disappear. We also let them know this: if we go into Honduras, we will join forces with the Salvadoran guerrillas. And we will even go to San José. What I mean is that if the conflict becomes international, all notion of borders will be obliterated. The idea was to force the gringos to enter an ant colony so that they wouldn't be able to just come in, strike a single blow, and take care of business in one week like they [later] did in Panama. The idea was that this would be a long-term situation that would go on indefinitely – a quagmire. They would not be doing battle with regular forces, which are at a huge disadvantage, where the other side would enjoy complete command of the air and seas. They would instead be forced to proceed on foot, conquering the territory 1 metre at a time. The price [that they would pay] would be very high.[66]

But the real war remained with the Contras. The damages suffered in the country between 1980 and 1988 totalled $17.8 billion, of which $9.8 billion was for economic damages, $1.9 billion for necessary increases in defence and security expenditures, and $1.8 billion for the dead and injured.[67] In 1984 Nicaragua brought (and later won) a lawsuit against the USA and Honduras in the International Court of the Hague, the judgment of which ordered the USA to pay Nicaragua the above-mentioned total monies in damages.[68] But this turned out to be nothing more than a moral victory. The USA refused to pay, and in 1990 the newly elected president Violeta Chamorro, who urgently needed to obtain bank credits from both the International Monetary Fund and the US government, simply forgave the damages.

The counterinsurgency campaigns of the EPS and the Special Forces of the Ministry of the Interior[69] had all of the characteristics typical of such campaigns, with violence and gifts being doled out in equal measure. In 1986, around 250,000 persons were forcibly displaced (Wheelock, 1990: 61). Their property was for the most part confiscated and transferred to the co-operative sector, with about 150 of the villages held by the Contras destroyed in reprisal (Bataillon, 1994: 196). According to official sources,[70] the death toll on both sides was about the same: more than 32,000 of the EPS personnel and civilian population and more than 29,500 of the Contras and civilians living in or near Contra bases.[71] The national death toll between 1980 and 1989 was officially calculated to be 61,826, with 60 per cent of these occurring between 1986 and 1989. The dead, the injured and the disappeared all left very deep traces in the nation's collective memory.[72] The conduct of the war against the Contra forces, the never-ending military campaigns, the economic damages and the victims in so many families, all became the subject of an ardent debate within the *dirección general.* The army commanders were absolutely unyielding in their defence of universal military service and the continuation of the war until the Contras were defeated. Most other comandantes – Henry Ruiz and even Tomás Borge – appealed for peace negotiations. The military wing of the Sandinista leadership prevailed and thus the war went on, as did the requirement of universal military service. The outcome of this debate reveals those who really held power when it came to making the most crucial decisions. It also demonstrates the autonomy that the army had acquired in relation to the party and the government.

In March 1988, a ceasefire was reached in Sapoa, a city on the border with Costa Rica, with Costa Rican diplomats serving as mediators, and in 1989 two preliminary disarmament agreements were signed by the Contras requiring that they disarm and reintegrate into Nicaraguan society and political life. Even after this, however, armed violence continued, although on a smaller scale, and shortly after the electoral victory of Violeta de Chamorro in 1990, a final agreement was reached: the Contras were to completely surrender their arms and the EPS would be recognized by the new government as the nation's only legitimate armed force. Although the military outcome of the Contra war was a Sandinista triumph, this was no more than a pyrrhic victory. In economic, social and political terms, the war had drained the lifeblood of the nation. The real-life utopia that seemed to be dawning at the time of the Sandinistas' initial triumph had ended in a nightmarish dystopia of post-war devastation and national disillusionment.

Electoral Defeat

The war had another consequence: 'The entire organization of the government was placed in the service of war, including the cooperation that we were able to secure from countries that expressed solidarity with Nicaragua.'[73] The war had affected the structure of the state, as well as plans for the social welfare and economy of the nation, which ended up heavily indebted. A pervasive poverty began to make itself felt during the years of the Contra War, and continued in its immediate aftermath.

During the years 1987–89, Nicaragua was a very poor country. Poverty was a defining characteristic of the nation, shared by a large majority of its citizens. Real income had fallen drastically. The rate of inflation had been very low throughout most of the Somoza era. Only in 1973 and 1974 had it reached double-digit levels (27 per cent and 13 per cent respectively). From 1979 onward, the inflation rate was always at least in double digits. At the beginning, it was more or less controlled: the annual average rate between 1979 and 1984 ranged from 23 per cent to 48 per cent. Beginning in 1985, there was triple-digit inflation: 219 per cent in 1985 and 747 per cent in 1986, and then a whopping 1,347 per cent in 1987. Thereafter, hyperinflation attained levels reminiscent of Weimar Germany, reaching 33,548 per cent in 1988, 1,689 per cent in 1989 and 13,490 per cent in 1990.[74]

The period of hyperinflation in Nicaragua lasted four years (from April 1987 to April 1991), one of the longest such periods in the twentieth century. In addition, the government introduced austerity measures during these years whose impact greatly increased the nation's overall poverty. First, they implemented 'Operation Berta' in 1988. A Swedish grant of $50 million was used to conduct a revaluation of all circulating currency. In an atmosphere of absolute secrecy, 'the new córdoba' was prepared; this new currency was to have a value of 1,000 'old' córdobas. This monetary conversion operation was carried out in twenty-four hours and resulted in all of the financial reserves of the Contras suddenly losing their value. But hyperinflation still continued because of the practice of inorganic issuance of currency, printing money without hard currency backing.[75] The second austerity measure had no beneficial social effects whatsoever: this consisted of the downsizing of the public sector, which involved the complete disappearance of government offices or the slashing of their budgets by 50 per cent. Public servants were fired en masse without severance pay or benefits of any kind. UN and ECLAC experts polled in 1988 felt that the austerity measures that had been instituted by the FSLN were among the most draconian in the Latin American region. The net result was a considerable increase in unemployment, which, ironically, hit FSLN members themselves the hardest of all.

During the final years of the government, the very notion of money had gradually disappeared. The córdoba had lost its utility as an exchange medium for goods and services. The salaries that people earned became less important than the public services that people actually received – for example, health and education. Provision of basic nutritional needs of the population was also a priority. The government rationed food in an equitable manner in order to meet the minimal nutritional requirements. They did this by means of distributing the 'AFA packet', which contained rice, beans and sugar (*arroz, frijoles y azúcar*) for each family. While all this was going on, the *dirección nacional* displayed open hostility towards its political adversaries, expropriating their belongings. Informal micro-entrepreneurs and *campesinos* who tried to sell their products in the streets were arrested for participating in the illegal economy. José Ángel Buitrago recalled those dark days:

> People became desperate. There were *campesinos* who were being treated like criminals. The lands of political opponents who complained were confiscated. By 1989 I had left the Ministry of External Cooperation and was heading the National Coffee Commission. I remember that I was invited by Arnoldo Alemán – at that time he was president of the Coffee Growers Union – Jaime Cuadra and Nicolás Bolaños, brother of Enrique,[76] to come to a meeting in Matagalpa. And the meeting began to take on an obviously anti-Sandinista tone. They even attacked me – they said terrible things about me.... After the meeting, I got a call from Jaime Wheelock, who said: 'I'm calling you to inform you that we've decided on account of what happened in Matagalpa to confiscate the lands of Arnoldo Alemán, Jaime Cuadra and Nicolás Bolaños.' And they went ahead and confiscated the land. And from that point on, I would say that the Frente began to feel the adverse effects of what it had done to Arnoldo Alemán – an obscure nonentity up to that point who now portrayed himself as a victim of the Sandinistas. After this event, Alemán's popularity began to increase enormously.[77]

Waning sympathy and wavering loyalty within the Nicaraguan population were now becoming clear in a way that could no longer be denied. The resistance against the Sandinista government was not limited to the Contra movement, the armed opposition of the northern *campesino* population and the indigenous peoples of the Atlantic coast. Now, there were also stirrings of discontent among residents of urban centres and within the Pacific coast region – sectors of the country that had previously supported the Sandinistas. And still, despite the discontent, the government continued to succeed in appealing to a considerable – although decreasing – proportion of the population. They continued organizing marches and meetings. On the day of the tenth anniversary of the Revolution, in July 1989, tens of thousands of sympathizers gathered for hours to await the arrival of Fidel Castro. When Castro failed to up, Daniel Ortega took the podium and received a warm l of applause.

In the final analysis, it was neither hyperinflation nor widespread poverty which led to the fall of the government. The dire state of the economy could be explained away – at least in comandantes' speeches and in the government-controlled media – as the result of the malevolent machinations of the Colossus of the North, the economic blockade and wartime privations. It was widespread despair as a result of the war's prolongation, battle deaths and injuries, along with the continued requirement of 'Patriotic Military Service' ('patriotic' meaning 'obligatory') without any end in sight that sounded the collective death knell of the Sandinista regime. The euphoria of the Revolution's first years was now but a distant memory and the prevalent mood was one of fatigue, disenchantment and uncertainty regarding the future.

In April 1989 an agreement was reached among all forces opposing the FSLN to form a broad-based political coalition including the Unión Nacional Opositora (UNO).[78] Violeta de Chamorro, widow of the venerated opposition leader Pedro Chamorro, who had been murdered by Somoza and who in 1979 had been a member of the Junta de Gobierno, was prevailed upon to lead the opposition campaign. Her son-in-law, Antonio Lacayo, acted first as her campaign manager and then as leader of the cabinet-in-waiting of the future government. In its zeal to remain in the good graces of the international community, the Sandinista government moved up the presidential elections from November 1990 to February of that same year. The majority of surveys and public opinion polls predicted an FSLN victory. In the Sandinista camp there was very little concern: no provision was made in the event of defeat at the polls. The election results surprised the majority of observers and analysts. In the end, it appeared that the costs of war weighed more heavily with the general populace than revolutionary ideals, and UNO won with 55 per cent of the vote versus 41 per cent for the FSLN.[79]

This defeat, which seemed to many to be the last gasp of socialism in the twentieth century, took place in the context of the fall of the Berlin Wall and the downfall of the Eastern European governments, and would be followed in due course by the disintegration of the Soviet Union. The imminent collapse of Soviet Communism was becoming evident to careful observers in 1989. Nevertheless, the electoral reverse came as a shock to the FSLN leadership. Vice-ministers and directors general were found crying in their offices. This lugubrious mood would endure in Sandinista circles for several years until an internal debate arose as to the causes of the defeat. Yet a serious and objective analysis was never published. One of the former members of the *dirección nacional*, Víctor Tirado, who continues to serve as an adviser to popular organizations that he himself helped create, and who over the years had distanced himself from the FSLN, provided the following personal reflections on the fall of the regime:

> I am by no means averse to providing an analysis of our mistakes. I am interested in seeking the truth as to the reasons for our defeat. The first mistake: we quickly found ourselves alone and isolated, with only our fellow socialists as allies. Having the Soviet Union instead of Central American and other Latin American governments as allies was the first mistake. Second: the stronger the ties with Cuba and the Soviet Union became, the more the USA intervened on behalf of the resistance. Third mistake: in the country, there were many small-scale producers. We expropriated these businessmen and evicted them from their lands. We confiscated. And [there were also] many producers who abandoned their lands, like the coffee growers. You know, all this created a crisis in production. An economy as weak as ours was not prepared to confront the USA.... Fourth: forgiving debts by extending additional credits. And this when Nicaragua was not producing. [Fifth:] there was also internal resistance, social resistance, on the part of displaced *campesinos*. We have to admit: this resistance was *Nicaraguan*. This wore us out internally. The people were also opposed to us. The silent disapproval and disgruntled whispers of the past three years began to be expressed openly. And we were defeated. An entire project was defeated. In sum, you know, the defeats were strategic in nature. It's true: we transferred power, and did so very smoothly. The Sandinista party, after the defeat of 1990 – pay close attention – an entire project was defeated as a result

> of these elections. The people showed that they were against the project that the Frente had underwritten.... But the Sandinista Frente never studied the reasons for this – for the defeat of the Sandinista project.[80]

The demise of the Sandinista government, and therefore of the Sandinista Revolution – had consequences that reached far beyond the borders of Nicaragua. The electoral defeat of the Sandinistas, along with the worldwide collapse of the Soviet-style communist parties, brought all hopes of revolution and the establishment of socialism in Central America to an abrupt end. Although there had never been a unified and coherent regional guerrilla project for Central America, the breakdown of the Nicaraguan revolutionary experiment had long-term consequences for the wars in El Salvador and Guatemala. The downsizing and 'de-partification' of the redoubtable Sandinista Popular Army and the Sandinista police immediately after April 1990 signified a considerable material and moral loss for the FMLN in El Salvador, and even for the URNG in Guatemala, which had never had nearly as intimate a relationship with the Sandinista Frente as their Salvadoran counterparts. In El Salvador, the Sandinista defeat helped pave the way towards pragmatic peace negotiations between the FMLN and the government and armed forces. After a half-hearted start in 1989, the real negotiation process was launched in 1990. In Guatemala formal peace talks began in 1991, by which time members of the *comandancia general* of the URNG had lost all hope of achieving total victory.

5

Negotiations, Peace and Post-war Reintegration

In public, both the armed forces and the guerrillas in Guatemala expressed a Spartan resolve to go on fighting until the bitter end – until victory or death. The leadership of the Sandinista Popular Army and that of the Contra forces in Nicaragua voiced this same uncompromising message. In private, however, discreet attempts were being made to seek a political solution: secret meetings between sides were being held well before the official commencement of peace negotiations. In El Salvador, highly regarded Cuban and Vietnamese advisers had always emphasized the necessity of a political solution.[1] In 1982 Guatemalan military dictator General Rios Montt had cautiously and via intermediaries sounded out envoys representing the URNG on the possibilities of agreeing some kind of amnesty.[2] But the terms offered were vague and the URNG never responded. The military politicians then decided to rely on Bismarck's formula of 'blood and iron' in order to achieve total victory. The longer the wars lasted, the higher the death tolls mounted, and the greater grew the throngs of internally displaced persons and refugees that fled the country, the guerrilla leadership and their political advisers began to resign themselves to the fact that there was no real possibility of final victory in sight. In Guatemala, deliberations ensued within the inner circle of the URNG leadership about the possibilities of an honourable settlement.[3] In Nicaragua, the political damage of the Contra War was openly acknowledged within the *dirección nacional* in 1989 and 1990. Several FSLN comandantes explicitly insisted on peace negotiations and peace agreements.[4] The Contra leadership agreed to a scheme of disarmament and reintegration in 1989 but their troops were still armed and combat-ready in the months leading up to the elections of 1990.

The disintegration of the Soviet Union and the downfall of the Eastern European satellite governments, along with the electoral defeat of the Sandinista government, together helped persuade the Salvadoran and Guatemalan guerrillas to the negotiating table. The Salvadoran guerrillas had waited for a final offensive to gain the upper hand in 1989, but when the hoped-for urban revolt did not take place, the *comandancia general* saw no other solution than a negotiated peace. The Guatemalan comandantes had already tested the waters in the last years of President Cerezo's government and, very soon after the election of his successor Serrano, agreed to an initial round of peace meetings in 1991. The regime change in Nicaragua in 1990 made resolute and pragmatic negotiations about the terms and conditions of peaceful transition a matter of urgent necessity.

This chapter has two sections: the first contains a detailed summary of the peace talks, while the second charts the course of the integration of the guerrilla organizations as political parties into the national arena. In the first section, I analyse the progress of the peace negotiations and show how agreements were actually reached in practice – generally through formal discussions attended by many leading figures on both sides of the conflict, but sometimes through secret bargaining and informal back channels. Conflict-study scholars emphasize the role of elite pacts as a way to bring long-standing conflicts to an end. The three successive Central American peace processes are the result of what could be viewed as nearly standard elite pacts. In the case of Nicaragua, the terms of agreement were reached in a one-to-one conversation between Antonio Lacayo, son-in-law of president-elect Violeta de Chamorro, and Sandinista chief negotiator Humberto Ortega; this tête-à-tête was mediated by former US President Carter. In the case of El Salvador, formal negotiations regarding the broad outlines of provisional agreements on specific subject matters and a final comprehensive pact took place between trusted top advisers of President Cristiani and a delegation of FMLN leaders. The hammering out of the actual provisions of the agreement took place in working groups, in meetings sometimes involving no more than four to six delegates – and at times as few as two. A United Nations undersecretary general acted as mediator in both the former and the latter meetings. This model was largely copied during the Guatemalan peace talks. These discussions involved negotiations between a government delegation – in which high-ranking military participated – headed by a trusted presidential delegate, and the *comandancia general* of the URNG. They were mediated first by the Archbishop of Guatemala and then by a personal delegate of the UN secretary general. Again, most discussions were held in small working groups. In the later stages of the process, the military establishment and the guerrilla leadership conducted secret negotiations that led to the final agreement.

Negotiations and Peace

In the 1980s, the presidents of Colombia, Costa Rica, Mexico and Venezuela had tried to pave the way for a negotiated solution of the wars. In El Salvador, the military categorically rejected any possibility of a negotiated solution. Three times between 1984 and 1989 President Duarte attempted to jump-start a dialogue between the two sides. Samayoa (2003: 45) characterized the first session as 'a dialogue of the deaf'. Other parties – high-ranking representatives of the Second Socialist International, Scandinavian heads of government, university rectors, and archbishops in the two countries – had acted as intermediaries among the government, the armed forces and the guerrillas in both El Salvador and Guatemala.[5] In the case of Nicaragua, Costa Rican diplomats functioned as mediators between the two sides. In 1983 the foreign ministers of Colombia, Mexico, Panama and Venezuela sponsored an international peace conference held on Contadora Island in Panama. There they established working groups on peace, democracy and regional security and invited their Central American colleagues to participate in a permanent dialogue on peace in the region. Argentina, Brazil, Peru and Uruguay accepted this invitation. The Central American presidents expressed their support; US spokesmen, however, refused to back the initiative. After the failure of the Contadora group to lay the groundwork for peace negotiations, Costa Rican president Arias convened a series of Central American presidential dialogues in Esquipulas, Guatemala (1986–87). It was there that agreements were reached that established the context for preliminary peace negotiations, ceasefire, international verification procedures, timetables for partial and final accords, and the definitive end of hostilities.

As a consequence of the Esquipulas accords, the UN Security Council agreed to form a United Nations Observation Mission to Central America (ONUCA). Emissaries of the UN secretary general visited El Salvador, Nicaragua and Guatemala. This mission comprised high-ranking delegates, special UN negotiation teams and peace and verification functionaries. The peace negotiations in Nicaragua were conducted bilaterally, between the government and the Contras, at the very beginning of the government period of Violeta de Chamorro. The presence of the UN verification missions ONUSAL (in El Salvador) and MINUGUA (in Guatemala) in each case made a decisive contribution to the de-escalation of the conflict, overseeing the disarmament of the guerrillas (in El Salvador) and preparing monthly reports on the implementation of the agreements in both El Salvador and Guatemala.[6]

By the end of 1989 the US administration of George H.W. Bush sent an unmistakable signal of a change in US foreign policy in the region. Bush instructed General Woerner, who as commander-in-chief of the US Southern Command was the official responsible for implementing US national security policy in Latin America, to announce Washington's support for democratic government in Central America. He famously called for the generals and military politicians to 'return to the barracks'. This message was highly resented in El Salvador[7] where the military, immediately after the guerrilla offensive in the same year, were still licking their wounds.

Nicaragua

It was not President Daniel Ortega but rather his brother Humberto who played a key role in the negotiations on peace and democratic transition. Humberto Ortega had headed the negotiation team in Sapoa that in March 1988 concluded the first de-escalation agreement with the Contras. Although in 1989 two more specific disarmament accords had been signed with the Resistencia Nacional, as the Contras were officially known, armed clashes continued to occur. In the summer of 1989, ONUCA was instrumental in securing the closure of all Contra encampments in Honduras. In exchange, the Sandinistas moved the elections forward from November to February 1990. Amid the prevailing confusion following the Sandinista electoral defeat in 1990,

> President Carter was instrumental in bringing about the first meeting between 'officials of the outgoing government' – these were his words – and 'officials of the incoming government', [which] took place forty-eight hours after the elections. The Frente Sandinista sent three persons. I and another person representing President Violeta [Chamorro] went and met with [officials of] the OEA and the UN, and with President Carter. There was an initial exchange which primarily focused on the future of the Contras – this was their principal concern. The following day, I held a private [conversation] in my house with General Humberto Ortega, who was the head of the [FSLN] delegation. The two of us spoke alone for a long time – about three hours. We ended up reaching agreement regarding fundamental objectives. One of these was the pacification of the country, ending the

> war. Another agreement had to do with the legal framework. We said that we were going to act in complete accordance with the [Sandinista] constitution – which was not something we had created, but which was the nation's constitution – and with all other laws. In exchange for this, we asked them to act in complete accordance with this same constitution, which clearly establishes that the armed forces are subordinate in power to the president of the republic. Upon her inauguration, Doña Violeta would be the supreme chief and this would mean that the armed forces would have to show their loyalty to the constitutional president and not to the Sandinista movement. Afterwards, we spoke for a while about the subject of property – specifically, about agrarian reform. I said that the land allotments provided for under the agrarian reform would be respected, with compensation made to the former owners. We agreed on an instrument that we called 'the transition protocol', which was published on 28 February 1990 in both *La Prensa* and in *El Nuevo Diario*.[8]

The fragile agreement[9] that grew out of these meetings formally recognized the Ejército Popular Sandinista (EPS) as the country's only armed institution, under the dual leadership of Generals Humberto Ortega and Joaquín Cuadra Lacayo, but with drastically reduced numbers of both officers and troops. President Violeta de Chamorro assumed the function of minister of defence, delegating *de facto* authority for this cabinet post to Minister-President Antonio Lacayo.[10] All formal relations between the EPS and the FSLN were abruptly ended; and the armed institution was renamed the Nicaraguan National Army. Comparable conditions obtained with respect to the reconstitution of the Sandinista police force – namely, its transformation into a national institution and the severing of previous organizational ties to the FSLN. René Vivas, the director general of the Policía Sandinista, remained in his position as head of the reorganized National Police before being asked to retire in 1992. Antonio Lacayo successfully concluded peace negotiations with the Contra leadership in March 1990. One month later, and two weeks after the inauguration of the new government, peace accords were formally signed and the disarmament process commenced under the auspices of the United

Nations and the OAS. In June 1990 the Contra forces were demobilized. Concomitantly, the reorganization of the Nicaraguan National Army was proceeding apace. In June 1990 around half of all army personnel, soldiers and officers were discharged; more than 200,000 reserve troops had previously been released from military service. Within a period of two years, the 80,000-man standing army was reduced to 12,500, transforming what had been Central America's largest army into the region's smallest national armed force (1992). In 2005 the Ejército de Nicaragua had 1,475 officers and 9,399 troops.[11] The fleet of Soviet helicopters, as well as the Soviet-made sophisticated radar defence systems, were sold to the Ecuadorian and the Peruvian armed forces, which were engaged in border clashes along their common frontier in 1992.[12]

The Sandinistas transferred power to the incoming Chamorro government in a fair and equitable manner. Nevertheless, in the transfer of state properties the senior FSLN leadership had apparently forgotten the difference between mine and thine. The *pacto* between the Sandinistas and the new government called for a legal solution for the property transfers that had been made during the Sandinista government. This provision was interpreted extremely liberally by the FSLN during the transition period between the elections and Chamorro's presidential inauguration (i.e. between February and April 1990). In the 1980s a significant transfer of individual rural assets to communal and co-operative property had been implemented. Under the optimistic assumption that the Revolution would be eternal, little attention had been paid to creating a legal basis for such a transfer. The government had also issued urban land plots to (former) *guerrilleros*, militia volunteers and ex-combatants as a reward for services rendered to the Revolution. Special legislation was immediately enacted to regulate the property titles (Wheelock, 1991; Zamora, 1996). Nevertheless, some of the most influential comandantes, as well as many Sandinista functionaries, used the opportunity to appropriate state property – houses, vehicles, furniture, and so on. At least one senior comandante created his own commune, providing the loyal ex-employees of his ministry with plots surrounding his own home – and with weapons as well. Some highest-ranking Sandinista officials appropriated government monies by using figurehead corporations; others became 'Sandinista entrepreneurs', and initially served in the role of trustees of FSLN holdings. This process came to be known as 'Daniel's piñata':[13] an opportunity for government officials, from high to low, to appropriate possessions of the state. Some ministries – Foreign Affairs, Interior, Economy, Industry and Commerce – were completely looted; in some cases, high cabinet officials of Chamorro's incoming government entered offices that were lacking desks and chairs.[14] A couple of days before the transfer of power, President Daniel Ortega enlarged the number of public servants and increased their salaries by an average of 300 per cent.[15] 'Daniel's piñata' tarnished the image of moral superiority and revolutionary purity that the Sandinistas had so assiduously cultivated.

El Salvador

In El Salvador the guerrillas had never been in power. Yet the FMLN was a force to be reckoned with. After ten years of war a military stalemate was reached. Thus, both sides reluctantly came to realize that peace would be achieved only through a political solution. El Salvador's first ARENA president, Alfredo Cristiani, had always remembered the good advice of his political mentor, Roberto D'Aubuisson: to provide the FMLN with a compelling reason to come to the negotiating table:

> It was important to offer the FMLN a way out via a golden bridge. It was obvious that finding a way forward to peace was going to be the first task of government. [First] we needed to suggest a negotiation process that would require that, once we had started, we would not leave the table until we had found a solution. [Second...] all of the guerrilla forces, or at least the large majority of them, had in some way tried to participate in elections in order to look for a way to attain power via electoral means. However, the military prevented them from doing this. Whether the military won or lost, in reality they always won

> [by appointing the president]. And this led to violent clashes between the opposing sides. So it was important to propose to the FMLN that we try to reach an agreement that would lead to peace; an agreement that would strengthen the nation's democratic institutions. For us, it was obvious that if we insisted on talking about economic issues, we would be painting ourselves into a corner. We would not be able to reach an agreement there. But on political issues, we could do so. If everyone – the right, the centre, the left – if we all believed in democracy, we would all win. What we sought to do first and foremost was to create an agenda in which the main issue was that of political space and the strengthening of democratic institutions in El Salvador.[16]

Cristiani asked Father Ellacuría, the Jesuit UCA rector, to act as an intermediary between him and the FMLN *dirección nacional.* Ellacuría came back with a categorical 'no': the FMLN leadership, preparing the 1989 offensive, only discussed a 'final insurrection' and was not particularly enthusiastic about being involved in peace negotiations before the popular uprising, which they expected to erupt at any moment. Nevertheless, Cristiani went ahead and announced his initiative during his inaugural address of 1 July 1989. The FMLN accepted the invitation and attended the peace talks, with the first round of talks being held in Mexico and the second round in Costa Rica. The Salvadoran Army Command – composed primarily of hardliners[17] – refused to attend the sessions. President Cristiani was forced to appoint a cabinet member, who was also a retired general, to represent the armed forces.

During the 1989 FMLN offensive that was launched after the first sessions of the peace negotiations, this organization withdrew its representatives from negotiations. The government envoys, meanwhile, continued to show up. The outcome of the offensive would have profound and long-lasting effects on the course of the struggle. The FMLN, in spite of an impressive show of firepower, was not able to ignite a popular insurrection. The army, on the other hand, successfully resisted but also emerged less than fully satisfied, in that they had come nowhere near achieving total victory. Additionally, the government forces were discredited in the eyes of the common people and the international community as a result of both atrocities they committed during counter-attacks and their cold-blooded murders of Father Ellacuría and five other Jesuit priests. Even the Reagan administration and the Pentagon expressed indignation.[18] During the two years of the negotiations preceding the signing of the peace agreements, both the military and the guerrillas began to show signs of battle fatigue. General Mauricio Vargas, deputy chief of staff, who was a member of the government delegation after the FMLN offensive, had enormous difficulties in convincing his military colleagues to engage in the peace process.[19] Ultimately it was the instinct of institutional self-preservation – the National Army's wish to avoid complete annihilation – that prodded the military leadership towards the negotiating table. Vargas recalls this tense period:

> Well, if we [i.e. the military] want to go on like this for another forty years, then OK. Let's drop an atomic bomb: out of the nation's 6 million people, 100,000 will survive. But their relatives [i.e. of the FMLN rebels] will live on, and thus the conflict will resume once again. Let's put a stop to this – for good. But the hardest thing of all for the armed forces to understand, in my opinion, is that the intoxication of power is ten times greater than that of liquor. And I can survive the hangover from getting drunk. But the hangover from the intoxication of power – I don't want to get it in the first place, let alone have to deal with its effects afterwards. To be at the summit of power – to be at the centre of the power that governs everyone and controls everything – overcoming this addiction is the most painful of all.[20]

Given the agreement of both sides on the necessity of a peace with honourable conditions, agreement was quickly reached on the framework of the negotiations that would take place: an agenda of political and democratic reforms: the reorganization and purification of the armed forces and the police, a reform of the judiciary, and the complete demilitarization of the state. Pragmatism prevailed on both sides. Proposals about far-reaching anti-capitalist reforms were swiftly withdrawn from the agenda.

Both sides had very large delegations. The UN monitoring and mediating mission, headed by UN deputy secretary general Alonso de Soto, was also sizeable, and delegates representing religious and the civilian organizations, as well as envoys of the 'friendly countries' of Colombia, Mexico, Spain and Venezuela – countries that would act as guarantors of any agreement reached – also included large numbers of people. The crucial issues, however, were resolved by two negotiating commissions, each consisting of three people. Representing the government were Oscar Santamaría, prime minister; David Escobar Galindo, university rector and Cristiani's personal adviser and text writer; and General Mauricio Vargas. Representing the FMLN were Schafik Handal, the formal delegation leader; Salvador Samayoa, the well-connected and prestigious senior diplomat of the Frente; and Ana Maria Guadalupe, the trusted comrade of Villalobos.[21] Out of meetings between these two three-member delegations emerged most of the agreements on political reforms, demobilization and the purging of the army, the creation of a new police force that would include former guerrillas, reform of the judiciary and the electoral system, and the institution of municipal democracy. David Escobar Galindo described the process as follows:

> The fundamental problem of the twenty-five sessions of the peace negotiations was that, for many years, it had been the army that had essentially administered the political system. And the FMLN was a political group that had risen up in arms. So the peace agreement did a good job, I think, of putting these two forces in their proper places. The armed forces [would become] an apolitical institution with weapons. The FMLN would become an unarmed political party.[22]

The final agreement was brokered by the United Nations and underwritten by the four 'friendly countries', with the USA acting as co-guarantor. Not long after the agreements, President Cristiani decreed a far-reaching amnesty. Hundreds of members of the armed forces, as well as some high-ranking FMLN leaders – especially those of the ERP, in Villalobos's inner circle – were officially pardoned. Although these pardons would remain the subject of heated discussion for many years, it cannot be denied that the amnesty decrees contributed to fostering a climate of moderation and reconciliation.[23]

Guatemala[24]

Although the Guatemalan guerrilla movement was undeniably forced onto the defensive after the counterinsurgency campaigns of 1982–83, the leadership of the URNG had never responded to the half-hearted amnesty scheme of Rios Montt in 1982. But the organization finally decided to test the waters when Vinicio Cerezo of the Christian Democratic Party (DC) became Guatemala's first civilian post-military president in January 1986. Miguel Ángel Reyes was a long-time friend of Cerezo who had previously served with him as a DC adviser to fledgling *campesino* organizations in the mid-1970s and later joined the ranks of the FAR, representing the Guatemalan guerrillas in Costa Rica. He and several other ex-DC members of the URNG consulted with the guerrilla leadership to explore the possibilities of peace negotiations with the president-elect. The first informal and off-the-record contact took place in the Cariari Hotel near San José.[25] There were later informal tête-à-têtes at El Escorial in Spain, where the Spanish Crown hosted talks between a URNG representative and civilian and military delegates. Guatemalan ambassador Danilo Barrillas, the head of the delegation in Spain and a close friend of President Cerezo, was assassinated upon his return to Guatemala 'under mysterious circumstances' – the standard Guatemalan expression in those days for politically motivated killings. Indignant officers within the military were outraged by the secret participation of military envoys in the peace talks and staged the first of two coups against Minister of Defence Gramajo.[26] Nevertheless, President Cerezo created a National Reconciliation Commission (CNR) headed by Msgr Quesada Turuño, Archbishop (and, later, Cardinal) of Guatemala; other members were politicians of the various parties, with a retired military politician serving as liaison between the

URNG and the generals. After holding a series of discussions with the political parties, entrepreneurs, professional associations and the military, the CNR organized a formal dialogue in Oslo in 1990 between representatives of the nation's legally sanctioned political parties – from the far right to the DC – and delegates of the URNG. The Oslo conference led to a series of bilateral discussions involving the URNG in the following months: in Spain (with the political parties), in Canada (with the entrepreneurial class), and twice in Mexico (first with the middle-class organizations and then with the trade unions and the popular organizations).

The old guard of the Guatemalan military hardliners, who were still in power, were extremely reluctant to engage in peace negotiations. In their eyes, they were winning the war. Why, then, should they negotiate? President Jorge Antonio Serrano Elías, who was elected in 1991, decided to take on the military establishment and, as supreme commander, explicitly instructed the recalcitrant generals to form a permanent military mission that would serve as an integral part of the government delegation.[27] As luck would have it, the senior colonels and junior generals appointed to this mission were soon thereafter promoted to high-level positions in the military hierarchy. This new generation of officers was finally convinced of the necessity of a negotiated end to the war. In military terms, the prevalence of the army over the guerrilla forces was evident. The younger Guatemalan military, however, had learned never to underestimate the political costs incurred as a result of endless counterinsurgency campaigns against guerrilla forces that were able to recruit from a seemingly endless pool of new combatants, and miring the nation indefinitely in conflict and bloodshed. The army command wanted to continue fighting, but gradually became convinced of the necessity of a negotiated settlement, provided that the important gains that they had achieved would be confirmed as part of any final accord. The Guatemalan guerrilla leadership, in contrast to their Salvadoran brothers-in-arms, who had opted for a pragmatic political solution after accepting the reality of an impasse with no end in sight, was prepared to continue fighting for another decade or more in the event that peace talks did not lead to a satisfactory outcome. They would continue talking but would lay down their arms if and only if some of their long-cherished objectives were achieved: far-reaching economic, social, cultural and political reforms that would justify the sacrifices, in terms of loss of life and suffering that had been made during the course of more than thirty years of war. It was under the burden of these historically laden expectations that negotiations proceeded fitfully between the years 1991 to 1996. These talks were presided over by three different heads of state, three delegation leaders, and two mediators – Msgr Quezada (conciliator) and UN delegate Jean Arnault (mediator).

President Serrano opted in May 1993 to suspend the constitution and to carry out a self-coup in a way that emulated Peruvian president Alberto Fujimori's accomplishment of the feat just one year previously. Serrano attempted to do this with the assistance of the army. In Guatemala, however, this coup attempt was immediately greeted by widespread popular protest. The army leadership, which in turn began to waver in its resolve, consulted the constitutional court, which declared the attempted overthrow unconstitutional. The failed self-coup led to the Guatemalan parliament appointing De León Carpio, at that time the nation's human rights ombudsman, as president. Shortly after taking office, De León Carpio purged the military hardliners from his cabinet and appointed instead more progressive ministers who were much more acceptable negotiating partners in the eyes of the guerrillas. A newly formed Asamblea de la Sociedad Civil (ASC), headed by Msgr Quesada Turuño and consisting of trade-union officials, journalists, Maya representatives and leaders of other popular movements, functioned as a kind of extra-parliamentary support group. Surprisingly, the Congress remained very quiet during these years. As a consequence of the first partial accord – concerning human rights – in 1994, a UN verification mission (MINUGUA) was established in Guatemala: its mission following the final peace agreement in 1996 was to monitor compliance with the terms of the settlement.

In April 1991, the first in a long series of peace talks took place in Mexico. The government negotiating team comprised civilian government appointees along with four military delegates. The guerrillas were represented by the four members of the URNG *comandancia general*, accompanied by their advisers. The formal negotiations carried on over the course of six years, during which time there were several interruptions when the URNG leadership thought it better to retire from the negotiating table. As in the case of El Salvador, the actual negotiations were for the most part conducted in small working groups of four to six persons. Equally, an initial agreement stipulated that all substantive accords would be suspended until the final peace agreement was signed. But in contrast to the case of El Salvador, where both parties basically negotiated about a solution of the armed conflict by means of political reforms, the Guatemalan peace talks were characterized by a gradually expanding agenda: political reforms, complete economic transformation of the country, special agreements on behalf of the indigenous population, and so on.

In December 1996, the final peace agreement was signed, making effective all previous partial accords. But all these wide-ranging partial accords – calling for revolutionary economic transformations, the definitive end of the second-class citizenship of the Maya peoples and other 'minorities', the radical reform of the judiciary, far-reaching educational and linguistic reform, and so on – were never actually put into practice. Even worse, when in May 1999, three years after the peace agreements, the government organized a plebiscite on the necessary constitutional reforms implied by the peace agreements of 1996 and other important administrative changes, it was soundly defeated: this negative vote dealt a heavy blow to the credibility of the peace process. The economic transformations and the constitutional reforms were postponed indefinitely. The extreme poverty of vast sectors of the nation was never resolved. About a third of the combatants on both sides – soldiers, paramilitary and guerrilla forces – migrated to the USA as either legal or undocumented immigrants to escape the desperate situation.[28] The ethnic rift that pervaded Guatemalan society remained essentially unhealed, the judiciary and the public sector was only partially modernized, and the notion of equal status for the twenty-plus Maya and other indigenous languages remained little more than a dead letter.

Nevertheless, the negotiated peace did bring the war itself to a definitive conclusion. Two Truth Commissions – one organized by the office of the archbishop and the other by the United Nations – published separate reports, in 1998 and 1999 respectively.[29] Some vital agreements involving the monitoring of human rights and the reform of the security sector were indeed implemented: specifically a transformation and radical reduction of the armed forces, the creation of a new national police and the demobilization of the URNG. It is fair to conclude that the success of the security-related agreements was the result of a gradual rapprochement between the army and the URNG.[30] The personalities of the two main protagonists, Asturias and Balconi, were decisive. During lunch or dinner breaks in the course of each two-week negotiating session, they developed a strong rapport and mutual trust. At one point each man agreed to keep the other informed about sensitivities and susceptibilities within his own camp in order to avoid unnecessary friction during the public sessions. In private conversations they exchanged impressions about how proposals on demobilization and disarmament, the reduction of the army, the abolishing of the various police organizations, the new security doctrines, and other matters, would be received by the other side. In early 1993 they worked together to establish a direct dialogue between the Army Command and the URNG. After initial sessions between Balconi and the four URNG leaders, the Army Command convinced President De León Carpio of the advisability of high-level discussions between an army delegation and the URNG leadership. The first session was held with little fanfare in Cancún, Mexico. When in 1996 newly elected President Arzú appointed Balconi as minister of defence, negotiations between army and guerrilla leaderships were intensified – with the full consent of the president. They asked each other, in confidence, 'What will happen to us after the peace'? At another session, the URNG suggested half-jokingly that the next session should be held in Cuba. Balconi accepted the challenge and organized – through intermediaries – a three-day session in Havana, under the auspices of Fidel and Raúl Castro. The Havana session marked the decisive reconciliation between the army and URNG. Immediately afterwards the URNG announced a unilateral ceasefire and Balconi ordered the disbanding of the hated paramilitary patrols. The army staff and the second-in-commands of the URNG worked out the timetable of disarmament of the guerrilla forces, and the peace was signed in December 1996.

Integration into Society

The demobilization process of the former guerrilla forces in El Salvador and Guatemala, and of the Contra fighters in Nicaragua, proceeded without difficulties and without violence. Most fighters returned to their neighbourhoods, villages and communities. The rural ex-combatants found employment with their families, generally sharing a very modest income. Most ex-combatants with an urban background ended up in the informal economy. In many Maya communities in Guatemala, war widows, their families and demobilized guerrilla fighters had to live in the same neighbourhoods as former paramilitary perpetrators of violence and their relatives. Despite this potentially combustible situation, large-scale violence did not occur. When disabled FMLN veterans returned from Cuba to El Salvador in wheelchairs after the final peace agreement, there was a widespread emotional reaction among the popular sectors, with some people weeping openly in the streets. It was only in Nicaragua that the problem of unemployment of the former Contras and the large contingent of demobilized army officers led to a series of short-term and localized armed conflicts in the mid-1990s.

In this section I present the country analyses in inverse chronological order, beginning with Guatemala, where the peace and reconciliation process started in 1996 and where the URNG encountered substantial difficulties in establishing itself in the political arena and among the organizations of civil society. In El Salvador, the party that emerged from the former FMLN organizations achieved an institutional position that nearly equalled the popularity of the party blocs of the right. In Nicaragua, the last country discussed in this section, I follow the fate of the transformation of the Sandinista party into a 'Danielista' party machine, ending the chapter with the inauguration of Daniel Ortega in 2007 following his election as president.

Guatemala

The day after the formal peace ceremony at the presidential palace, General Balconi, URNG coordinator Ramírez de León and Nobel laureate Rigoberta Menchú planted a ceiba tree, a Maya symbol of reconciliation. One important figure was absent from these festivities: Asturias, the charismatic and internationally recognized URNG leader. A couple of weeks before the signing of peace agreements an elderly and wealthy widow, Olga de Novella, had been kidnapped for ransom. Military intelligence established the involvement of an ORPA commando.[31] President Arzú was furious and wanted to suspend the peace arrangements. His trusted political secretary and former EGP associate Gustavo Porras was sent with Balconi – whose good relations with the comandantes was well known – to meet with the URNG leadership in Mexico City. These men had not been informed by Asturias of the planned kidnapping, however: they felt betrayed and accused him of imperilling all formal and informal agreements. Asturias scapegoated his second-in-command Isaías as the person responsible for the assault. The incident was extremely inconvenient for the URNG and quite opportune for Asturias's enemies. This episode eventually cost Asturias his reputation within the URNG; he had to accept a secondary role in the party hierarchy for many years to come. Even worse, Arzú immediately rescinded all standing gentlemen's agreements with the URNG. The episode almost certainly contributed to the URNG not being immediately recognized as a formal political party, whereas the Salvadoran FMLN had been recognized a couple of months after the peace accords.

The structure of the URNG, whose *dirección general* of four members made all of the organization's important decisions (e.g. re military operations, peace negotiations, relations with the outside world), was extremely centralized during the war. Afterwards, without internal elections or membership conventions, the three former URNG military leaders continued to command the embryonic party. The URNG cadres referred to this leadership model as *comandantismo*. It was no secret that the comandantes had antagonistic relations among themselves. Things only grew worse with the death in 1998 of Ramírez de León (Rolando Morán), the EGP leader who had always acted as mediator. Jorge Soto (Pablo Monsanto), an implacable hardliner, succeeded him as secretary general of the URNG. The cumbersome legal procedures of formal registration of the organization as a legally constituted political party were delegated to Celso Morales (Tomás) of the EGP and Santiago Santa Cruz of the ORPA; this process lasted two years. Alba Estela Maldonado (Lola) explains:

> We had a very tough beginning – it lasted two years – in order to form a political party. At that time, it was necessary to gather a certain number – something like a little over 4,000 signatures – in order to be recognized. I'm going to say something now that is very hard, but it's the truth: the signing of the peace meant for us that after so many years underground – for some 10 years, for others 20 or 30 years, even up to 36 years – that we returned to the [social] class from which we had originally come. This means, for example, that someone who had been a poor *campesino* was once again a poor *campesino*. And someone who had come from the petite bourgeoisie went back to being part of the petite bourgeoisie. There were also people from a much more well-to-do class – better off even than the bourgeoisie. For example, someone who, on account of his class, had undergone academic study and then had joined [the movement] and had gone underground – there was a big difference between the possibilities of such a person and someone who had learned how

> to read and write when he was a member of a guerrilla unit, and whom the government considered as having completed the third or the sixth grade – let's say the third grade. There's really quite a difference.... Many male and female comrades were left to their own devices: some searched the cemeteries for their dead relatives – the children and parents who had been massacred. Others tried to find out if they still had been left some plot of land, or part of some plot of land. Men and women looked for their wives and husbands only to find that they had found other partners. This is a very profound human drama – a subject that was never discussed but that we carry in our hearts. Those who had been working in the revolutionary organization for so many years, but who were left to their own fate – we really have no right to ask that they dedicate so much time and effort to forming a political party. Another factor is that we had to spread out across the country. This was because our ranks comprised people from all over: from the north, south, east and west, and sometimes in remote, inaccessible places. I think that it also had to do with a certain profound despair, certain uneasiness on the part of the fighters and militants with the peace agreements themselves, you know.[32]

The URNG, with its small nucleus of both committed cadres and rank-and-file members, and having only the most tenuous of connections with the newly emerging Maya movements,[33] opted for a political alliance with other leftist parties, some of them sectarian splinter groups. The alliance that emerged, Alianza Nueva Nación (ANN), participated in a broader electoral centre-left party coalition that acquired 12 per cent of the votes in the 1999 elections. After this meagre performance, a fair number of party cadres, disillusioned by the *comandantismo*, left the URNG. An even more crucial parting of the ways occurred between the URNG and the social movements, popular organizations and Maya federations that had been arising in the pre-peace period in the years of formal democracy, between 1985 and 1996. The URNG even helped hasten the demise of the COPMAGUA, the national confederation of Maya movements.[34] The party simply failed to attract a new generation of either the nation's Maya population or progressive-minded Ladinos.[35]

Tensions between the three party factions – EGP, ORPA and the FAR – increased. Relations between the two veteran leaders of URNG, Soto and Asturias, escalated; this ultimately led to a rupture along the former factional lines. In 2001 a public scandal involving incest allegations against a young emerging leader of the URNG's Executive Committee, Arnoldo Noriega,[36] and the subsequent internal party tribunal, marked the beginning of the end of party unity:

> There were discussions about Noriega, about whether or not to stand by him. Afterwards, we had to withdraw our support. But the split had already begun to form during the discussions. In the national [party] assembly, two different platforms were presented: one from FAR that was called The Revolutionary Current, stating that they would save us – the classic ploy whenever there is any kind of schism. It came to where there was open conflict. We won the internal elections, and then the actual split occurred. The Revolutionary Current withdrew, and later renamed itself ANN.[37]

Most of the former FAR members left the URNG to join the newly created Alianza Nueva Nación (ANN), an alliance between the FAR faction led by Jorge Soto and the movement around Nineth Montenegro, a human rights activist with an urban following. In 2003, ANN obtained six seats in parliament (two for Soto, four for Montenegro). Afterwards, the alliance split and Montenegro formed her own political party, Encuentro por Guatemala. The URNG, the redoubt of the former EGP and ORPA members, participated in these elections with Asturias as presidential candidate. They obtained less than 3 per cent of the votes and its one seat in parliament was occupied by EGP Comandante Lola. Asturias died in June 2005. He spent his last years lonely and destitute, having spent his life savings – $3,000 – on the URNG presidential campaigns. The funeral cortège of 3,000 people made a stop at URNG headquarters before gathering at the cemetery, shouting, '¡Compañero Gaspar, para siempre!' (Comrade Gaspar, forever!) In his graveside eulogy, Jorge Soto (Pablo Monsanto) waxed rhapsodic about the unity of the Guatemalan left.

El Salvador

A couple of months before the signing of the peace agreements, Eduardo Sancho (1991a, 1991b), a member of the *comandancia general* of the FMLN, published a two-part essay about the challenges of post-war El Salvador. In the first part, he bade farewell to traditional 'bureaucratic' socialism. In the second part, he pondered the prospects of a 'democratic revolution' with self-management experiments and co-operativism within a free-market economy. This very moderate action programme could have been that of a centre-left party in any country of the present-day European Union. There was no mention of the path to socialism by the armed revolutionary masses. Sancho's proposals reflected the general pragmatism of the FMLN on the eve of the post-conflict period. In fact, the peace accords had left the structure of the national economy intact. In post-war El Salvador two important economic changes took place: the transformation of the traditional coffee-producing elites into an urban banking-and-shopping-mall bourgeoisie,[38] and the massive migration of poor Salvadorans to Mexico and the USA as legal or undocumented migrant workers.[39] The role of the FMLN was negligible in both of these great events.

Their diminished role in Salvadoran politics notwithstanding, the FMLN rose like a phoenix from the fire and ashes of the war that had devastated the country. In contrast to the frustratingly slow legalization of the URNG in Guatemala, the formal legalization of the FMLN by the electoral tribunal was achieved in three months. Religious leaders of all Christian denominations were invited as honorary witnesses to the proceedings marking the FMLN's legalization.[40] The leadership structure reflected the old politico-military organization of the civil war. As in Guatemala, *comandantismo* prevailed in the leading positions; for the middle cadre positions 'guerrilla experience' was required (Zamora, 1998: 216 ff.). In contrast to Guatemala, at least some special funds were allocated to facilitate the social and economic integration of 600 FMLN members into leadership and cadre positions;[41] for the rank and file, the 'normal' integration route was the national informal labour market and remittance-migration to either Mexico or the USA.

The immediate electoral prominence of the FMLN in 1994, when the party participated for the first time in national elections, was a surprise to both the right and the left. ARENA had underestimated the strong electoral nucleus – the so-called *voto duro* – of the former guerrillas, and expected to win easily. ARENA won the 1994 presidential election – and they have won every presidential election since then – but they needed a second round to defeat the FMLN. The Christian Democrats were reduced to the status of a fringe party.[42] In subsequent municipal elections FMLN candidates have been even more successful. The party consolidated its gains, and within the Salvadoran political scenario a kind of two-party equilibrium emerged, with ARENA and the FMLN being the stable electoral organizations of the right and left respectively. Since then, however, a fifteen-year process of leadership drainage, purges and expulsions in both parties has resulted in a landscape of many dwarf parties across the political spectrum.

In fact, the marriages of convenience of the constituent parties under the umbrella structure of the FMLN, whose internal differences and conflicts had been swept under the rug during the war, disintegrated during the post-war decade. Slowly but surely the old cadres, and even the senior comandantes, disappeared from the party leadership, to the dismay of the loyal middle cadres.[43] Within the FMLN, the sequence of internal divisions resulted in the emergence of two competing currents: the *ortodoxos* and the *renovadores*, entangled in power struggles that masqueraded as ideological debates. Eventually, in 1997 Schafik Handal, FMLN's first general coordinator (1993–94), succeeded in becoming FMLN's parliamentary leader, being re-elected as such twice and controlling the party from this power position. Internal democracy is not the most outstanding party characteristic; every now and then emerging *renovadores* are purged. In 2004 Handal was the party's presidential candidate. This former leader of the Communist Party who in 1980 unenthusiastically joined the FMLN remained the staunch leader of the organization's orthodox wing. He was the party's presidential candidate in 2004; he died in January 2006 of a heart attack.

The leadership drainage was also felt at the level of municipal government. Héctor Silva, a doctor who was twice elected FMLN mayor of San Salvador, sketches the fault lines:

> when you are serving in office, the question is: where is the money going to come from? Then you have to start implementing a fiscal policy, you have to create a rational leftist agenda. There's the concept of the 'vanguard of the proletariat'. Of course there is the assumption that the party – the Communist Party, because there is no other party worthy of the name – is the sole repository of Truth, that it can make any kind of alliance and that it can do whatever it wants – but if others do the same thing, then they're traitors. At the end of my second term, we were already having a lot of conflicts. If we wanted to undertake projects, we would have to raise taxes. What are the fairest kinds of taxes? Another problematic issue: urban planning. Afterwards there was the most problematic issue of all: the renewal of slum areas. The renewal of slum areas requires money, investment and technical assistance. It also requires cooperation with the central government. I'm giving an abbreviated version here of a much longer story. And the last problematic issue was the health workers' strike. We all participated in this movement. When the president withdrew the privatization bill from Congress, I proposed to the party that we take advantage of the opportunity to bring the conflict to an end. [But] the party ascribed greater importance to another Marxist concept: 'the sharpening of contradictions' and 'the crisis of the bourgeois system'. So I left the party in 2002.[44]

There is an interesting contrast between the impact of leadership change in ARENA, the successor organization of the military dictatorship, and in the post-war FMLN, the successor party of the revolution.[45] A couple of years before the peace ARENA, the party of the military and the death squads under ex-mayor D'Aubuisson, was taken over by Cristiani, who represented the more respectable face of the entrepreneurial elite. A couple of years after the first post-war elections, Schafik Handal, the only non-combatant member of the *dirección general* of the FMLN during the war, usurped power in this organization after the departure of three of the four 'historical' comandantes with troops and a following. In the case of ARENA, the leadership transition led to a broadening of its membership base: from urban and rural radicals to a mass following with a strong rural prominence. In contrast, the FMLN is mostly represented in the larger cities. ARENA has a hold over the majority of municipalities, but the population of the (fewer) municipalities where the FMLN controls the city councils represents more than 50 per cent of the electorate. The FMLN is an urban party, while ARENA's base is in El Salvador's rural areas. This political bipolarity has prevailed ever since the peace agreements of 1992.

Nicaragua

After losing the elections in 1990, Daniel Ortega announced that he would 'govern from below'. It was both a threat and a promise. In the first years of the 1990s he twice instigated urban unrest that brought the government to the brink of collapse. With respect to his implied promise of acquiring government power, he had to wait seventeen years until his inauguration for a second presidential term, but it cannot be denied that between 1990 and 2007 Ortega exercised a great deal of *de facto* political power in Nicaragua. Streetwise but lacking charisma in public, his ability to outwit rivals within his own party and his unscrupulous willingness to make a deal with any politician holding power, allowed him to function as something of a 'co-president' during the administrations of Violeta de Chamorro (1990-97), Arnoldo Alemán (1997-2002) and Enrique Bolaños (2002-07). The FSLN controlled a considerable segment of the neighbourhood organizations; the unions of transport workers, the paramedics and the teachers; and the student movement. Lacayo, Chamorro's minister president and political factotum, had to depend on an unstable partnership with the Sandinistas when his heterogeneous UNO (Unión Nacional Opositora) alliance quickly collapsed. In order to make it unmistakably clear that he expected to be taken very seriously, Daniel Ortega instigated urban unrest on two separate occasions. In each instance, the government had to seek the intervention of the army, commanded by his brother Humberto.[46] When the president announced Humberto's departure as army commander in August 1993, the two Ortega brothers visited her office and threatened her advisers.[47] Joaquín Cuadra succeeded Humberto in early 1995 for a period of five years. He consolidated the army's position as a constitutional and apolitical institution, even confronting the armed opposition of former Contras and former EPS members, who had revolted. Between 1993 and 1997 this kind of social banditry plagued the country:[48]

> A group of *recompas*, including former captains, took Estelí, the nation's third largest city. Declaring that the Revolution had been betrayed, and that it was necessary to begin anew, they robbed banks and distributed the stolen money to the common people, just like Robin Hood. This was a clear challenge to the army's authority. Daniel Ortega and others in the FSLN were tolerant of these *recompas* – they referred to them as 'confused comrades'. We decided to fight them. We mounted a military operation to retake Estelí, which we did after three days of fighting and twenty-eight rebel deaths. This marked a crucial turning point. It was the [new] army's 'trial by fire', and won them the respect of the entire country. After this, the *recompas* and *recontras* were standing in line to hand over their weapons and disarm.[49]

By the mid-1990s the political landscape in Nicaragua was changing. Arnoldo Alemán, coffee farmer turned opposition politician after the confiscation of his farm in 1989,[50] reconstituted Somoza's Liberal Party. In the polls – and in the subsequent elections – the Liberals appeared as a powerful right-wing political force. The UNO had already disintegrated into a variety of splinter parties. Daniel Ortega, assisted by his associates Arce, Borge and Cerna, gained prominence within the FSLN. Ortega's authority, however, was not uncontested.[51] In 1993 the FSLN faction in parliament split into two groups: Sergio Ramirez and Dora

María Tellez led a breakaway faction that eventually called itself the Movimiento de Renovación Sandinista (MRS), which they characterized as a political alternative to *Danielismo* (Ortega's party dominance) within the FSLN. Notwithstanding the ongoing exodus of the prominent leaders of the 1980s, all efforts to form a political alternative with a substantial following were fruitless, as was the case in El Salvador. And, as was also the case in El Salvador, Nicaraguan politics began to look more and more like a two-party system, with a strong right (the Liberal Party) and a strong left (the FSLN), each with a stable and powerful base.

The departure of decent comandantes and cadres was due to either party purges or personal disillusionment. Daniel Ortega's intrigues against respected adversaries and the suspicion of fraudulent management of the party's financial assets gave abundant cause for concern. In 1990 the Frente had entrusted forty-eight party enterprises to the management of Arce, Ramirez and Wheelock. Ramirez and Wheelock recognized their lack of entrepreneurial capacities and transferred their assets to the party. But in 1993, the highly respected Henry Ruiz declared before a disconcerted FSLN audience that he was the party's 'treasurer without treasures'. Asked about the particulars of the party's trust fund, Daniel Ortega coldly answered that the FSLN had never possessed properties. Nevertheless, I interviewed some managers of these apparently non-existing former party enterprises. Meanwhile, Arce is a multi-millionaire. Formally, Daniel Ortega is only a party leader with a modest income. He is, however, surrounded by a group of 'Sandinista entrepreneurs', several of them prominent members of the Hombres de Negocio del Evangelio, a kind of secret fundamentalist Christian entrepreneurial society. According to persistent rumours, the economic empire around Ortega and his wife Rosario Murillo comprises investments in radio and television stations, telecom enterprises, shopping malls and supermarkets.[52] In fact, Ortega and his associates are a part of the nation's current economic elite, an amalgam of the old oligarchy and the new post-1990 entrepreneurs, including some who had lived in Miami during the 1980s. As in El Salvador and Guatemala, a large segment of Nicaragua's poor migrated to Mexico and the USA, keeping their families afloat with periodic remittances.[53]

Another setback to Ortega's reputation occurred when his relationship with his stepdaughter Zoilamérica was made public in 1998.[54] Zoilamérica accused him of molestation and sexual harassment when she had been a young girl. The relationship allegedly lasted a very long time. The case caused an enormous scandal when Ortega's stepdaughter began giving interviews in the national press and on the radio and television, visiting foreign embassies one by one, and initiating a lawsuit at the Inter-American Human Rights Court in San José, Costa Rica. Daniel Ortega's wife, Rosario Murillo, defended her husband. Ortega's parliamentary status precluded his being formally prosecuted. Afterwards, a gentlemen's agreement between Ortega and President Alemán[55] provided protection for both politicians. Alemán was handled with kid gloves following his involvement in a mega-million-dollar corruption case and Ortega was accorded protection against backlash from the Zoilamérica case. This *pacto* also resulted in the division of spheres of influence between the two major political parties: equal representation on the Supreme Court, the Electoral Tribunal and the Constitutional Court, as well as within the Office of the Comptroller. For many, the situation appeared to be a return to the informal *pacto* between the Liberal Party and the Conservative Party during the Somoza era.[56]

Yet Ortega continued to amass political capital. In the 1990s both the FMLN in El Salvador and the FSLN had won important municipal elections. In the 1990s the FSLN lost the municipal elections in Managua, but after 2000 well-liked FSLN figures like Herty Lewites and Dionisio Marenco held the post of mayor in the nation's capital. Other strategic municipalities were also administered by elected FSLN mayors. In 2005 the FSLN won a surprising number of municipal elections nationwide: 80 of the 153 municipalities, including the most populous, were controlled by the party. After a split in the Liberal Party, Ortega signed a *pacto* with President Bolaños (Alemán's successor) in 2005 while maintaining his alliance with Alemán. The deals with Alemán and Bolaños resulted in a change in electoral legislation.[57] The only one who could benefit from this agreement was Ortega.[58] Ortega's wife Murillo arranged an understanding, even a political friendship, with former adversary Cardinal Obando; this prelate consecrated their marriage in a religious ceremony in 2005 and dismissed the father-stepdaughter relationship as a 'family affair'. Ortega manoeuvred the cardinal's alleged son[59] into the presidency of the Electoral Tribunal, after an apparent corruption scandal in which the new magistrate was involved. Murillo even engineered a kind of reconciliation between Ortega and his stepdaughter. Ortega concluded another alliance, this time with the Contra leadership, appointing former Contra leader and confidant of both the CIA and Alemán, Jaime Morales Carazo, as his running mate for the elections in 2006. His brilliantly engineered, but ultimately vacuous, electoral campaign, under the heading of 'Peace and Reconciliation', which took as its anthem John Lennon's 'Give Peace a Chance', was supervised by Murillo, the second most powerful figure in the FSLN.[60]

In 2006, the Movimiento de Renovación Sandinista (MRS), a political movement of ex-members of the FSLN, comprising many of the leading Sandinista political actors of the 1980s, acquired a new lease of life when Herty Lewites, former mayor of Managua and hitherto a personal friend of Daniel and a loyal FSLN cadre, challenged the Ortega leadership and launched a successful opposition campaign as leader of the MRS, obtaining 30 per cent of the national vote in opinion polls. However, Lewites died suddenly a couple of months before the elections of November 2006 and his party ended up obtaining only 6 per cent of the final vote. Ortega won with 38 per cent of the vote, assuming office for the second time in January 2007 as president of Nicaragua.

Whatever the final judgement of history turns out to be regarding the second government term of Ortega, at least he proved that he could manage a comeback after electoral defeats and seventeen years of grim opposition, secret agreements, and tacit understandings with all possible former adversaries. Yet his political triumph came at a high price: most of the comandantes who had retained a strong sense of moral integrity had left the party, leaving the present party leadership of former state employees and middle party cadres under the control of a stubborn caudillo couple, man and wife who together administer a political machine with a glorious past and a meagre political programme, albeit one that retains all the symbols and rhetoric of the 1970s and the 1980s.

The Salvadoran FMLN acquired political capital, even respectability, preparing for a generational change in its leadership. Probably the Salvadoran path to integration in society has been the most successful of the three guerrilla organizations. The Salvadoran guerrillas obtained long-term government experience as a result of winning a number of mayoral elections and, in spite of all *comanditismo*, the party is nurtured by a relatively loyal and stable electorate. This loyalty of party supporters is a characteristic shared with the Nicaraguan FSLN. The evolution of the URNG, however, has been an irredeemable tragedy: *comandantismo* plagued this party as well, but furthermore the leadership and the small party cadre lost the ties with the popular movements, old and new, and they also lost the confidence of the Maya peoples. The party split, forming splinter groups around the two surviving members of the *comandancia general*. With the Guatemalan left thus divided, nobody can seriously assert that the URNG and the ANN can look forward to better times in any foreseeable future.

6

Legacies and Ambivalences

'The war is an armed plebiscite ... between a people divided.' This is what Cardinal Goma wrote about the Spanish Civil War.[1] This simple characterization of the complexities and resentments of the ruthless struggle between the rebel forces of the far right and those of a fledgling republic supporting progressive reforms also neatly encapsulates the essence of the three Central American insurrections considered here. In El Salvador, Guatemala and Nicaragua the guerrilla leaderships also initiated and justified an armed conflict in desperate attempts to force armed plebiscites against dictatorships and ruling elites. For many Central Americans who came of age between the 1960s and 1980s the solution to mass poverty, discrimination and social exclusion lay in taking up arms against the entrenched structures of authoritarian militarism and oligarchic elites. These were the ideals of the guerrilla movements in Central America that emerged from the radicalizing Christian Base Communities and student movements, and from some young military officers and former members of the semi-clandestine communist parties.

More than ten years after the guns fell silent, following a generation of bitter war and negotiated peace in the region, an analysis of the legacies of the guerrilla movements is still not easy. Any examination of these wars' long-time effects tends to raise more questions than it answers, and is necessarily fraught with ambiguity. The Salvadoran, Guatemalan and Nicaraguan comandantes justified their armed opposition against the state as a righteous war against repressive military domination, the persistence of mass poverty, and the exclusion of ethnic minorities and marginalized social classes. Raw capitalism, financially and militarily sustained by US imperialism, was to be transformed into more humane economic and societal structures, creating new socialist orders of full participatory democracy. This transformation was to be instituted by means of armed insurrection carried out by a politico-military vanguard comprising the comandantes and political leaders of the guerrilla movements, along with supporting popular organizations.

The lowest estimate of the combined death toll in all three countries is 330,000; the actual number of fatalities may well have reached 500,000. The number of those officially classified as having 'disappeared' swells this toll by at least another 20 per cent. And then there are the hundreds of thousands of internally displaced persons and external refugees. In Nicaragua, where no Truth Commission or comparable institution was created, the large majority of deaths in the campaigns of the 1970s were without doubt caused by the brutal counterinsurgency operations of the Somoza regime against the civil population in 1977-79.[2] Victims of the Contra war in the 1980s are attributed more or less equally to operations of EPS regular forces and Contra troops. Most victims of the rebel campaigns during the 1990s were the *re-contras* and the *re-compas* killed in action. The Salvadoran and Guatemalan Truth Commissions (Comisión de la Verdad, 1993; CEH, 1999) attribute the large majority of the victims to aggression by the state; the combined guerrilla forces in these two countries were deemed to be responsible for less than 10 per cent of total deaths.

This is in line with the conclusions of similar reports written about the consequences of decades of military dictatorships in Latin America. The only report of a Truth Commission with a distinctly different conclusion was that of Peru.[3] The terrifying armed actor during the civil war in this country was without doubt Shining Path, a macabre Maoist guerrilla organization that in the use of systematic terror against the entire population is reminiscent of the regime of Pol Pot in Kampuchea (Cambodia) or the great purges in Stalinist Russia or in Maoist China. The Central American guerrilla movements have committed atrocities as well, but, in comparison with those carried out by the armed forces and their paramilitary clients in El Salvador and Guatemala or by the Somoza regime in Nicaragua during its waning days in power, they are on a far smaller scale.

There is not, and there is never likely to be, a computable index of 'justified numbers of deaths' in civil wars. As is always the case with human tragedies, it is impossible to justify individual deaths or mass fatalities in terms of 'historical necessity'. The duration of the conflict, the long years of low-intensity warfare, and the daily individual killings and intermittent massacres in the three countries not only destroyed the lives of men and women but ruined part of the economic, social and political order of three countries. Not only did many individuals lose their lives, but entire societies were pervaded with fear, permeated with anxiety, and plunged into mourning.

During the years when peace agreements were being hammered out (Nicaragua, 1990; El Salvador, 1992; Guatemala, 1996) Jorge Castañeda (1994) wrote and published a seminal book on the post-Cold War Latin American left. Analysing several decades of leftist popular movements and political parties, he concluded that the institutionalized armed left of Cuba, the Latin American insurrections in the 1960s and 1970s, and the Central American guerrilla movements of the 1970s and 1980s belonged to the past. The previous chapter described the integration of the former Central American guerrilla organizations as political actors in a national multi-party system. The former Cuban guerrilla movement was long ago transformed into a ruling single-party political and military juggernaut. In Colombia, two guerrilla forces remain: the ELN and the FARC.[4] Both are on the defensive and both are, as are all non-state armed actors in Colombia, contaminated by the narco-trafficking that has helped finance their continued operations. Even the insurgent Zapatista movement in Chiapas and other southern Mexican regions – launched in 1994 – did not evolve like the other Mesoamerican guerrilla movements of the past. After initial skirmishes the Zapatista leadership began conducting their campaigns in a way that did not directly challenge the federal authority, and the Mexican government in turn, having learned the lessons of the Central American wars, suspended major counterinsurgency operations. The scenario of entrenched military conflict which most observers expected was quickly replaced by negotiation rounds, debates, meetings, marches and even public appearances of the Zapatista leadership aimed at gaining national and international support.

Legacies

The guerrilla forces in El Salvador, Guatemala and Nicaragua aimed at bringing an end to dictatorship by force; halting massive poverty and exclusion of the poor, the underprivileged and the indigenous; establishing a morally superior socialist order instead of the existing raw capitalist economy and society; and replacing US imperialism with a robust national welfare state. With more than a decade having transpired since the end of hostilities in the three nations, to what extent can the insurgent forces be said to have achieved these ambitious goals?

The *military dictatorships* vanished, and their disappearance can at least in part be attributed directly to the interventions of the guerrilla movements. In Nicaragua a victorious guerrilla force took over power and overthrew the Somoza regime in 1979. In El Salvador a sort of military stalemate was reached. The Salvadoran army maintained considerable political influence during the term of civilian President Duarte (1984-89). In the opinion of most of the FMLN leaders, Duarte was in fact a hostage of his military entourage and was thus prevented from working towards an equitable solution to the Salvadoran civil war. Even President Cristiani could not convince the members of the military establishment to participate fully and openly in peace negotiations. Only after the national and international outrage sparked by the 1989 murders of six Jesuit priests did the military begin to participate reluctantly in the peace talks. As a direct result of the peace negotiations a complete demilitarization of the state was reached, with the reorganization and purification of the armed forces and the disbanding of police forces. In Guatemala, democracy was re-established ten years before the signing of the peace agreements, but the governments of presidents Cerezo (1986-91), Serrano (1991-93) and De León Carpio (1993-96) were civilian governments under the considerable – but slowly eroding – tutelage of the military establishment. As a result of the peace agreements, the police forces were entirely rebuilt and the armed institution was considerably reduced.[5] In 2004 President Berger (2004-08) ordered a final cutback to 15,000 effectives. The waning political power of army and police forces in the three countries was, in an abrupt reversal of posture, also supported by the US government. During the Cold War, the United States had been a staunch supporter of Latin America's dictatorships as a bulwark against Communist infiltration and influence. With this threat having disappeared following the fall of the Berlin Wall, the region was no longer a Cold War battleground, and the importance of the region in US foreign policy dropped precipitously.

No conclusive verdict is possible with regard to the role of guerrilla forces in *reducing national poverty*. Present-day Central America is, with the exception of Costa Rica, still the same Balkanized region of small states with severe economic and social inequalities and significant segments of poor and extremely poor people. According to the most recent CEPAL (2007: 36) study El Salvador, Guatemala and Nicaragua are still classified as countries with an 'extremely unequal income distribution' in comparison with other Latin American countries. Similarly, the Human Development Indexes and poverty indicators are among the highest on the continent. In Nicaragua the poverty indicators even increased slightly under the government of President Bolaños (2002–07).[6] Nicaragua is a nonchalantly governed country, living on external credit. The dependency on foreign donors was initiated in 1979; until now, successive governments have been generously subsidized by the international donor community. Under President Bolaños some fifty donor countries and multilateral institutions provided around 20 per cent of the national budget; the most prominent donors form a Budget Support Group, which is presided over by the World Bank. In 2007, President Ortega succeeded in adding Iran and Venezuela to the country's list of creditors.

A more positive trend, which is at least indirectly attributable to the intervention of the guerrilla movement, is the gradual reduction of the immense *social exclusion* of the Maya peoples in Guatemala. After the municipal elections of 1993 a third of the elected mayors were of Maya descent, a result impossible before the war and even during the 1980s. In Quetzaltenango Rigoberto Quemé Chay, the first Maya mayor of the second largest Guatemalan city, was re-elected after a successful first term of municipal government. Given the long-standing and widespread practice of discrimination and exclusion of Maya peoples in Guatemala, the fact that a Maya could mount a successful campaign for the mayor's office in the nation's capital, or even run for president, as Nobel laureate Rigoberta Menchú would later do, is something that would have been unthinkable in this country throughout most of the twentieth century.

Gender equality was a concern that formally had a high priority in the guerrilla programmes. During the guerrilla campaigns Latin America's traditional gender roles did change in so far as the equality of men and women fighters was being emphasized. Gender equality was officially propagated by the FSLN during the years of its rule, and by the FMLN in the territories that it controlled during the war. But afterwards the gender issue lost its high official priority. In the aftermath of the war – with so many war widows and female-headed household due to the massive migration of men to the United States and Mexico – more female employment has been generated in the informal economy by bitter necessity than as the result of the promotion of gender equality on the part of the guerrilla comandantes. During the 1980s around 30 per cent of the members of the Ejército Popular Sandinista were women. At present, there are only four women serving as officers in the entire National Army in Nicaragua. Only in the higher echelons of the National Police are men and women represented in approximately equal numbers.

The ideological undercurrent of the Central American guerrillas has always been *anti-imperialism* and, specifically, an effort to escape *US economic and political domination*. However, the massive migration to the USA, especially after the wars, along with the dependence of 10 to 25 per cent of the households of El Salvador, Guatemala, and Nicaragua on remittances from relatives residing in the USA, demonstrates the weakness of Central American economies. Post-war Central America is tangled up in a new dependency on the United States, expressed in a substantial and continuing emigration to that country and increasing dependence on remittances from family members residing in the USA, either legally or illegally. Even the relatives of many of the guerrilla leaders found refuge in North America or in Western Europe. No Central American government, whatever its political orientation, can risk provoking the ire of a US government capable of regulating the residential status of their illegal and semi-legal immigrants and, thus, of interrupting the indispensable remittance stream of $3 billion a year per country – a stream that attenuates the poverty in each nation and that provides at least a minimally acceptable standard of living for a considerable proportion of their citizens.

As for the institution of *socialist structures*, the transformation of the national economy into non-capitalist societies was not a significant precondition during either the pragmatic peace negotiations in El Salvador or the painstaking and protracted peace talks in Guatemala. The route towards socialism was somehow irretrievably detoured during peace negotiations. The governments holding power since the conclusion of talks, while democratically elected and not overtly repressive, have generally served the interests of the moneyed classes in these two nations. The Nicaraguan experiment ended in a war economy and war society where the voice of the military became decisive and the management of the national economy was a prelude to hyperinflation and economic disaster. The Sandinista management of economic and social transformation ended with an electoral defeat in 1990 after a decade of civil strife and economic catastrophe. The governments that followed essentially reconsolidated the Nicaraguan economy and society in accordance with the Washington Consensus, with little attention to the poor and underprivileged.

Anti-imperialism and socialism were ingrained ideals within the guerrilla movements. Nevertheless, the eradication of the dependency on the United States, and the end of US imperialism in Central America – whether expressed in the form of overt military involvement or implemented through diplomatic channels – was a distant dream that would be unattainable in the near-term future. 'Socialist accumulation within peripheric economies', a strategy propagated by the Sandinista government and their economic advisers, ended up being an illusion. 'Socialism' was always the ideal social order as expressed by the comandantes in their official booklets and brochures and in the collected interviews published by Marta Harnecker (1984, 1992). As I remarked in Chapter 2, for most of the comandantes the notion that revolution and socialism are two sides of the same coin was an article of faith. However, in all my interviews, nobody wanted to go into details on the subject of a socialist economy and society. Most of the Salvadoran and Guatemalan guerrilla leaders frowned on Soviet-style communism. Many years after final peace agreements were concluded in El Salvador and Guatemala, a couple of the guerrilla comandantes even went so far as to express their distaste regarding the Communist Party's control over daily life in Cuba. What explains, then, the lack of clarity regarding the essential nature of the future society that they were fighting for? In retrospect I assume that most comandantes and their political advisers were absorbed by the day-to-day conduct of the war, and that questions about the final objectives of the guerrilla campaigns had slowly receded from their immediate awareness. Those with whom I discussed the future society tried to explain to me that revolutionary socialism was qualitatively different from Western European social democracy. However, a comparison between El Salvador, Guatemala and Nicaragua, on the one hand, and their Central American neighbour country Costa Rica, on the other, is instructive. Costa Rica has never been governed by decades-long military dictatorships or ultra-conservative elites, and its political culture has never favoured the rise of autocratic strongmen. The victors of the short Costa Rican guerrilla campaign in 1948 chose a prudent path of electoral social democracy as a political solution and a modest welfare state as the consensus ideology for its economy and society. Considering comparative economic and political performance during the last half of the twentieth century, Costa Rica is without a doubt better off than El Salvador, Guatemala and Nicaragua. Costa Rica embarked upon its successful path in different times and within a different context, but the different result is nonetheless remarkable.

By and large, the Central American revolutions were inconclusive. The revolutionary ideals of the guerrilla generation dwindled away. The guerrilla leadership, apart from the fact that they can claim credit for important short-term accomplishments, ultimately failed to achieve significant and sustainable economic and social transformations. Yes, there was an agrarian reform in Nicaragua, and there was a similar reform attempted in El Salvador. However, in the post-war years, most members of the agricultural co-operatives and other collective forms of rural property individualized their land titles and a significant proportion of these members sold their possessions in the 1990s. The collective agricultural property in Nicaragua fell from 25 per cent in 1988 to 5 per cent in 2001.[7]

In Guatemala, the country where the guerrilla forces finally failed after thirty-six years of gruesome warfare, peace was restored after the signing of agreements that had been the subject of deliberation over the course of many years. The fate of the Guatemalan peace accords is that of covenants that ended up never being implemented – with the exception of the army and police reforms and the demobilization of the guerrilla fighters. Rigoberto Quemé Chay, then mayor of Quetzaltenango and political leader of the Maya Xeljú movement, commented bitterly:

> The peace agreements were signed by representatives of the traditional political system, who invaded the [Maya] region to fight out their war with Maya soldiers, Maya *guerrilleros* and Maya victims. Nobody signed the peace. They signed a treaty in which the defeat of the URNG was camouflaged. They signed another agreement about a future multi-ethnic society; it was signed without previous consultation with the Maya representatives.[8]

The peace accords probably constitute a perfect programme of action for a visionary government. Unfortunately, there is no government to put into practice the far-reaching economic and social transformations required. The peace agreements are, tragically, nobody's business: not of the Guatemalan right, not of the Guatemalan centre and not of the Guatemalan left. Even worse, there is no organized Guatemalan left ten years after the signing of the peace accords.

Ambivalences

In Nicaragua the Sandinista government turned over power to its political opponents after being defeated in the 1990 Nicaraguan elections. Central American guerrilla movements were transformed in peacetime into political parties and acquired their place in a multi-party democracy. Mao Zedong famously wrote that 'political power comes from the barrel of a gun'. Does this mean that fully participatory democracy and fair and equitable social arrangements can also only come from the barrel of a gun? More to the point in the present context: are guerrilla comandantes capable of exercising democratic leadership once they are in a position to do so?

The Leninist vanguard thesis,[9] whose influence I discussed in Chapter 2 and which had been incorporated into the storehouse of conventional revolutionary wisdom that nearly all comandantes had digested, seemed to be invalid under peacetime conditions. All politico-military organizations incorporated in the three umbrella guerrilla consortia – FSLN, FMLN and URNG – had been founded as 'vanguard parties', headed by vanguard elites who were to develop the overall strategy both in the military and the political sense. This self-appointed intellectual, military, political and moral leadership was probably very functional during the years of clandestine existence and during the war. However, in peacetime its organization interfered with the development of democratic leadership. The post-war management model of the FSLN, the FMLN and the URNG was previously characterized as *comandantism*:[10] namely, maintenance of the same closed command structure as had prevailed under conditions of guerrilla struggle, with an insistence on ideological orthodoxy. In the 1990s and afterwards, the younger and upcoming party members in El Salvador, Guatemala and Nicaragua tried to convince the old comandantes to revitalize the leadership by yielding decision-making powers to the younger generation while remaining in the background as highly respected figures. The old comandantes categorically refused to transfer power. It is precisely this tendency of leaders to hold on to power that was identified by early-twentieth-century sociologist Robert Michels (1911) in the context of oligarchic tendencies and the obstacles to recruiting new generations – and new ideas – in leadership positions within the German left before World War I.

In fact in all three new political parties – FSLN, FMLN and URNG – a kind of power struggle emerged, revealing a split between an 'orthodox' wing, on the one hand, and a 'moderate', 'social democratic' or *renovador* tendency, on the other. Within the FMLN and the FSLN, the two parties that acquired a significant and loyal segment of the Salvadoran and Nicaraguan electorate respectively, those who favoured changes left the party, a process that was initiated in the 1990s and that is still continuing. The first two presidential candidates of the FMLN, of 1994 and 1998, considered to be moderates, left or were ostracized. Of the five 'historical' comandantes, four are alive and three of them left the party. Of the eight members of the Sandinista *dirección nacional* during the 1980s who are still alive, only three – Daniel Ortega, Bayardo Arce and Tomás Borge – are still members of the party. Both in El Salvador and in Nicaragua, those who left or were sent away and opted for a political career outside, ended up leading only very small successor parties with one or two seats in parliament and with no future prospects. In Guatemala the URNG eventually became a dwarf party. There is only one 'historical' comandante still alive as of this writing. He, Jorge Soto (Pablo Monsanto), is the presidential candidate of another dwarf party, Alianza Nueva Nación (ANN), the redoubt of his ex-guerrilla group FAR. His former second-in-command, Arnoldo Villagrán (Daniel Ruiz), headed ANN's list in the 2007 elections.

Yet there are some signs of movement in a progressive direction. In the Nicaraguan FSLN some mayors of the country's principal municipalities are considered to be moderates, and, after they have been re-elected once or twice, have claimed in interviews that 'good governance' at the municipal level requires close cooperation with political opponents. Several of the moderates within the FMLN are also highly popular and efficient mayors of the larger Salvadoran cities. They gained administrative experience being re-elected twice or three times and advocate explicitly the necessity of multi-party alliances and of sharing power with members of opposition parties. After the death of Schafik Handal in 2006, former FPL comandante Sánchez Cerén took over the coordination of the FMLN in parliament. Considered to be an orthodox party member, he expressed himself rather cautiously when asked about the FMLN's chances of victory in the presidential elections in 2009 and the tradition of party orthodoxy: 'Socialism cannot be imposed from above', he said, adding that, 'you have to move with the tide of the popular preferences'.[11]

In many of my interviews I asked for an appraisal of the final achievements in relation to the original ideals. Was the balance positive? Some interlocutors mentioned the reforms carried out during the war years or while being in government; others talked with nostalgia about the revolutionary fervour of their comrades or the gaining of the sympathy and trust of the local population. Most comandantes recounted their war memories with gusto and recalled episodes of military heroism. 'We could teach them a trick or two', was the comment of the leading Salvadoran comandantes, comparing their campaigns with the Cuban (1959) and the Nicaraguan (1979) revolutions. It is the soldier in them that prevails. Many of them took great pains to explain their tactics and military decisions in some detail. Only one or two embellished their deeds and sang their own praises. The majority were relatively modest. Not infrequently, they presented a critical appraisal of what happened during and after the war years. 'To be honest: there were no good guys and bad guys; all parties committed atrocities', said Facundo Guardado, reflecting on the costs of the war and the wounds that are slowly healing in El Salvador.[12] He is the most outspoken of all, but he is not alone. Rodrigo Asturias prepared the official document asking pardon on behalf of the URNG in 1999 for all acts of violence committed in the thirty-six years of war in Guatemala. In Nicaragua Henry Ruiz, without vilifying the anti-Sandinistas, emphasized the necessity of a fair history research project on the role of the opposition fighters in the Contra War.[13]

Then there is the issue of the lifestyle of some of the comandantes. In El Salvador and in Guatemala they live the plain and simple life of the modest urban middle class. In El Salvador most members of the former guerrilla leadership and of the peace negotiating team are members of parliament, parliamentary advisers or professors at provincial universities. Their homes, offices and workplaces are completely lacking in ostentation. In Guatemala, the lifestyle of former comandantes has been rather austere; by the standards of the European Union, most of them would have been classified as poor. What they do earn they give to their parties and spend on party campaigns. By contrast, most of the former Nicaraguan comandantes live amid material comfort. They were the aristocratic members of the revolutionary family that was in power for more than ten years, and received choice town houses when the possessions of Somoza were allotted in 1979. A couple of comandantes and former FSLN members live fairly modestly; some gave away what they had received and live below the local middle-class standards. There are, however, a few prominent FSLN members who, after the 1990 *piñata*, became members of the economic elite. Arce, Borje and Daniel Ortega are the most well known. Daniel's brother Humberto Ortega became a prominent businessman both in Costa Rica and in Nicaragua.

Of course, in Nicaragua the FSLN has come full circle. The movement took over power by means of arms in 1979 after a successful guerrilla campaign. In 1990, after a bitter civil war and an economic debacle, it handled over power to the newly elected opposition government. After seventeen years of dogged opposition and the conclusion of informal agreements with right-wing forces, Daniel Ortega once again became president in January 2007 following a cleverly conceived campaign. But the revolutionary FSLN of 1979 was transformed in the 1990s into a political machine headed by a caudillo who – with the help of his wife – built alliance after alliance with corrupt politicians, former arch-enemies, members of the economic elite and the reactionary old guard of the Catholic Church hierarchy. Seventeen years of political intriguing and campaigning to maintain the FSLN united has been rewarded with a devoted and loyal following among a third of the Nicaraguan electorate and a handful of dissatisfied voters of the right and the centre. Past accommodations and secret agreements concluded by Ortega with conservative presidents leading to a dual control over the judiciary and the public sector – only the army and the police maintained their institutional autonomy – were smoothed away under the banner of 'peace and reconciliation': 'peace' after what and 'reconciliation' between whom?

The more orthodox members of the FSLN and the FMLN always maintained good relations with the old and new emerging leaders of the Latin American left, like Fidel Castro, Hugo Chávez and, more recently, Rafael Correa in Ecuador and Evo Morales in Bolivia. Schafik Handal offered Chávez the assistance of former guerrilla fighters of the FMLN 'in case of necessity'. This offer was received with tongue-in-cheek comments and cost him an electoral defeat. He died in 2006 of a heart attack at the San Salvador airport after returning from the inauguration of Evo Morales as president. Daniel Ortega dedicated his presidential victory in November 2006 to Fidel Castro, then seriously ill. Hugo Chávez attended his inauguration as president in January 2007 after being inaugurated for his own second presidential term that same day. Still, despite the rhetoric and fanfare surrounding the expressions of solidarity among these politicians, the domestic reform and anti-poverty polices that Ortega unveiled in the early days in office can be characterized as timid and lacklustre rather than revolutionary. His government style is in any case not a radical break with that of his right-wing predecessors Alemán and Bolaños. The former revolutionary left of Guatemala can only express hopes for the long-term future. In the early months of 2007, there were attempts on both sides to establish an electoral alliance between the URNG and the ANN. The efforts failed, this time because the URNG would not permit the inclusion in any alliance of certain ex-military members of the ANN with a 'dubious past'.[14] They hope for better times and a possible government alliance with the larger electoral blocks of the centre-left, and perhaps of the centre-right.

Although they are undeniably a significant part of the region's recent history, the Central American guerrilla movements are a legacy, not a reality for politics and economics in present-day Latin America. 'No way', responded most of the senior members of the

FMLN, the URNG and the FSLN when asked in 2004, 2005, 2006 and 2007 about the possibilities of a new guerrilla generation in the near future.

In the second half of the first decade of the twenty-first century the political landscape of the continent has changed. In Brazil President Lula da Silva was re-elected in October 2006 with a 60 per cent victory. In Mexico left-wing candidate López Obrador very narrowly lost the 2006 presidential elections. In Argentina, Bolivia, Chile, Ecuador, Peru, Venezuela and, finally, in Nicaragua, a candidate of the centre-left or left was invested with presidential authority after free elections. That proves that in twenty-first-century Latin America, at present a continent with a post-war and post-dictatorship tradition of civilian government, reformist and left-wing reform programmes can be realized by electoral means. Nicaragua, Guatemala and El Salvador endured decades of war to end dictatorship. These countries have enjoyed rather less success than some of their larger neighbours to the north and south when it comes to electoral success of leftist parties. Still, if the goals of halting massive poverty and giving a voice to large swathes of previously disenfranchised persons are to be achieved, or even approached, this will probably happen as the result of the electoral success of the moderates and reformists of the generation succeeding the guerrilla comandantes who took up arms to achieve these same goals.

Appendices

1. Politico-military Organizations

El Salvador

The Frente Farabundo Martí de Liberación Nacional (FMLN) was founded as a revolutionary guerrilla organization in October 1980 and then constituted as a political party in September 1992.

In October 1980 four politico-military organizations with their respective popular organizations unified under the banner of the FMLN. The Communist Party joined the organization later that same year. The constituent politico-military organizations were:

- The *Fuerzas Populares de Liberación 'Farabundo Martí'* (FPL), founded in April 1970 and headed by Cayetano Carpio. After the suicide and murder of the two founding members, in 1983, the organization was led by Salvador Sánchez Cerén. The related federation of popular organizations was called the Bloque Popular Revolucionario (BPR), led by Facundo Guardado.
- The *Ejército Revolucionario del Pueblo* (ERP), founded in March 1972 and headed by Joaquín Villalobos (its original name was

Partido de la Revolución Salvadoreña [PRS]). Its corresponding federation of popular organizations was called Las Ligas Populares 28 de Febrero (LP-28).

- The *Resistencia Nacional* (RN), a secession of the ERP, formed in May 1975 after the execution of the poet-*guerrillero* Roque Dalton and headed by Eduardo Sancho. Its corresponding federation of popular organizations was called the Frente de Acción Popular Unificada (FAPU).
- The *Partido Revolucionario de los Trabajadores Centroamericanos* (PRTC), founded in January 1976 and headed by Francisco Jovel. Its corresponding federation of popular organizations was the Movimiento de Liberación Popular (MLP). The PRTC eventually joined the Frente in December 1980.
- The *Partido Comunista de El Salvador* (PCS), founded in 1930 and in the 1970s headed by Schafik Handal. Its corresponding federation of popular organizations was called the Unión Democrática Nacionalista del Partido Comunista de El Salvador (UDN).

In January 1980 the Coordinadora Revolucionaria de Masas (CRM) was founded. This organization represented a merger of the Bloque Popular Revolucionario (BPR), the Ligas Populares 28 de Febrero (PL-28), the FAPU, the MLP and the UDN.

The political unification process of the FMLN was more complicated.[1] In December 1979 the LPF, the RN and the PCS signed an accord to form the Coordinadora Político-Militar (CPM). The following non-guerrilla parties on the political left formed the Frente Democrático Revolucionario (FDR) in April 1980: the social-democratic Movimiento Nacional Revolucionario (MNR), headed by Guillermo Ungo, and the Social Christian Movimiento Popular Social Cristiano (MPSC), a secession of the Partido Demócrata Cristiano (PDC or DC), and headed by Ruben Zamora, founded at the same time as the Coordinadora Revolucionaria de Masas CRM. In May 1980 a Dirección Revolucionaria Unificada (DRU) was formed that comprised the FPL, EPR, RN and PCS.

This organization was the immediate predecessor of the FMLN. In October 1980 the FMLN was formed and in December 1980 the remaining PRTC formally became its fifth member party. In June 1985 the *comandancia nacional* took the initiative to transform the FMLN into a political party after the peace accords, formally creating a party alliance between the FMLN and the FDR, thus joining the guerrilla and the non-guerrilla political left of El Salvador. In September 1992 the FMLN was officially founded as a political party.

In 1994 the FMLN participated in presidential elections with Rubén Zamora as presidential candidate. Facundo Guardado was the presidential candidate during the 1999 elections. Between 1994 and 2006 the FMLN was always the primary opposition party, losing the presidential elections but winning the mayoral elections in the most important municipalities. Meanwhile three of the five members of the *comandancia general* and half of the members of the original board left the party. None of the disassociated splinter groups achieved substantial electoral success. Until his death in January 2006, Schafik Handal controlled the party machinery, with Sánchez Cerén as his second-in-command; Sánchez Cerén succeeded him as the FMLM coordinator in parliament.

Guatemala

The Unidad Revolucionaria Nacional Guatemalteca (URNG) was founded in February 1982 and constituted as a political party in 1999.

The URNG was originally an organization that served as a coordinating body among three guerrilla groups and (a splinter faction of) the Communist Party.[2] The constituent politico-military organizations were:[3]

- The *Fuerzas Armadas Revolucionarias* (FAR), the successor organization of a leftist military movement founded in 1960 (Movimiento Revolucionario 13 de Noviembre [MR-13]) and headed by Luis Turcios Lima and Marco Antonio Yon Sosa. It was originally allied with the Communist Party but in 1968 formally broke away from it and took the name of FAR. In the early 1970s Jorge Ismael Soto became the *comandante-en-jefe*, with Arnoldo Villagrán serving as his second-in-command.

- The *Ejército Guerrillero de los Pobres* (EGP), founded in January 1972 and headed by Ricardo Ramírez de León,[4] with Celso Morales serving as his second-in-command in the 1980s and 1990s.
- The *Organización del Pueblo en Armas* (ORPA), which began operating in 1971 under the name of *La Organización* but was officially renamed ORPA in September 1979 and was headed by Rodrigo Asturias.[5]
- The *Partido Guatemalteco de Trabajadores* (PGT), with Ricardo Rosales as secretary general; after 1986 he participated as the fourth member of the *comandancia general* of the URNG.

Although not participating as such in the URNG, the Comité de Unidad Campesina (CUC), founded in April 1978, was a mass organization of *campesinos*, rural workers, landless indigenous and Ladino peoples, closely associated to the EGP (and also supported ORPA). The organization was persecuted by the successive governments of military presidents Fernando Romeo Lucas García, Efraín Ríos Montt and Óscar Humberto Mejía Víctores.

In 1997, after the peace accords, the FAR, EGP, ORPA and PGT officially merged, forming the Unidad Revolucionaria Nacional Guatemalteca. Ricardo Ramírez de León was the first secretary general of the provisional board and Jorge Soto the vice secretary general. After the death of Ramírez de León in 1998, Soto became the new secretary general and under his leadership the party started splitting along the lines of FAR versus EGP and ORPA. In 2001 the Alianza Nueva Nación (ANN), headed by Jorge Soto (ex-FAR), broke away from the URNG, led at the time by Rodrigo Asturias (ex-ORPA) with Celso Delgado (ex-EGP) as sub-secretary general.

Nicaragua

The Frente Sandinista de Liberación Nacional (FSLN) was founded in 1961 by a group headed by Carlos Fonseca Amador, and then reconstituted in March 1979, transformed into a political party in July 1979.

Before the reunification of the Frente in March 1979 there were three separate revolutionary factions or 'tendencies':

- the *Guerra Popular Prolongada* (GPP), headed by Tomás Borge, Henry Ruiz and Bayardo Arce;
- the *Tendencia Proletaria* (TP), headed by Luis Carrión, Jaime Wheelock and Carlos Nuñez;
- the *Tendencia Tercerista* or *Insurreccionista*, headed by Daniel Ortega, Humberto Ortega and Víctor Tirado.

After July 1979 the members of the *dirección nacional* of the FSLN were the *comandantes de la revolución* Bayardo Arce, Tomas Borge, Luis Carrión, Carlos Nuñez (coordinator del Consejo de Estado [1980-84]), Daniel Ortega (coordinator of the Junta de Gobierno de Reconstrucción Nacional [1979-84] and president of Nicaragua [1984-90]), Humberto Ortega, Henry Ruiz, Víctor Tirado and Jaime Wheelock.

The civilian Grupo de los Doce ('group of the twelve') was coordinated by Sergio Ramirez (member of the Junta de Gobierno de Reconstrucción Nacional [1979-84] and vice-president of Nicaragua [1984-90]), and consisted of Ernesto Castillo and Joaquín Cuadra Sr (lawyers); Emilio Baltodano and Felipe Mantica (entrepreneurs); Fernando Cardenal and Miguel d'Escoto (priests); Carlos Tunnerman (academic) and Sergio Ramirez (academic, novelist and writer); Casimiro Sotelo (architect); Arturo Cruz (banker) and Carlos Gutierrez (dentist).

After 1990 the FSLN participated in all presidential elections, always obtaining a stable vote of 30-35 per cent of the national vote and generally gaining important posts of municipal mayor. The FSLN suffered from internal splintering; meanwhile, Daniel Ortega became the party leader, surviving all opposition attempts and eliminating all competitors. In 1995 Sergio Ramírez and Dora Maria Tellez formed the Movimiento de Renovación Sandinista (MRS); in 2005 former Sandinista minister and mayor of Nicaragua

Herty Lewites challenged Ortega with a modernizing Sandinista alliance (with a leadership comprising Sergio Ramírez and former *comandantes de la revolución* Luis Carrión, Henry Ruiz, Victor Tirado, and *comandantes guerrilleros* Monica Baltodano, Dora Maria Tellez, Victor Hugo Tinoco and Hugo Torres). After the death of Lewites in April 2006, former ambassador Edmundo Jarquín took over command. Daniel Ortega's electoral campaign manager was his wife, Rosario Murillo. Ortega won the 2006 presidential elections with 38 per cent of the national vote.

2. Demographic Data on Central America

Population and urbanization of El Salvador, Guatemala and Nicaragua, 1950-2005

	El Salvador	Guatemala	Nicaragua
Population (m)			
1950	2.0	3.1	1.2
1955	2.2	3.6	1.4
1960	2.6	4.1	1.6
1965	3.0	4.7	1.9
1970	3.6	5.4	2.2
1975	4.1	6.2	2.6
1980	4.6	7.0	3.0
1985	4.8	7.9	3.5
1990	5.1	8.9	4.0
1995	5.7	10.0	4.5
2000	6.3	11.2	5.0
2005*	6.9	12.6	5.5
Urbanization (%)			
1950	36	25	35
1955	37	28	37
1960	38	31	40
1965	39	34	43
1970	39	35	47
1975	41	37	48
1980	44	37	50
1985	46	39	52
1990	49	41	53
1995	54	43	55
2000	58	45	56
2005*	60	47	58

Note: * estimate.

Source: Extrapolation of UN Secretariat data (UN, 2003, 2004).

3. List of Interviews

Costa Rica

Rodrigo Carreras, at the Embassy of Costa Rica in Nicaragua, Managua, 27 February 2006. Rodrigo Carreras is a former vice-minister of foreign affairs of Costa Rica and was at the time of the interview ambassador of Costa Rica to Nicaragua.

Luis Guillermo Solis, in his office at the secretariat general of FLACSO (Facultad Latinoaméricana de Ciencias Sociales), San José de Costa Rica, 20 and 21 February 2006. Luis Guillermo Solis is a former vice-minister of foreign affairs of Costa Rica and a roving ambassador to Central America. At the time of the last interview he was the academic director of the FLACSO system.

El Salvador

Rafael Alemán, in his office at the Instituto de Ciencias Políticas y Administrativas 'Farabundo Martí', Colonia Escalón, San Salvador, 26 and 28 July 2005. Rafael Alemán fought with the urban guerrillas of the Fuerzas Populares de Liberación (FPL) and was at the time of the last interview the director of the Instituto Farabundo Martí.

Manlio Argüeta, in his office at the Biblioteca Nacional, Centro Histórico de San Salvador, 29 July 2005. Manlio Argüeta, writer and novelist, was at the time of the interview the director of the Biblioteca Nacional de El Salvador.

Federico Bermúdez, at the Instituto de Ciencias Políticas y Administrativas 'Farabundo Martí', Colonia Escalón, San Salvador, 26 and 28 July 2005. Frederico Bermúdez was at the time of the last interview a staff member of the Instituto Farabundi Martí.

Roberto Cañas López, in his office at the Universidad Evangélica de El Salvador, San Salvador, 10 August 2005. Roberto Cañas, a former member of the *dirección nacional* of the Resistencia Nacional, was later an international spokesman for the FMLN and a peace negotiator (1989-92). At the time of the interview he was in charge of the postgraduate centre of the Universidad Evangélica.

Humberto Corado Figueroa, at the residence of his son, Ciudad Merliot, San Salvador, 15 August 2005, and at the Holiday Inn, San Salvador, 31 May 2007. General Humberto Corado was chief of staff of the advisory board of President Cristiani (1989–92) and then minister of defence (1992–96). At the time of the last interview he was a retired private citizen, planning to write his memoirs.

Alfredo Cristiani, at the headquarters of Droguería Santa Lucía, Colonia Roma, San Salvador, 18 August 2005. Alfredo Cristiani was president of El Salvador from 1989 to 1994; the peace agreement was signed during his term of office. At the time of the interview he was one of the leading Salvadoran entrepreneurs.

Héctor Dada, at the library of FLACSO de San Salvador, Colonia Escalón, San Salvador, 29 July 2005. Héctor Dada was minister of foreign affairs in 1979–80 and a member of the second transition junta in 1980. He is the former director of FLACSO de San Salvador and at the time of the interview was an independent member of parliament.

David Escobar Galindo, in his office at the Universidad Dr José Matías Delgado, San Salvador, 10 August 2005 and 31 May 2007. David Escobar is a poet and a legal adviser. He was the speechwriter for President Cristiani (1989–94) and was a member of the government delegation at the peace negotiations (1989–92). At the time of the last interview he was rector of the Universidad Dr José Matías Delgado.

Facundo Guardado Guardado, at the residence of his daughter, Calle Motocross, San Salvador, 9 and 18 August 2005, and in his office, 83 Avenida Norte, 30 May 2007. Comandante Facundo Guardado was secretary general of the Bloque Popular Revolucionario and a senior member of the *dirección nacional* of the FMLN. In 1999 he was the FMLN presidential candidate. At the time of the last interview he was the director of a social welfare NGO.

Dagoberto Gutiérrez, at the Casa de la Mujer, Colonia Buenos Aires, San Salvador, 12 and 22 August 2005. Comandante Dagoberto Gutiérrez was a member of the Fuerzas Populares de Liberación (FPL) and a member of the FMLN peace negotiation team. At the time of the last interview he was a professor of law at the Universidad Luterana.

Francisco Jovel, in his office at the Asamblea Legislativa, Centro de Gobierno, San Salvador, 24 August 2005. Comandante Francisco Jovel (Roberto Roca) was secretary general of the Partido Revolucionario de Trabajadores Centroamericanos (PRTC) and a member of the *comandancia general* of the FMLN. At the time of the interview he was an adviser to the parliamentary fraction of the FMLN.

Oscar Ortiz, in his office at the City Hall of Santa Tecla, 22 and 26 August 2005, and 31 May 2007. Comandante Oscar Ortiz was the last commander of the Special Forces of the FMLN. At the time of the last interview he was serving his third term as the (FMLN) mayor of Santa Tecla.

Gerardo Potter, in the parish hall of the Iglesia del Rosario, Centro Histórico de San Salvador, 29 August 2005. Father Gerardo Potter was a priest in the Salvadoran refugee camps in Honduras in the 1970s and 1980s and at the time of the interview was a parish priest at the Iglesia del Rosario.

Carlos Ramos, in his office at FLACSO de San Salvador, Colonia Escalón, San Salvador, 25 July and 25 August 2005. Carlos Ramos is a political analyst and at the time of the interview was academic director of FLACSO de San Salvador.

Salvador Samayoa, in his office at the Comisión Nacional de Desarrollo, Colonia Escalón, San Salvador, 23 August 2005, and at the Holiday Inn, San Salvador, 30 May 2007. Salvador Samayoa, philosopher, was minister of education during the first transition junta (1979–80). He was also a senior member of the *comisión político-diplomático* of the FMLN and a peace negotiator. At the time of the last interview he was the president or member of three presidential commissions, including the National Development Council and the National Security Council.

Salvador Sánchez Cerén, in his office at the Asamblea Legislativa, Centro de Gobierno, San Salvador, 26 August 2005 and 30 May 2007. Comandante Salvador Sánchez Cerén (Leonel González) was a member of the *comandancia* of the FMLN on behalf of the Fuerzas Populares de Liberación (FPL). He was the coordinator of the FMLN (2001-04) and at the time of the last interview was the FSLM coordinator in parliament.

Eduardo Sancho, in his office at the Universidad Francisco Gavidia, San Salvador, 23 August 2005. Comandante Eduardo Sancho (Fermán Cienfuegos), a poet and a sociologist, was secretary general of Resistencia Nacional (RN) and a member of the *comandancia general* of the FMLN. At the time of the interview he was professor of sociology at the Universidad Francisco Gavidia.

Héctor Silva, in his office at the Asamblea Legislativa, Centro de Gobierno, San Salvador, 16 August 2005. Héctor Silva, a medical doctor who served twice as (FMLN) mayor of San Salvador, was at the time of the interview an independent member of parliament.

Maria Marta Valladares, in her office at the Parlamento Centroamericano, Centro de Gobierno, San Salvador, 19 August 2005. Comandante Maria Marta Valladares (Nidia Díaz) was a member first of the Ejército Revolucionario del Pueblo (ERP) in Guatemala and after 1976 of the Partido Revolucionario de Trabajadores Centroamericanos (PRTC) in El Salvador. She also was a member of the FMLN peace negotiating team (1989-92). At the time of the interview she was an FMLN member of the Central American parliament.

Omar Arturo Vaquerano, in his office at the Colegio de Altos Estudios Estratégicos, San Salvador, 30 May 2007. General Omar Arturo Vaquerano was at the time of the interview the director of the Salvadoran Defence Study Centre.

Mauricio Vargas, in his office at Carnes Marejo, Colonia Buenos Aires, San Salvador, 19 August 2005 and 30 May 2007. General Mauricio Vargas was chief of operations (1986-88) and chief of staff (1990-92) of the Salvadoran Armed Institution. He also was, on request of President Cristiani, a member of the government peace negotiating team (1989-92) and after the peace the presidential commissioner who oversaw the implementation of the peace agreements (1992-94). At the time of the last interview he was running a meat-processing business.

Rubén Zamora, at his residence, Colonia Vista Hermosa, San Salvador, 26 July and 16 August 2005. Rubén Zamora, a sociologist, was prime minister (*ministro de la presidencia*) during the first transition Junta (1979–80). After the constitution of the FMLN as a political party in 1992, he was the first presidential candidate of the FMLN (1994). Since the late 1990s he has worked alternately as a professor at Columbia University and as an UNDP consultant on civil-military relations in the Horn of Africa.

Guatemala

Rodrigo Asturias, at his residence in Zona 2, Guatemala City, March 1999, February 2002, March and April 2005. Comandante Rodrigo Asturias (Gaspár Ilóm) was the *comandante-en-jefe* of the Organización del Pueblo en Armas (ORPA) and a member of the *comandancia general* of the URNG. In 2004 he was the presidential candidate of the URNG. Until his death in May 2005 he was also the secretary general of this party.

Enrique Álvarez, at the office of the NGO Incidencia Democrática, Zona 1, Guatemala City, 13 April 2005. Enrique Álvarez was a member of the *dirección nacional* of the Fuerzas Armadas Revocutionarias (FAR) and of the *consejo político* of the URNG. He was the co-secretary of the Comisión de Acompañamiento de los Acuerdos de Paz after 1996. At the time of the interview he was director of the NGO Incidencia Democratica.

Julio Balconi, at his residence in Zona 15, Guatemala City, March 1999, March 2002, December 2003; at Casa de Protocolo #14, Havana, Cuba, October 2004; his residence in Zona 15, Guatemala City, April 2005, July 2006, May and July 2007. General Julio Balconi was a member of the Estado Mayor Nacional in the 1980s, and commander of the elite Brigada Mariscal Zavala in the 1990s. In 1996 he signed the peace agreements as minister of defence. At the time of the last interview he was the coordinator of the Guatemalan National Security Council.

Sergio Camargo, in his office in Zona 15, Guatemala City, 11 July 1994. General Camargo Carmargo, former deputy chief of the Estado Mayor Presidencial of President Marco Vinicio Cerezo (1986–90), was at the time of the interview commander of the elite Brigada Mariscal Zavala.

Pablo Ceto, 15 April 2005, at the office of the NGO Fundemaya, Zona 7, Guatemala City, 13 May 2004 and 7 April 2005. Comandante Pablo Ceto was a member of the *dirección nacional* of the Ejército Guerrillero de los Pobres (EGP) and of the URNG. He also is a founding member of the Comité de Unidad Campesina (CUC). In 2004 he was the vice-presidential candidate of the URNG. At the time of the last interview he was the director of the NGO Fundemaya, assisting Maya associations.

'Uncle' Cros, Finca Santa Anita, at the foot of the volcano Tajamulco, San Marcos, March 1999. 'Uncle' Cros, a small coffee farmer in San Marcos, was one of the first Maya members of the Organización del Pueblo en Armas (ORPA); his residence served as the first ORPA headquarters. At the time of the interview he was a member of the Santa Anita coffee co-operative, founded by ex-combatants of the URNG.

Víctor Ferrigno, in his office at USAID, Guatemala City, 11 August 2000; at Hotel Oud London, Zeist (the Netherlands), 28 April 2005; in his office at the Comité de Unidad Campesina (CUC), Guatemala City, 18 July 2005; at Las Colinas Country Club, Quetzaltenango, 13 July 2006. Víctor Ferrigno was a founding member of the Comité de Unidad Campesina (CUC) and a member of the *dirección nacional* of the Ejército Guerrillero de los Pobres (EGP). At the time of the last interview he was the general adviser of the board of the Comité de Unidad Campesina (CUC) and a consultant on the indigenous (Maya) legal system.

Rafael Gonzáles, at the office of the Comité de Unidad Campesina (CUC), Guatemala City, 18 July 2005. Rafael Gonzáles was at the time of the interview a member of the board of the Comité de Unidad Campesina (CUC).

Héctor Alejandro Gramajo, in his office in Zona 9, Guatemala City, and afterwards in the general's car driving from Guatemala City to his weekend country residence and back, 13 July 1994. General Alejandro Gramajo was minister of defence during the administration of President Marco Vinicio Cerezo (1986–90). He earned an M.A. from Harvard in public administration, and was one of the founding members of the Centro ESTNA, the National Stability Studies Centre, and a senior consultant on civil-military relations. He died in 2005.

René Juárez Poroj, in his office in Zona 3, Quetzaltenango, 12 July 2006; at his residence in Zona 1, 14 July 2006. René Juárez Poroj, a lawyer, was during the 1990s first a founding member of Xelju and then a member of the municipal council of Quetzaltenango. At the time of the interview he was a professor at the Universidad Nacional San Carlos and a legal adviser to Maya rights organizations.

Suruma Lima, at her residence in Zona 1, Quetzaltenango, 14 July 2006. Suruma Lima, a medical doctor, was a founding member of Xelju and a member of the municipal council of Quetzaltenango in the 1990s. At the time of the interview she was an independent consultant on indigenous and women's rights.

Alba Estela Maldonado, in her office at the Palacio de Cultura, Zona 1, Guatemala City, 13 December 2006 and 29 May 2007. Comandante Alba Estela Maldonado (Lola) was a senior member of the Ejército Guerrillero de los Pobres (EGP) and a member of the *comisión política* of the URNG from 1986 to the present. She lived underground from the 1960s to 1996. At the time of the last interview she was the only URNG member of parliament.

Celso Humberto Morales, in his office at the URNG, Zona 2, Guatemala City, 20 April 2005. Comandante Celso Humberto Morales (Tomás) was the second-in-command of the Ejército Guerrillero de los Pobres (EGP) and a member of the *comisión política* of the URNG. Between 1997 and 1999 he was (with Luis Santiago Santa Cruz) in charge of organizing the URNG as a legal political party. At the time of the interview he was in charge of the political office of the URNG.

Daniel Pascual, in his office at the Comité de Unidad Campesina (CUC), Zona 7, Guatemala City, 18 July 2005. As a teenager, Daniel Pascual served in the Ejército Guerrillero de los Pobres (EGP). At the time of the interview, he was serving as secretary general of the Comité de Unidad Campesina (CUC).

Ricardo Peralta Méndez, at his residence in Zona 14, Guatemala City, 13 July 1994. General Peralta Méndez served as commander of the elite Guardia de Honor during the administration of President Julio César Méndez Montenegro (1966–70). In 1978 he was the presidential candidate of the Democracia Cristiana, losing the election to general Romeo Lucas García. At the time of the interview he was a private citizen, finishing his memoirs.

Edgar Ponce, at the Centro ESTNA, Zona 10, Guatemala City, 7 July 1994. Edgar Ponce was at the time of the interview the academic director of the civil-military Centro ESTNA (National Stability Studies Centre).

René Poitevin, in his office at the UNDP, Edificio Europlaza, Zona 14, Guatemala City, 14 April 2005. René Poitevin, a political scientist, was the director of FLACSO de Guatemala between 1989 and 2001 and vice-rector of the Universidad Landívar between 2001 and 2004. At the time of the interview he was a UNDP consultant; he died in May 2007 as the director of the Soros Foundation in Guatemala.

Gustavo Porras, at the Café Vienes, Hotel Camino Real, Zona 10, Guatemala City, 12 April 2005. Gustavo Porras was a member of the *dirección política* of the Ejército Guerrillero de los Pobres (EGP) and served in 1996 as coordinator of the presidential Peace Commission (COPAZ). After 1996 he was the private secretary of President Arzú. At the time of the interview he was an independent consultant and political analyst.

Rigoberto Quemé Chay, in his office at the City Hall, Quetzaltenango, 26 February 1998. Rigoberto Quemé Chay, an anthropologist, was twice elected as the mayor of Quetzaltenango between 1997 and 2003. He was mayor of Quetzaltenango at the time of the interview.

Jaime Rabanales, in his office in Zona 1, Guatemala City, 12 July 1994. General Jaime Rabanales was the senior commander during the counterinsurgency operations against the Ejército Guerrillero de los Pobres (EGP) in the department of El Quiché in the 1980s. At the time of the interview he was a member of the board of the Centro ESTNA, the National Stability Studies Centre.

Miguel Ángel Reyes, at his residence, Zona 11, Guatemala City, 18 April 2005. Miguel Ángel Reyes, a lawyer, was a member of the *comisión política-diplomática* of the URNG between 1986 and 1996. At the time of the interview he was an independent consultant on legal affairs.

Héctor Rosada-Granados, at the presidential palace, Zona 1, Guatemala City, 14 July 1994; at his office, Zona 11, 28 February 1999, 24 June and 28 August 2000, and 1 April 2005. Héctor Granados-Rosada, an anthropologist and sociologist, was a cabinet member and the national peace negotiator (1993–96). At the time of the last interview he was an independent consultant on peace programmes and border disputes.

Luis Santiago Santa Cruz, at Hotel Ibis, Brussels, 22 June 2006; at Malie Hotel and the author's residence, Utrecht, 30 June and 1 July 2006. Comandante Luis Santiago Santa Cruz (Santiago) was the last commander of the Frente Unitario of the URNG and a member of the *comisión política* of the URNG. Between 1997 and 1999 he was (with Celso Morales) in charge of organizing the URNG as a legal political party. At the time of the last interview he was a private citizen, having recently published his memoirs.

Catalina Soberanis, in her office at the OAS, Torre Europlaza II, Zona 14, Guatemala City, 5 April 2005. Catalina Soberanis was the president of Congress during the administration of President Marco Vinicio Cerezo (1986–90). In 1999/2000 she was the presidential candidate of the Frente Democrático Nuevo Guatemala (FDNG). At the time of the interview she was a consultant for the Organization of American States.

Silvia Solórzano, at the Hotel Crown Plaza, Managua, 24 October 2006. Silvia Solórzano was at the time of the interview in charge of International Relations for the Unidad Revolucionaria Nacional Guatemala (URNG).

Jorge Soto, at the office of the Comisión de Acompañamiento de los Acuerdos de Paz, Zona 1, Guatemala City, 9 August 2000; at the office of Alianza Nueva Nación (ANN), Zona 1, 28 May 2007. Comandante Jorge Soto (Pablo Monsanto) was the *comandante-en-jefe* of the Fuerzas Armadas Revolucionarias (FAR) and a member of the *comandancia general* of the URNG. At the time of the last interview he was the presidential candidate of Alianza Nueva Nación (ANN).

Ricardo Stein, at the office of the Soros Foundation, Guatemala City, 8 and 26 August 2000, and 8 April 2005. Ricardo Stein, a political scientist, was between 1996 and 2001 a cabinet member and the director of the Comisión de la Paz (COPAZ). At the time of the last interview he was the director of the Soros Foundation in Guatemala.

Edelberto Torres-Rivas, at his residence, Zona 9, Guatemala City, 3 April 2005 and 27 May 2007. Edelberto Torres-Rivas was the secretary general of FLACSO between 1986 and 1994. At the time of the last interview he was an UNDP consultant.

Edmundo Urrutia, at Hotel Las Américas, Zona 14, Guatemala City, 8 April 2005. Edmundo Urrutia was a member of Octubre Revolucionario and in 2003–04 minister of home security (Secretario de Análisis Estratégico). At the time of the interview he was a private citizen, preparing for a career as a security consultant.

Rafael Vásquez, in his office at the Comité de Unidad Campesina (CUC), Guatemala City, in 18 July 2005. Rafael Vásquez was at the time of the interview a member of the board of the Comité de Unidad Campesina.

Arnoldo Villagrán, in his office at the NGO Incidencia Democrática, Zona 1, Guatemala City, 14 April 2005, and in the office of Alianza Nueva Nación (ANN), Zona 1, 28 May 2007. Comandante Arnoldo Villagrán (Daniel Ruiz) was the second-in-command of the Fuerzas Armadas Revolucionarias (FAR) from the mid-1980s to 1996. At the time of the last interview he was leading the electoral campaign of Alianza Nueva Nación (ANN).

Zully de Asturias, at her residence, Zona 2, Guatemala City, March and April 2004, 18 July 2005 and 13 December 2006. Zully de Asturias (Manuela) fought with the urban guerrillas of the Organización del Pueblo en Armas (ORPA) and is the widow of Rodrigo Asturias. At the time of the last interview she was the staff supervisor of a Guatemalan NGO working with victims of domestic violence.

Nicaragua

Joop Amse, at his office at the Ministry of Agriculture and Forestry (MAGFOR), Managua, 25 April 2006. Joop Amse, an economist, was an adviser to the Fondo Nicaraguënse de Inversiones (1987–90), the research unit of the Central Bank. At the time of the interview he was a senior consultant at the Ministry of Agriculture and Forestry.

Carlos Argüello, in his office at the embassy of Nicaragua, The Hague, 27 March 2006. Carlos Argüello served as ambassador to the Netherlands and to the International Court of Justice in the mid-1980s and was at the time of the interview again serving as Nicaragua's ambassador to The Hague.

Carlos Arroyo Borgen, in his office at the Ministry of Defence, Managua, 5 May 2006. Carlos Arroyo was at the time of the interview director general of policies at the Ministry of Defence.

Nestor Avendaño, at his residence in Villa Fontana, Managua, 26 April 2006 and 1 June 2007. Nestor Avendaño, an econometrist, was vice-minister of planning (1980-85) and adviser on donor coordination and international cooperation during the presidencies of Violeta Barrios de Chamorro (1990-96) and Arnoldo Alemán (1996-2001). At the time of the last interview he was the senior partner of his consultancy firm on economic policy.

Mónica Baltodano, at the Managua office of the Movimiento de Renovación Sandinista (MRS), Managua, 11 May 2006. *Comandante guerrillero* Mónica Baltodano served as minister of regional development in the 1980s and (FSLM) member of parliament in the 1990s. At the time of the interview she was a member of the electoral team of the Movimiento de Renovación Sandinista.

Pedro Antonio Blandón, at the Holiday Inn, Managua, 2 March 2006. Pedro Antonio Blandón was minister of the Fondo Internacional para la Reconstrucción (FIR) (1993-94) and vice-minister of external cooperation in charge of the relations with the capitalist countries between 1985 and 1990. At the time of the interview he was an UNDP consultant.

Tomás Borge, in his office, Barrio Bello Horizonte, Managua, 24 February 2006. *Comandante de la revolución* Tomás Borge, one of the co-founders of the FLSN, was minister of the interior (1979-90) and was at the time of the interview an FSLN member of parliament and sub-secretary general of this party.

José Ángel Buitrago, in his office, Barrio Altamira, Managua, 5 December 2006. José Ángel Buitrago was the president of the

National Coffee Export Organization (1979-84), vice-minister of external cooperation in charge of relations with the socialist countries (1985-89), and president of the Comisión Nacional del Café (1989-90). At the time of the interview he was the manager of his coffee farm.

Roberto Cajina, in his residence in the Centro Histórico de Managua, 2 May 2006. Roberto Cajina, a military historian, was with the Ministry of Defence (1984-90). At the time of the interview he was the adviser to the Minister of Defence.

Fernando Cardenal, in his office at Fé y Alegría (Faith and Joy), Managua, 9 May 2006. Father Fernando Cardenal S.J. served as a member of the Comisión de los Doce and as Minister of Education (1984-90). At the time of the interview he was the national director of Fé y Alegría, a Latin American Jesuit NGO.

Marta Isabel Cranshaw, during a car drive between Estelí and Achaupa, 6 May 2006. Marta Isabel Cranshaw, a senior guerrilla member in the 1970s and appointed a member of the *segunda promoción de militantes del FSLN* (1979-90), was at the time of the interview the managing director of a migrant support NGO.

Joaquín Cuadra Lacayo, in his office, Las Colinas, Managua, 10 and 16 May 2006. *Comandante guerrillero* and general, Joaquín Cuadra was chief of staff of the Ejército Popular Sandinista (1979-90) and of the Ejército Nacional (1990-95). From 1995 to 2000 he was the commander-in-chief of the Ejército Nacional. At the time of the interview he was managing his coffee farm.

Miguel d'Escoto, in his office, Villa Fontana, Managua, 11 May 2006. Father Miguel d'Escoto, a Maryknoll priest, served as a member of the Comisión de los Doce and minister of foreign affairs (1979-90). At the time of the interview he was living at the Maryknoll convent.

Clemente de Jesús Gonzáles Quiñónes, in his home in El Portillo, 7 May 2006. Clemente Gonzáles, nephew of a colonel who served under General Sandino in the 1920s and 1930s, was affiliated with the FSLN. At the time of the interview he was retired and living on his farm.

José Adán Guerra, in his office, Barrio Bolonia, Managua, 12 May 2006. José Adán Guerra was the private secretary of President

Violeta de Chamorro (1990–96), vice-minister of foreign affairs (1997-2000) and minister of defence (2000–05). At the time of the interview he was the senior partner of his law firm.

Carlos Manuel Irías Martínez, at the Hotel Miraflor, Estelí, 6 May 2006. Carlos Irías has been a member of the FSLN since 1959. His last military function was *official de armas* of the Brigada de Ocotál (1990). At the time of the interview he was working as an artisan.

Paul Kester, at la antigua casa de Chema Castillo, 26 April 2006. Paul Kester, a development official in Nicaragua during most of the 1980s, was at the time of the interview a consultant on micro-enterprises with the Deutscher Entwicklungsdienst.

Antonio Lacayo, at his residence at the Carretera Sur, Managua, 11 May 2006. Antonio Lacayo, an entrepreneur before and after he entered politics, served as prime minister (*ministro de la presidencia*) and acting minister of defence during the presidency of his mother-in-law Violeta de Chamorro (1990–97). At the time of the interview he was the managing director of several enterprises.

Maria López Vigíl, in her office at the Universidad Centroamericana, Managua, 27 October 2006. Maria López, a journalist and the biographer of Msgr Romero, is the editor-in-chief of *Envío*, a leading Nicaraguan monthly journal of politics and society, published since 1981.

Vilma Núñez de Escorcia, in her office at the Nicaraguan Human Rights Centre (CENIDH), Barrio de Altagracia, Managua, 10 May, 17 October and 20 November 2006. Vilma Nuñez, a lawyer who was also with the FSLN during most of the 1970s, was appointed a member of the *segunda promoción de militantes del FSLN*, and then vice-president of the Supreme Court (1979–87) and National Commissioner of Human Rights (1987–90). At the time of the last interview she was the president of the board of CENIDH.

Orlando Nuñez, in his office at CIPRES, Universidad Nacional de Ingeniería, Managua, 27 February 2006. Orlando Nuñez, a sociologist and between 1979 and 1990 in charge of the research institute of the Ministry of Agriculture and Land Reform (MIDINRA) and a leading FSLN ideologue from the mid-1970s to the present, was at the time of the interview the director of CIPRES, a rural development institute.

Lola Ocón Nuñez, in her office in the Centro Histórico de Managua, 12 December 2006. Lola Ocón, an economist and a former FSLN member, was between 1979 and 1990 an adviser to President Daniel Ortega as a member of the Presidential Secretariat. At the time of the interview she was an independent consultant on development programmes.

Humberto Ortega Saavedra, at his residence, Carretera a Masaya, Managua, 15 May 2006. *Comandante de la revolución* and general, Humberto Ortega was minister of defence and commander-in-chief of the Ejército Popular Sandinista (1979-90) and the Ejército Nacional (1979-95). At the time of the interview he was a leading entrepreneur with business interests in both Costa Rica and Nicaragua.

Manuel Ortega Hegg, in his office at the Centro de Análisis Sociocultural (CACS), Universidad Centroaméricana (UCA), Managua, 28 February and 14 December 2006. Manuel Ortega is a political scientist at the UCA. At the time of the last interview he was the director of the CACS.

Carlos Palacios, in his office at the Nacional Office of the Policía Nacional, Managua, 20 November 2006 and 1 June 2007. Carlos Palacios joined the Policía Sandinista in 1979. At the time of the last interview he was Comisionado General and the second-in-command of the National Police.

Edén Pastora, at his residence, Centro Histórico de Managua, 25 April 2006 and 1 June 2007. *Comandante guerrillero* Edén Pastora (Comandante Cero) was one of the co-founders of the FLSN. In 1979 he was appointed vice-minister of the interior, in charge of the Sandinista militias. He left the FSLN in 1981 to become the chief commander of ARDE, the Southern Contra movement. At the time of the last interview he was, after participating in the presidential elections of 2006 as the candidate of a small Social Christian political movement, a private citizen.

Silvia Porras, at the Netherlands Embassy, Managua, 9 November 2006. Silvia Porras was the manager of CODEHUCA (Commission for Human Rights in Central America) in Costa Rica (1984-94) and afterwards worked as an independent consultant on popular movements and human rights in Nicaragua. At the time of the interview she was a staff member of the Netherlands embassy in Managua.

Jan-Kees de Rooy, at Rostipollos Restaurant, Managua, 8 and 11 May, and 7 and 14 November 2006. Jan-Kees de Rooy, formerly a television and film executive, was at the time of the last interview an adviser to the Banco de Desarrollo Financiero BDF.

Henry Ruiz, at his residence, Los Robles, Managua, 13 December 2006. *Comandante de la revolución* Henry Ruiz (Modesto) was minister of planning (1979-85) and of external cooperation (1985-90). Between 1990 and 1994 he was the treasurer of the FSLN. He left the FSLN in 2001. At the time of the interview he was a member of the board of the Movimiento de Renovación Sandinista.

José Santos Gutiérrez, at the Hotel Miraflor, Estelí, 6 May 2006. José Santos was an officer in the Ejército Popular Sandinista (EPS) after 1982. He held the rank of second lieutenant at the time that he was wounded and crippled in 1984. At the time of the interview he was living as a *campesino*.

Dora María Téllez, at her residence, Pancasán, Managua, 4 May and 14 November 2006. *Comandante guerrillero* Dora María Téllez was minister of public health in the 1980s. She is a founding member of the Movimiento de Renovación Sandinista (1995-present). At the time of the last interview she was an independent consultant on development programmes.

Víctor Hugo Tinoco, in his office at the Casa de Campaña of the Movimiento de Renovación Sandinista (MRS), Las Colinas, Managua, 4 May 2006. *Comandante guerrillero* Víctor Hugo Tinoco was vice-minister of foreign affairs (1979-90) and an FSLN member of parliament in the 1990s. At the time of the interview he was a member of the electoral team of the Movimiento de Renovación Sandinista.

Víctor Tirado López, at the Hotel Villa Americano, Carretera a Masaya, Managua, 3 March 2006. *Comandante de la revolución* Víctor Tirado López, a founding member of the FSLN, was in charge of the Sandinista popular organizations between 1979 and 1990. At the time of the interview he was an adviser to the (independent) labour movement.

Hugo Torres, at his residence, Las Colinas, Managua, 8 May 2006 and 1 June 2007. *Comandante guerrillero* and general, Hugo Torres was chief of state security and vice-minister of the interior (1979–82) and secretary of the Consejo del Estado (1980–82), director of the political directorate of the Ejército Popular Sandinista (1982–90) and director of personnel and defence intelligence of the Ejército Nacional (1990–95, 1995–99). At the time of the last interview he was a leading member of the Movimiento de Renovación Sandinista and the manager of his coffee farm.

Oscar René Vargas, at his residence, Barrio Los Robles, Managua, 28 February 2006. Oscar René Vargas has been a leading ideologue of the FSLN since its inception. At the time of the interview he was a personal adviser to *comandante de la revolución* Daniel Ortega, secretary general of the FSLN.

René Vivas, in his office at SERVIPRO, Rotunda Santo Domingo, Managua, 3 May 2006. *Comandante guerrillero* René Vivas served as national director of the Policía sandinista (1979–90) and director general of the National Police (1990–92). At the time of the interview he was the managing director of a private security company.

Jaime Wheelock, in his office at Instituto para el Desarrollo y la Democracia (IPADE), Carretera a Masaya, Managua, 9 May 2006. *Comandante de la revolución* Jaime Wheelock was during the 1980s minister of agriculture and land reform (MIDINRA). Afterwards he obtained a Harvard M.A. (public administration) and at the time of the interview he was the president of IPADE, a research NGO.

Rosa Marina Zelaya Velásquez, in her office, Carretera Sur, Managua, 2 May 2006. Rosa Marina Zelaya was a magistrate at the Corte Electoral (1979–90) and the president of the Corte Electoral during the government of President Violeta de Chamorro (1990–97). At the time of the interview she was an independent legal consultant.

Notes

Foreword

1. On 7 August 1987, five Central American presidents signed an accord titled 'Procedures for Establishing a Just and Enduring Peace in Central America'. Two of the signatories, Duarte and Azcona, have since died; two others, Arias and Ortega, are once again presidents of their respective countries.

Introduction

1. Comisión de la Verdad, 1993.
2. ADHAG, 1998; and CEH, 1999.
3. Called the *comandancia general* in El Salvador and Guatemala, and the *dirección nacional* in Nicaragua.
4. Comandante Fermán Cienfuegos (Eduardo Sancho), member of the *comandancia general* of the FMLN, and university rector David Escobar Galindo, speech writer of and adviser to president Cristiani; see Sancho and Galindo, 1996.
5. Facultad Latinoamericana de Ciencias Sociales.

Chapter 1

1. The most complete history of Central America is the six-volume collection *Historia General de Centroamérica* under the general editorship of Torres-Rivas (1993b). A fine single-volume political history is Dunkerley, 1988. Pérez-Brignoli (1989), who was also editor

of volumes 3 and 5 of the *Historia General de Centroamérica*, has written another first-class general history of Central America. An excellent general overview is edited by Bethell, 1991.

2. For a recent account, see Sanford, 2003.
3. Data presented in Dunkerley, 1988: 217. The most recent data are 3 million for Guatemala City (2006), 1.7 million for Managua (2004) and 2 million for Metropolitan San Salvador (2006).
4. As the percentage of the industrial workforce of the economically active population.
5. Both estimates are published in Vilas, 1994: 80.
6. Systematic data on Central America's poverty in the 1980s and 1990s are collected by a FLACSO study group headed by Rafael Menjívar. The final studies were published as Menjívar and Trejos, 1992; and Menjívar, Kruijt and Van Vucht Tijssen, 1997. A case study on Nicaragua's post-war poverty is Renzi and Kruijt, 1997; the most recent publication is Avendaño, 2007. A recent study on the urban poverty in El Salvador is Ávalos-Trigueros and Trigueros Argüello, 2005.
7. The current remittances stream that helps alleviate present-day poverty in El Salvador, Guatemala and Nicaragua provides annual revenues of US$2.5 to 3 billion to each country (2006).
8. See Luján Muñoz, 2004: 224-419.
9. See Gleijeses, 1992 for the definitive study on the period 1944-54.
10. Author's interview with Héctor Alejandro Gramajo in the general's car driving from Guatemala City to his weekend country residence and back, 13 July 1994.
11. This relationship continued into the 1990s. When General Quilo, then vice-minister of defence, prepared to stage a coup in 1994, President Ramiro de León was alerted by the Israelis. For more details on the Israeli-Guatemalan intelligence collaboration, see *NACLA Report*, 1987.
12. Analysed in detail in ADHAG, 1998.
13. *Report on Guatemala*, 1985: 26-7.
14. Author's interview with Héctor Alejandro Gramajo.
15. The tradition of military dictatorship in El Salvador in fact began in the nineteenth century. For a history of the violence and repression in El Salvador between 1840 and 1940, see Alvarenga, 1996; and Ching, 1997.
16. For a short biography, see Arias Gómez, 2002.
17. See González, 2004: 36.
18. For details of the 1944 revolt, see Parkman, 2003.
19. The Partido Revolucionario de Unificación Democrática (1949) mutated into the Partido de Conciliación Nacional (1961), which was to govern to October 1979.

20. See Baires Martínez, 1994 for the early history of the party. Galeas (2004) published a detailed political biography of D'Aubuisson.
21. Author's interview with Salvador Samayoa, San Salvador, 23 August 2005.
22. Author's interview with Roberto Cañas, San Salvador, 10 August 2005.
23. Author's interview with Rubén Zamora, San Salvador, 26 July 2005. A death squad killed Mario Zamora, at the time serving as attorney general, on 23 February 1980.
24. See Menjívar Ochoa, 2006: 203–22; Dunkerley, 1985; and Comisión de la Verdad, 1993: 172–80.
25. See McClintock, 1985: 196 ff., for details.
26. Comisión de la Verdad, 1993: 181, author's translation. The report mentions especially the role of ex-major D'Aubuisson, who refused cooperation but who was considered one of the leading actors of the death squads.
27. Anastasio Somoza García (Tacho) was assassinated in 1956. His son and successor Luis Somoza Debayle died in 1967 of a heart attack. His brother Anastasio Somoza Debayle (Tachito) fled the country on 17 July 1979 and was assassinated in Paraguay on 17 September 1980 by an Argentine guerrilla commando.
28. For a history and analysis of the National Guard, see Millett, 1977. Recent publications, more eulogistic than scholarly in nature, are Boza Gutiérrez, 2002; and Pérez, 2004.
29. Between 1945 and 1960 Guatemala received 59 per cent of the total US military aid to Central America. This pattern was more or less unaltered until the mid-1970s. During the Carter administration the military aid volume was equally distributed between Costa Rica, Honduras and Nicaragua. In 1980, US military aid was mainly directed to El Salvador (data published in Weaver, 1994: 132, 181).
30. The USA had been landing troops in Nicaragua since 1853, and was the dominant force in this semi-protectorate since at least 1910. For US involvement between 1857 and 1979, see Pérez Baltodano, 203: 243–574. For military involvement between 1926 and 1993, see Boot, 2003: 231–52.
31. The classic biography of Sandino is written by Selser, 1979. The Frente Sandinista de Liberación Nacional (FSLN) in Nicaragua was named in his honour, while Martí's name was incorporated into the Frente Farabundo Martí de Liberación Nacional (FMLN) in El Salvador. Martí fought as a colonel in Sandino's guerrilla army and served as his political secretary. The two leaders parted ways with respect to party discipline, Sandino becoming the more nationalist and Martí the institutional communist hero.

32. See Walter, 2004 for a detailed history of the founder of the dynasty.
33. Between 1946 and 1956, for instance, the total number of soldiers and officers gradually increased, the former from 3,635 to 4,391, the latter from 345 to 526 (Walter, 2004: 342).
34. Author's interview with Marta Isabel Cranshaw, during a car drive between Estelí and Achaupa, 6 May 2006.
35. I consulted the following sources in preparing this section. On Guatemala: Loveman and Davies, 1997: 181-208, 337-83, 385-425; Le Bot, 1997; Sesereses, 1992; and Gramajo, 2003: 484-604. On Nicaragua: Flakoll and Alegría, 2004. On El Salvador: Corr and Prisk, 1992; Montgomery, 1995; Menjívar Ochoa, 2006.
36. Author's interviews with Eduardo Sancho and Francisco Jovel, San Salvador, 23 and 24 August 2005.
37. See his Central American diary (Guevara, 2002). The fall of Árbenz and the necessity of building up strong defences is a theme he continually returns to in his later writings as well.
38. A Guatemalan brother-in-arms, 'el patojo Cáceres' was influential in the emergence of the first guerrilla waves and in the origin of ORPA, the movement under the command of Asturias (author's interview with Rodrigo Asturias, 31 March 2005.
39. Guatemala and Nicaragua were used as CIA bases for the training of counter-revolutionary Cubans for the Bay of Pigs invasion.
40. Paz Tejada had been chief commander of the armed forces during the government of Arévalo (1944-50) and minister of planning during the Árbenz administration (1950-54).
41. Author's interview with Jaime Rabanales Reyes, Guatemala City, 12 July 1994. Other military sources even mentioned 100,000.
42. From mid-1981 to early 1982 intelligence operations led to the destruction of twenty-eight safe houses of the URNG in Guatemala City.
43. Data published by the Ministry of Defence; see *El Periódico* of 13 May 2004.
44. REDSAL, 2005: 194, 198, www.resdal.org/libros/Archivo/atlas-libro.htm (consulted 11 August 2006).
45. See Luciak (2001: 88-93) for the figures. An URNG source (*Diagnóstico URNG*, 1997) mentions around 4,000, of which 71 per cent were ethnic Maya. More than 80 per cent were male, 58 of them being married or living in free union. Of the demobilized, 16 per cent were illiterate.
46. In 1959 Pedro Joaquín Chamorro, editor of the journal *La Prensa* and husband of the future president Violeta Barrios de Chamorro (1990-97), and Tomás Borge participated in a guerrilla group based in Costa Rica. Chamorro separated and invaded Nicaragua with a

group of 100 insurgents. The Guard easily defeated the rebel group and imprisoned their leaders.

47. Also Carlos Fonseca was killed in combat in 1976.
48. See for this period Arias, 1981; Baez, 1979; Borge, 1983; and Cabezas, 1985.
49. Edén Pastora, the leading commander (Comandante Cero) acquired here international fame.
50. The Frente Interno, commanded by Joaquín Cuadra Lacayo.
51. The Grupo de los Doce, coordinated by Sergio Ramirez and the cradle of the future civilian cabinet members in the 1980s. They were: Ernesto Castillo and Joaquín Cuadra Sr (lawyers), Emilio Baltodamo and Felipe Mantica (entrepreneurs), Fernando Cardenal and Miguel d'Escoto (priests), Carlos Tunnerman and Sergio Ramírez (academics), Casimiro Sotelo (architect), Arturo Cruz (banker) and Carlos Gutierrez (dentist) (Dunkerley, 1988: 264).
52. The politician behind the scenes was Costa Rican President José Figueres Sr, arch-enemy of the Somoza dynasty. Somoza Debayle invaded Costa Rica twice, in 1949 and 1955. Figueres liberally supported the cause of the FSLN and finally secured his cabinet's approval for transport of weaponry to the Frente Sur of Humberto Ortega and Edén Pastora (author's interviews with Luis Guillermo Solis, San José, on 20 and 21 February 2006, and with Rodrigo Carreras, Managua, 27 February 2006).
53. Estimates made by the comandantes Joaquín Cuadra Lacayo, Humberto Ortega, Edén Pastora, Víctor Tirado and Jaime Wheelock (author's interviews, Managua, 10 May 2006, 15 May 2006, 25 April 2006, 3 March 2006 and 9 May 2006).
54. I discussed the origins of the politico-military organizations at length with Carlos Ramos (author's interviews with Carlos Ramos, San Salvador, 25 July and 25 August 2005).
55. The Ejército Revolucionario del Pueblo (ERP), headed by Joaquín Villalobos (René Cruz) and Ana Guadalupe Martínez, with the Ligas Populares '28 de Febrero'; the Resistencia Nacional, headed by Eduardo Sancho (Fermán Cienfuegos), with the Frente de Acción Popular Unido (FAPU); the Partido Revolucionario de Trabajadores Centroamericanos (PRTC), after 1981 headed by Francisco Jovel (Roberto Roca) with various labour organizations. Note: there is always confusion between Francisco Jovel and Ernesto Jovel, the *nom de guerre* of the first leader of the RN, who died in 1980 in an air crash.
56. See Menjívar Ochoa, 2006 for a detailed account of the events between 1979 and 1981.
57. Author's interview with Faculdo Guardado, San Salvador, 9 August 2005.

58. A semi-official historical account of the war reflecting the version of the Reagan administration was published by Manwaring and Prisk (1988).
59. Author's interview with Mauricio Vargas, San Salvador, 19 August 2005. The newly formed battalions were BIRI (Batallones de insurgencia y de reacción inmediata) and BIAS (Batallones de infantería antiterroristas).
60. REDSAL, 2005: 186, www.resdal.org/libros/Archivo/atlas-libro.htm (consulted 13 August 2006).

Chapter 2

1. Dalton, 1966.
2. Within a Latin American context, the Spanish term *Cristiano* is often used to refer to Catholic Christians. The term *Evangélico* is frequently used for Protestant Christians.
3. The emergence of the first military-led guerrilla movement in Guatemala is described in Gott, 1972: 39–118. See also Gramajo, 2003: 484–604. For the grudges and long-term resentments within the young Guatemalan military, see Wer, 2003.
4. Author's interview with Francisco Jovel, San Salvador, 24 August 2005.
5. Author's interview with Monica Baltodano, Managua, 11 May 2006.
6. Author's interview with Celso Morales (Tomás), Guatemala City, 20 April, 2005.
7. Rafael Menjívar Larín was regarded as an intellectual guide by the *comandancia general* of El Salvador (Sancho, 1993: 8; confirmed by the author's interview with Francisco Jovel, San Salvador, 24 August 2005). In the 1980s he was a spokesman for the Frente Revolucionario Democrático (FDR), the umbrella organization of the non-military organizations of the FMLN (see also Menjívar Ochoa, 2006: 17, 272–96).
8. Author's interview with Edelberto Torres-Rivas, Guatemala City, 3 April 2005.
9. Author's interview with Santiago Santa Cruz, Brussels, 22 June 2006.
10. Central America has three Jesuit universities. The name of the Jesuit universities in both El Salvador and Nicaragua is the Universidad Centroamericana (UCA), while Guatemala's is called the Universidad Rafael Landívar. The three national universities are the Universidad de El Salvador (UES), the Universidad de San Carlos (USAC) in Guatemala, and the Universidad Nacional de Nicaragua (UNAN).
11. Samayoa and Galvan, 1979; Sancho, 1991; Villalobos, 1986, 1989a, 1989b.

12. See Zamora, 2003: 57.
13. A considerable number of the comandantes and other guerrilla leaders wrote their memoirs, sometimes with the assistance of ghostwriters. I consulted Belli, 2001; Borge, 1983, 1990; Cabezas, 1985; [Ernesto] Cardenal, 2004; Díaz, 2005; Gutiérrez, 2004; Montes, 1999; Morán, 2002; Ortega Saavedra, 2004; Payeras, 1987, 1991, 1992, 2002; Ramírez, 1999; Rico Mira 2004; Sancho, 2003; Santa Cruz Mendoza, 2004; Samayoa, 2003; Torres, 2003. At the time of the interviews, Fernando Cardenal and Facundo Guardado were finishing their memoirs.
14. I thank my Dutch and Belgian colleagues Jan Ooyens and Toon Thyberghin, in the late 1960s both students at COPAL, for providing information about the study programme there.
15. See, for instance, Gutierrez et al., 1986. See also Eagleson, 1975. See Löwy, 1996 for the evolution of liberation theology.
16. Miguez Bonino, 1979: 2-3.
17. See Montgomery, 1995: 83-93; and Cabarrús, 1983: 142 ff.
18. Romero et al., 1979.
19. Author's interview with Gerard Potter, San Salvador, 29 August 2005.
20. See Chapter 1 n51.
21. Author's interview with Fernando Cardenal, Managua, 9 May 2006.
22. Le Bot, 1997: 148. Also Santa Cruz Mendoza (2004: 280) mentions men and women inspired by liberation theology who were killed in action.
23. Interview with Daniel Ortega, www.cnn.com/specials/cold.war/episodes/ 18/ interviews/ortega (consulted 23 August 2006).
24. Author's interview with Dagoberto Gutiérrez, San Salvador, 12 August 2005.
25. Author's interview with Roberto Cañas, San Salvador, 10 August 2005.
26. Turcios Lima's Castroism and Yon Sosa's Trotskyism led to a split in the Guatemalan guerrilla movement in 1965. In 1962–63 a short-lived Troskyist guerrilla group had existed under the leadership of Hugo Blanco in the Valle de La Convención in Peru; see Blanco, 1972. And of course the Shining Path in Peru was Maoist in orientation.
27. Sancho (Fermán Cienfuegos), 1993: 10.
28. See Harnecker, 1981, then already in its 51st edition.
29. An innovative study on the nature and significance of 'popular intellectuals' can be found in Baud and Rutten, 2005.
30. Most interviews with ex-comandantes were conducted in their homes or offices. With the exception of Dora Maria Tellez, nobody had a volume of Marx or of one of the leading Marxists on their bookshelves.

I know that Rodrigo Asturias and Luis Santiago Santa Cruz had read about Marxism extensively; in general, ORPA placed a heavy emphasis on the education of all its guerrilla members.

31. Author's interview with Jaime Wheelock, Managua, 9 May 2006.
32. I use the following sources on Che Guevara: Anderson, 1997; Castañeda, 1997; Taibo II, 1997. A more hostile biography containing an interesting analysis of Guevara's Bolivian campaign is James, 2001. Loveman and Davies (1997) provide a fine annotated edition of his writings on guerrilla warfare. See also Dosal, 2003; Guevara, 1972, 1994; and Debray, 1999. For Fidel Castro I used the classic text of Szulc (1986) and the most recent interview-biography by Ramonet, 2006.
33. For a recent history of Cuba's military, see Klepak, 2005.
34. For a detailed history, see Murga Armas, 2006.
35. Santa Cruz, 2004: 262–3.
36. Author's interview with Luis Santiago Santa Cruz, Utrecht, 1 July 2006.
37. Author's interview with Victor Ferrigno, Zeist, 28 April 2005.
38. Author's interview with Victor Ferrigno, Zeist, 28 April 2005.
39. He also wrote on revolutionary strategy; see Dalton, 1970.
40. For a detailed analysis of the different politico-military organizations in El Salvador and the antagonisms between them, see Ramos, 1993; and Gonzalez, 1994.
41. Author's interview with Eduardo Sancho, San Salvador, 23 August 2005.
42. Humberto Ortega, interviewed in *La Prensa*, 18 July 2006.
43. Author's interview with Rodrigo Asturias, Guatemala City, 4 April 2005.
44. For a more detailed analysis, see Morales Carbonell, 1994.
45. Author's interview with Francisco Jovel, San Salvador, 24 August 2005. Sánchez Cerén confirms this version (author's interview with Salvador Sánchez Cerén [Leonel Gonzalez], San Salvador, 26 August 2005).
46. The Guerra Popular Prolongada (GPP) tendency, headed by Tomás Borge, Henry Ruiz and Bayardo Arce versus the Tendencia Proletaria (TP), headed by Jaime Wheelock, Luis Carrión and Carlos Núñez.
47. Headed by Daniel Ortega, Humberto Ortega and Víctor Tirado.
48. Personal communication of Margarita Vannini, director general of the Instituto de Estudios de Nicaragua y Centroamérica at the UCA, where the archives of the former Instituto de Estudios Sandinistas are deposited (Managua, 27 April 2006). When I interviewed Oscar René Vargas, FSLN ideologue and between 1980 and 1990 secretary of the *dirección nacional* (Managua, 28 February 2006) about the

same controversy, he referred me to the same Instituto de Estudios de Nicaragua y Centroamérica, 'where all archives are'; the subject was too complicated to explain in one hour, he said.

Chapter 3

1. Of course, it is not only guerrilla armies that make use of volunteer soldiers. See for instance Stevenson (2004: 198 ff.) on the participation of volunteers during World War I; and Beevor (2001) on the volunteer republican armies and international brigades during the Spanish Civil War.
2. Author's interview with Víctor Tirado, Managua, 3 March 2006.
3. Ortega, 1978; later incorporated in Ortega, 1981.
4. Author's interview with Joaquín Cuadra Lacayo, Managua, 10 May and 16 May 2006.
5. Author's interview with Joaquín Cuadra Lacayo, Managua, 10 May 2006.
6. See for details Flakoll and Alegría, 2004: 313 ff.
7. Author's interview with Joaquín Cuadra Lacayo, Managua, 16 May 2006.
8. See Barreto, 1980 for details.
9. Author's interview with Joaquín Cuadra Lacayo, Managua, 16 May 2006.
10. For an account, see Stanley, 1996: 221–2.
11. Author's interview with Facundo Guardado, San Salvador, 9 August 2005.
12. Benítez Mataút (1989) provides an early overview of the strategy and tactics of the war. For a detailed analysis of the internal military organization of the FMLN, see Moroni Bracamonte and Spencer, 1995: 43–92.
13. For an account of the Salvadoran FMLN Special Forces, see Spencer, 1996.
14. Author's interview with Oscar Ortiz, Santa Tecla, 22 and 28 August 2005.
15. See for an FMLN account Gutiérrez, 1993; for an account based on US sources Moroni Bracamonte and Spencer, 1995: 120 ff.; and Spencer, 1996: 121 ff. See also Stanley, 1996: 245–7.
16. Author's interview with Francisco Jovel, San Salvador, 24 August 2005.
17. For a detailed analysis, see Doggett, 1993; and Whitfield, 1998.
18. Author's interview with Alfredo Cristiani, San Salvador, 18 August 2005.
19. About the kidnapping of US ambassador Mien, see Sandoval, 1997: 131 ff.

20. The establishment of the military *Proyecto Nacional* of long-term political domination and counterinsurgency mobilization is analysed by Rosada-Granados, 1999, and details of the counterinsurgency regimes are presented by Schirmer, 1998, 2002.
21. Author's interview with Rodrigo Asturias, Guatemala City, 6 April 2005.
22. See www.nacion.com/CentroAmerica/Archivo/1996/marzo/22/guatemala.html. Villagrán (Ruiz), second-in-command of the FAR, corrects this number: in the early 1980s the FAR had two battalions operating in El Petén, with a total 2,000 *guerrilleros* (author's interview with Arnoldo Villagrán, Guatemala City, 14 April 2005).
23. The history of the CUC has never been written and most of the archives of the organization were destroyed by the military. Adams (1993: 201) mentions the origin of the CUC. The information presented here is based on this author's interviews with Pablo Ceto, Managua, 15 April 2005; with Víctor Ferrigno, Zeist, 28 April 2005, Quetzaltenango, 13 July 2006; with Daniel Pascual and Víctor Ferrigno, Guatemala City, 18 July 2006; with Rafael Gonzales, Guatemala City, 18 July 2006; and with Rafael Vásquez, Guatemala City, 18 July 2006 (during a day-long VPRO radio programme on 18 July 2006 at the CUC office).
24. Former army soldiers in the Maya regions whom the army charged with the responsibility of controlling indigenous villages.
25. Author's interview with Daniel Pascual, Guatemala City, 18 July 2005.
26. The complete destruction of the urban networks within one month and the near-capture of Asturias himself led over the next ten years to suspicions of internal treason. The existence of the computer program that detected the localities of the guerrillas was revealed by Vatican diplomats to the URNG leadership during peace talks in the early 1990s (author's interview with Rodrigo Asturias, Guatemala City, 21 February 2005).
27. Author's interview with Rodrigo Asturias, Guatemala City, 7 April 2005.
28. Comité Coordinador de Asociaciones Agrícolas, Comerciales, Industriales y Financieras, the Guatemalan entrepreneurial association.
29. Author's interview with Rodrigo Asturias, Guatemala City, 7 April 2005; and with Arnoldo Villagrán, Guatemala City, 14 April 2005.
30. Author's interview with Rodrigo Asturias, Guatemala City, 7 April 2005; and with Arnoldo Villagrán, Guatemala City, 14 April 2005.
31. Sancho, 2003: 134-4.
32. Author's interview with Humberto Ortega, Managua, 15 May 2006.
33. Author's interview with Rodrigo Asturias, Guatemala City, 4 and 7 April 2005; with Celso Morales, Guatemala City, 20 April 2005; and

with Arnoldo Villagrán, Guatemala City, 14 April 2005.

34. Inside El Salvador, a relationship of trust and cooperation developed – between Villalobos and Jovel, and between Sanchez Cerén and Sancho – due to the fact that in each case the men became territorial neighbours following the partition of regional commands implemented shortly after the failed offensive against San Salvador in 1981 (author's interview with Francisco Jovel, San Salvador, 24 August 2005).
35. Author's interview with Tomás Borge, Managua, 24 February 2006; with Humberto Ortega, Managua, 15 May 2006; and with Joaquín Cuadra Lacayo, Managua, 16 May 2006.
36. Author's interview with Roberto Cañas, San Salvador, 10 August 2005.
37. For an overview of the FMLN logistics, see Moroni Bracamonte and Spencer, 1995: 175 ff.
38. Vietnam provided the FMLN with US weaponry, seized from the former South Vietnamese armed forces.
39. See López Vigil, 1991; and Henríquez Consalvi, 2003.
40. Author's interview with Facundo Guardado, San Salvador, 5 August 2005.
41. Author's interview with Eduardo Sancho, San Salvador, 23 August 2005.
42. Author's interview with Facundo Guardado, San Salvador, 5 August 2005.
43. That is, from Nicaragua's reconstituted army. Sandinista officers were placed in positions of command of the national army under the terms of the 1990 peace agreement.
44. Author's interview with Francisco Jovel, San Salvador, 24 August 2005.
45. Author's interview with Rodrigo Asturias, Guatemala City, 4 April 2005.
46. Author's interview with Rodrigo Asturias, Guatemala City, 7 April 2005. The vital role of the US volunteers is confirmed by Santa Cruz Mendoza, 2004: 250–52.
47. Santa Cruz Mendoza, 2004: 281–3.
48. Author's interview with Arnoldo Villagrán, Guatemala City, 14 April 2005.
49. Author's interview with 'Uncle' Cros, Finca Santa Anita, San Marcos, March 1999.
50. Author's interview with Dagoberto Gutierrez, San Salvador, 12 August 2005; and with Santiago Santa Cruz, Utrecht, 1 July 2006. See also Moroni Bracamonte and Spencer, 1995: 184 ff.
51. Regarding (personal) relations between the Salvadoran NGO circuit

and the FMLN, see Sollis, 1995; Biekart, 1999; and Van der Borgh, 1999: 78 ff.

52. Author's interview with Rodrigo Asturias, Guatemala City, 21 February 2005; and with Santiago Santa Cruz, Utrecht, 1 July 2006.
53. Author's interview with Marta Isabel Cranshaw, in a car on the road between Estelí and Achaupa, 6 May 2006.
54. Author's interviews with Oscar Ortiz, Santa Tecla, 22 and 28 August 2005.
55. Author's interview with Santiago Santa Cruz, Utrecht, 1 July 2006.
56. Author's interview with Mónica Baltodano, Managua, 11 May 2006.
57. Author's interviews with Santiago Santa Cruz, Utrecht, 1 July 2006.
58. Author's interviews with Dagoberto Guttiérrez, San Salvador, 12 August 2005.
59. Author's interviews with Santiago Santa Cruz, Utrecht, 1 July 2006.
60. Moroni Bracamonte and Spencer, 1995: 67–71.
61. Author's interview with Dagoberto Guttiérrez, San Salvador, 12 August 2005.
62. Author's interview with Facundo Guardado, San Salvador, 9 August 2005.
63. Author's interview with Clemente de Jesús Gonzáles Quiñónez, El Portillo, 7 May 2006.
64. Author's interview with Rodrigo Asturias, Guatemala City, 21 February 2005; with Santiago Santa Cruz, Utrecht, 1 July 2006; and with Arnoldo Villagrán, Guatemala City, 14 April 2005.
65. Author's interview with Alba Estela Maldonado (Lola), Guatemala City, 15 December 2006.
66. Author's interview with Rodrigo Asturias, Guatemala City, 18 April 2005.
67. Author's interviews with René Juárez Poroj and with Suruma Lima, Quetzaltenango, 14 July 2006.
68. Rodrigo Asturias in Kruijt and van Meurs, 2000: 39.

Chapter 4

1. Author's interview with Orlando Núñez, Managua, 27 February 2006.
2. Author's interviews with Jan-Kees de Rooy, Managua, 8 and 11 May and 13 October 2006.
3. Ernesto Cardenal later clashed with the poet Rosario Murillo (Murillo, 1990), wife of Daniel Ortega. Cardenal called her 'an intellectual mediocrity' who 'seized control of the association [of writers and artists] by means of a fraudulent election, for the purpose of becoming the cultural arbiter of the nation' (Cardenal, 2004: 462).

4. See Wellinga, 1994 for a detailed analysis of Sandinista cultural policy.
5. According to official sources, the crusade reached 592,059 persons aged 10 or older.
6. See Musset, 2007, and López Vigil, 2006, for details.
7. The nine members of the *dirección nacional* were the *comandantes de la revolución* Bayardo Arce, Tomás Borge, Luis Carrión, Víctor Tirado, Carlos Núñez (coordinator of the State Council), Daniel Ortega (coordinator of the junta), Humberto Ortega, Henry Ruiz and Jaime Wheelock.
8. Humberto Ortega, interviewed in *La Prensa*, 18 July 2006.
9. Author's interview with Dora María Téllez, Managua, 4 May 2006.
10. Author's interview with Tomás Borge, Managua, 24 February 2006.
11. Author's interview with Henry Ruiz, Managua, 13 December 2006.
12. Marti, 1994: 42–3.
13. Dora María Téllez, Mónica Baltodano and Leticia Herrera.
14. Author's interview with Marta Isabel Cranshaw, on the road between Estelí and Achaupa, 6 May 2006.
15. Other *comandantes de la revolución* held positions as vice-ministers of defence or of the interior.
16. Edén Pastora, who had clashed with Humberto Ortega, was transferred to the Ministry of the Interior with the rank of vice-minister in charge of organizing the popular militias, a subordinate position that carried no real weight.
17. Author's interview with Tomás Borge, Managua, 24 February 2006.
18. Author's interview with Dora María Téllez, Managua, 4 May 2006.
19. Here are the complete Spanish names of the organizations listed: ATC (Asociación de Trabajadores del Campo); ANE (Asociación Nacional de Educadores); AMPRONAC (Asociación de Mujeres ante la Problemática Nacional), afterwards AMNLAE (Asociación de Mujeres Nicaragüenses 'Luisa Amanda Espinosa'); ASTC (Asociación Sandinista de Trabajadores de la Cultura); BPS (Brigadistas Populares de Salud); EPA (Ejército Popular de Alfabetización); CDC (Comités de Defensa Civil), afterwards CDS (Comités de Defensa Sandinistas); CST (Central Sandinista de Trabajadores); FETSALUD (Federación de Trabajadores de la Salud); Juventud Sandinista 19 de Julio; MPS (Milicias Populares Sandinistas); UNE (Unión Nacional de Empleados); UNAG (Unión Nacional de Agricultores y Ganaderos); UNE (Unión Nacional de Empleados); and UPN (Unión de Periodistas de Nicaragua).
20. Author's interviews with Joaquín Cuadra Lacayo, Managua, 10 and 16 May 2006.
21. Author's interview with Hugo Torres, Managua, 8 May 2006. Roberto

Cajina, an adviser to both Humberto Ortega and Torres, became the 'Sandinologist' of the regime and wrote the textbooks of political instruction for the new army (author's interview with Roberto Cajina, Managua, 2 May 2006). See also *Preparación Politica* (undated), the political manual for officers and soldiers of the EPS; 40 per cent of the text is devoted to the ethics and ideological legacy of Sandino.

22. Author's interview with Humberto Ortega, Managua, 15 May 2006; and with Tomás Borge, Managua, 24 February 2006. These data were confirmed by Pedro Blandón and José Ángel Buitrago (author's interviews of 2 March 2006 and 5 December 2006 respectively).
23. Lenin Cerna, cited in Trobo, 1983: 85.
24. Author's interview with Tomás Borge, Managua, 24 February 2006.
25. Author's interview with René Vivas, Managua, 3 May 2006.
26. Prepared by lawyers who were members of the Group of Twelve: Joaquín Cuadra Sr, Ernesto Castillo and Rodrigo Reyes.
27. Decree no. 3 of the Junta of National Reconstruction, 20 July 1979.
28. See Centro de Investigación políticos nacionales, 1986, for an evaluation.
29. 'Manzana' refers to a unit of land measure equalling 129 m sq.
30. Author's interview with Jaime Wheelock, Managua, 9 May 2006. Families of comandantes were also affected, as in the case of Luis Carrión Montoya. 'My children were right, and I was wrong', he told Tina Rozenberg (1992: 321) in 1990 when he was elected to the National Assembly – as a Sandinista congressman.
31. Nuñez Soto (1998: 435) reached 48 per cent in 1988. The agrarian reform had the blessing of Fidel: 'It is not true that Cuba was able to influence us to copy their model. On the contrary. Fidel advised us to be very careful in applying some of the models [i.e. the Cuban models]. He told us that part of what had happened in Cuba had to do with things that were beyond the control of the Cuban revolution.' According to Jaime Wheelock, Fidel had said, while travelling with him in 1984: 'I would have liked this model, a mixed model in which all of the elements of society are represented. This is a flexible revolution, with broad-based international support' (author's interview with Jaime Wheelock, Managua, 9 May 2006).
32. The overseeing adviser to the economic cabinet was Valpy Fitzgerald, who at that time was professor at The Hague and who later taught at Oxford. See Fitzgerald, 1982a, 1982b, 1985, 1986, 1987a, 1987b.
33. Author's interview with Henry Ruiz, 13 December 2006.
34. Author's interview with Néstor Avendaño, 26 April 2006.
35. See 'Grandes Disparates' (*La Prensa Magazine* 58, 7 May 2006: 27) for a list of failed mega-projects. Kinloch Tijerino (2006: 325) also concludes: 'many of these state-financed mega-projects were charac-

terized by a squandering of scarce national resources, as well as by improvisation, yielding results that fell far short of the goals projected by the engineers of the Ministry of Agricultural Development.'

36. Data supplied to the author by Néstor Avendaño, 26 April 2006.
37. Author's interview with Miguel d'Escoto, Managua, 11 May 2006.
38. Author's interview with Víctor Hugo Tinoco, Managua, 4 May 2006. See also Zamora, 1990, on Nicaraguan foreign policy between 1979 and 1990.
39. Author's interview with Henry Ruíz, Managua, 13 December 2006; with Pedro Antonio Blandón, Managua, 2 March 2006; and with José Ángel Buitrago, Managua, 5 December 2006.
40. Author's interview with José Ángel Buitrago, Managua, 5 December 2006.
41. Author's interview with Edén Pastora, Managua, 25 April 2006. Regarding Pastora's actions, see Eugarríos, 1979; Bardini, 1984.
42. Consejo Superior de la Empresa Privada (Higher Council on Private Enterprise), founded in 1972.
43. Antonio Lacayo, who in 1990 was prime minister in the government of Violeta de Chamorro, was a manager of one of the enterprises in which Robelo held a minority interest – GRACSA. Between 1984 and 1987, he took the case all the way to the Supreme Court of Justice. In his opinion, it was 'the only case in which a confiscated company was returned to its legitimate owners during the years of the Sandinista government' (author's interview with Antonio Lacayo, Managua, 11 May 2006).
44. Miguel d'Escoto as minister of foreign affairs, Ernesto Cardenal as minister of culture, Fernando Cardenal as minister of education and Edgar Parrales as vice-minister of labour.
45. See Ezcurra, 1983: 33 ff., about the development of this conflict.
46. FSLN, 1981.
47. Terms used in author's interviews with Tomás Borge, Managua, 24 February 2006; and Jaime Wheelock, Managua, 9 May 2006.
48. Asociación de Mujeres Nicaragüenses Luisa Amanda Espinoza, the Sandinista women's organization.
49. Author's interview with Jaime Wheelock, Managua, 9 May 2006.
50. Secondary sources consulted for this section include Nuñez, 1998; Bardini, 1988; Bataillon, 1994; Bendaña, 1991; Benítez, 1987; Brown, 2000, 2001; Dickey, 1985; Kornbluh and Byrne, 1993.
51. Author's interview with Hugo Torres, Managua, 8 May 2006.
52. White, 1984: 54–5. The advisers published an operations manual for Nicaragua (CIA, 1985). For more on the training provided, see Eich and Rincón, 1984.
53. Author's interview with Marta Isabel Cranshaw, on the road from Estelí to Achaupa, 6 May 2006.

54. Fuerzas Democráticas Nicaragüenses and Unión Nicaragüense Opositora. In 1985 the UNO was led by Adolfo Calero, Arturo Cruz and Alfonso Robelo. Its armed wing was RN (Resistencia Nicaragüense).
55. For a US-based source, see *US Assistance to Nicaraguan Guerillas*, 1988). On internal support within Nicaragua, see Bardini, 1988. *Testimonios de cien días* (1984) is an account of the first counter-insurgency campaigns. The journalists who wrote this account saw in the Sandinista army soldiers a reflection of the morale and spirit of the original guerrilla columns: 'And thus is born in Nicaragua the New Man.'
56. Author's interview with Rodrigo Carreras, Managua, 27 February 2006.
57. Author's interview with Edén Pastora, Managua, 25 April 2006.
58. Author's interview with Hugo Torres, Managua, 8 May 2006.
59. Author's interview with Joaquín Cuadra Lacayo, Managua, 10 May 2006.
60. Author's interview with Joaquín Cuadra Lacayo, Managua, 10 May 2006.
61. Author's interview with Hugo Torres, Managua, 1 June 2007. As a part of this process, there arose a discrepancy between the Sandinista hierarchy and the Cuban advisers and Fidel Castro regarding strategy (see López Cuba, 1999: 33–4; Ramonet, 2006: 300). Ramonet quotes Castro: 'Perhaps the highest price of the [American] "dirty war" was paid by the Sandinistas, because they had to establish [compulsory] military service, something that we ourselves never had to do, in order to fight the armed bands of the "dirty war". The time came when they got carried away with academic disputes, something which leads people to stray from revolutionary principles.'
62. Author's interviews with Joaquín Cuada Lacayo, Managua, 10 and 16 May 2006. The development of this strategy is confirmed by Hugo Torres (author's interview with Hugo Torres, Managua, 8 May 2006); and by Jaime Wheelock (author's interview with Jaime Wheelock, Managua, 9 May 2006): 'The application of this Plan was very important. Joaquín Cuadra, as a delegate of the EPS, worked on it, as did Mónica Baltodano, who represented the Frente Sandinista. I myself was the coordinator. If we had only had enough time, we would have been able to straighten everything out.'
63. www.bcn.gob.ni (consulted 10 November 2006).
64. *Gastos de defensa, 1980–1987*, 1987: 6.
65. www.gwu.edu/~nsarchiv/NSAEBB/NSAEBB210/index.htm#docs (consulted 3 December 2006); see document 3: CIA, Memorandum from DDI Robert M. Gates to DCI William J. Casey, 'Nicaragua', SECRET, 14 December 1984. Gates argued that the Contra War was 'an essentially half-hearted policy' and recommended initiating a

'comprehensive campaign openly aimed at bringing down the regime' with 'the use of air strikes' against Nicaraguan military targets. 'The fact is that the Western Hemisphere is the sphere of influence of the United States...'

66. Author's interview with Joaquín Cuadra Lacayo, Managua, 16 May 2006; information related during this interview was confirmed by Hugo Torres (author's interview, Managua, 8 May 2006).
67. According to data presented in The Hague. Not covered were the further damages caused by the war. Father d'Escoto, foreign minister, asked ECLAC to begin calculating the damages more conservatively (author's interview with Miguel d'Escoto, Managua, 11 May 2006). These calculations were made available to the author by Néstor Avendaño (author's interview, 26 April 2006).
68. See International Court of Justice, 1984 for the claim against the US government.
69. See Lotton, 2002.
70. Of the Presidential Office, 1990, cited in Núñez Soto, 1998: 295.
71. There is no systematic documentation regarding the fate of the injured and disabled. There is a similar lack of documentation about those who were captured or kidnapped. Some human rights organizations tried to bring some cases to trial (author's interviews with Vilma Nuñez de Escorcia, Managua, 10 May and 17 May 2006). Regarding the fate and treatment of some of the Contra comandantes who were captured, see Pereira and Bilbao, 1991; one of these comandantes was placed in a full body cast for an entire year in order to prevent him from escaping.
72. See *Hablan los desmovilizados*, 1995, and Castillo Guerrero, 1997, for soldiers' war recollections.
73. Author's interview with José Ángel Buitrago, 5 December 2006; and with Henry Ruiz, 13 December 2006.
74. Data from the Central Bank and from the Nicaraguan Investment Fund, its research unit during the 1980s (data provided to the author by Joop Amse, Managua, 25 April 2006, and by Néstor Avendaño, Managua, 26 April 2006). Amse was a member of a team that calculated the rates of inflation. See also www.bcn.gob.ni (consulted 10 November 2006).
75. I remember, negotiating in 1989 with functionaries of the new Ministry of Budget and Planning, that the latter sometimes made mistakes with regard to groupings of zeros (resulting in errors in the hundreds of thousands or even millions) due to projections of rampant hyperinflation. Their desperation can be seen in the pages of *Nicaragua: The Economic Situation* (1989) and in *Plan económico 1990* (1989), neither of which mentions any concrete measures to control hyperinflation

or take a different course with respect to economic development. At one point, when minister Luis Carrión visited Costa Rica in May or June 1989 to try to convince Costa Rican entrepreneurs to invest in Nicaraguan businesses, I asked him after his meeting if Nicaragua still had a mid-range economic plan. He responded that, honestly, the FSLN and the government were living hand-to-mouth, as they had back when they were engaging in guerrilla warfare (personal communication of Comandante Luis Carrión to the author).

76. Arnoldo Alemán and Enrique Bolaños later became president of Nicaragua, Alemán from January 1997 to January 2002 and Bolaños from January 2002 to January 2007.
77. Author's interview with José Ángel Buitrago, Managua, 5 December 2006.
78. For more on the formation of UNO and the subsequent election campaign, see Martí y Puit, 1997: 115-61; Lacayo Oyanguren, 2005: 13-164. See also Cortés Domínguez, 1990.
79. According to Tomás Borge: 'State security officials were all over the place ... We were so well positioned that, when we lost the election [in 1990], the observers of the other political parties, who were State Security agents, called us and said; "What are we going to do? We're losing." I asked that the following message be sent to them: "If we lose, we lose. We must respect the voice of the people." We had it in our power to commit electoral fraud. Because at all of the polling stations, the vast majority of the observers – of the Liberal Party, of the Conservative Party – were State Security agents.'
80. Interview with Víctor Tirado, Managua, 3 March 2006. See also Tirado, 2007.

Chapter 5

1. Author's interviews with Jovel, Sancho and Sanchez Cerén, San Salvador, 24, 23, 26 August 2005.
2. Author's interview with Edgar Ponce, Guatemala City, 7 July 1994; Ponce, in 1982 president of the national engineers' association, was one of the envoys.
3. Author's interview with Miguel Ángel Reyes, Guatemala City, 18 April 2005.
4. Author's interview with Henry Ruiz, Managua, 13 December 2006.
5. A systematic analysis of the Central American peace process is provided by Arnson, 1999; and Spence, 2004.
6. For the transition of the Central American armies, see Dunkerley and Sieder, 1996. An early analysis of the political transitions in Central America is Goodman, LeoGrande and Mendelson Forman, 1992. Domínguez and Lindenberg (1997) published a series of political

analyses in the mid-1990s. The collection edited by Sieder (1996) covers the judiciary and the role of the United Nations as well.

7. Personal communication of General Frederick F. Woerner Jr at the Inter-American Defense College, Washington DC, 31 March 1995.
8. Author's interview with Antonio Lacayo, Managua, 11 May 2006.
9. Monitored during the first year by a bipartisan commission of three FSLN members (Humberto Ortega, Joaquín Cuadra, Jaime Wheelock) and three UNO ministers (Antonio Lacayo, Carlos Hurtado and Francisco Mayorga) (Lacayo, 2005: 113). Some of those interviewed mentioned the names of other ministers who were also involved.
10. Lacayo thus officially served in this capacity as a *delegado presidencial*: this was due to an anomaly in the Nicaraguan constitution that, from 1990 until the present day, has created confusion regarding the boundaries between the formal authority of the president and the appointed minister of defence. In 2007 Daniel Ortega, assuming his second term as president, again appointed a *delegado presidencial* instead of a minister of defence.
11. RESDAL, 2005: 232. The reduction process is extensively analysed in Cajina, 1997.
12. Most of the revenues from these sales were used to finance a pension scheme for the Nicaraguan National Army.
13. A *piñata* is a *papier-mâché* figure full of small gifts at a children's party.
14. Personal communication to the author by Maria Hurtado de Vigil, in 1990 director general of the Ministry of Economy, Industry and Commerce; her husband was the minister of government (ex-interior) (Managua, May 1990).
15. Data of www.bcn.gob.ni (consulted 17 November 2006).
16. Author's interview with Alfredo Cristiani, San Salvador, 18 August 2005.
17. This group of leading generals and colonels was called the *Tandona*, an extended year-group (*tanda*) of former cadets.
18. Juhn (1998: 69, 1998) and Samayoa (2003) provide a detailed analysis of the negotiation process.
19. About the role of the Salvadoran armed forces during the peace negotiations and thereafter, see Walter, 1997; Williams and Walter, 1997; Córdova Macías, 1999.
20. Author's interview with Mauricio Vargas, San Salvador, 19 August 2005.
21. Sometimes the groups were reduced to four, or even two, members. Escobar and Samayoa, for instance, worked out the subject of political participation after the peace (author's interview with David Escobar Galindo, San Salvador, 10 August 2005).

22. Author's interview with David Escobar Galindo, San Salvador, 10 August 2005.
23. See Sprenkels, 2005: 82–5.
24. In this paragraph I used two sources written or co-written by persons who were directly involved in the events: Rosada-Granados, 1998; Balconi and Kruijt, 2004. I also interviewed Rodrigo Asturias and Julio Balconi extensively in 1999, 2003 and 2005 on the peace negotiations.
25. Author's interview with Miguel Ángel Reyes, Guatemala City, 18 April 2005.
26. See Chapter 1 n14 and n15.
27. See McCleary, 1999 for the military politics under Serrano.
28. Estimates of the Guatemalan Ministry of Defence in 2005.
29. Auxiliary bishop Juan Gerardi, under whose authority the first Truth Commission had worked, was assassinated 'under mysterious circumstances' the day following the publication of the 1998 report.
30. For details, see Kruijt and van Meurs, 2000; Balconi and Kruijt, 2004.
31. The FAR also captured the son of Arzú's private secretary; they subsequently set him free.
32. Author's interview with Alba Estela Maldonado, Guatemala City, 15 December 2006.
33. Coordinadora de Organizaciones del Pueblo Maya. See Álvarez, 2003: 6 ff.
34. See Álvarez, 2003: 3–5; Santa Cruz Mendoza, 2004: 285 ff. Álvarez provided details of this development in an interview (author's interview with Enrique Álvarez, Guatemala City, 14 April 2005).
35. About all these ethnic and popular movements, see Brett, 2006.
36. See Hernández Pico, 2005: 456–62, for an analysis.
37. Author's interview with Rodrigo Asturias, Guatemala City, 18 April 2005.
38. Analysed in detail in El Bloque Empresarial, 2002.
39. See Andrade-Eekhoff, 2003 on the issue of migrant remittances.
40. For the legal structure, see FMLN, 1993.
41. Villalobos, 2000: 40–47, 99–117.
42. See Béjar and Roggenbuck, 1996; González, 2003; Zamora, 1997, 1998, 2003; Artiga-González, 2004; Toll, 2005.
43. See Wood, 2003: 257 ff.
44. Author's interview with Héctor Silva, San Salvador, 16 August 2005.
45. I discussed this section extensively with Carlos Ramos (author's interview, San Salvador, 25 August 2005).
46. The presidential team called Joaquín Cuadra Lacayo, the army's second-in-command, who convinced Humberto Ortega to intervene.

47. Lacayo's version of the events (Lacayo Oyanguren 2005: 533 ff.) is not very detailed and the study by Close (2005) on the Chamorro-Lacayo government is rather vague, but the account here is based on the recollections of persons present when decisions were made.
48. The former Contras as *re-contras* and the former Sandinista officers as *re-compas* (*compa*, from *compañero*).
49. Author's interview with Joaquín Cuadra, Managua, 16 May 2005.
50. See Chapter 4 n75.
51. The following persons were interviewed extensively regarding internal party disputes: Monica Baltodano (Managua, 11 May 2006), Maria Lopez Vigil (Managua, 27 October 2006), Vilma Nuñez de Escorcia (Managua, 10 May, 17 October and 20 November 2006), Lola Ocón (Managua, 12 December 2006), Henry Ruiz (Managua, 13 December 2006), and Víctor Tirado (Managua, 3 March 2006).
52. Brother Humberto Ortega is also a wealthy businessman with considerable interests in real estate and shopping malls in Costa Rica.
53. See Fyjnzylber and López, 2007.
54. Zoilámerica Narvaez's legal representative was Vilma Nuñez de Escorcia.
55. Known as the *pacto* between Alemán and Ortega; Alemán's daughter took a photo during the private meeting that ended up being published in the Nicaraguan press.
56. Author's interview with Rosa Marina Zelaya Velásquez, Managua, 2 May 2006.
57. The new legislation stipulated victory without recourse to a second round for any candidate gaining at least 35 per cent of the votes, when the advantage over the second-place party was at least 5 per cent.
58. Ortega had participated in 1996 and 2001, and had obtained 37 per cent and 43 per cent of the vote, respectively. Political scientists and pollsters had calculated that Ortega had a stable base of 30 to 40 per cent of the electorate but also that his adversaries had a stable base of at least 45 per cent. Ortega Hegg mentioned the details of the strategy during an interview with the author (Managua, 14 December 2006).
59. Roberto Rivas, always referred to officially as the son of the private assistant of the cardinal.
60. Ortega's associate Arce is the third most powerful person in the party after Ortega and his wife.

Chapter 6

1. Mentioned by Beevor (2001: 279). Cardinal Goma was the moral authority behind the Franco regime.
2. See the discussion in Chapters 1 and 4.
3. See CVR, 2003, 2004; Degregori, 2008.

4. *Ejercito de Liberación Nacional* and *Fuerzas Armadas Revolucionarias de Colombia*.
5. See Chapters 1 and 5 for details about the post-war army reductions in El Salvador, Guatemala and Nicaragua.
6. Avendaño (2007: 83) cites the World Bank data.
7. See Baumeister and Fernández (2002: 15, 28) for an analysis of rural property transformation in Nicaragua.
8. Author's interview with Rigoberto Quemé Chay, Quetzaltenango, 26 February 1998; see also Kruijt, 2000: 27-8.
9. Lenin, 1969; see Becket, 1937 for a criticism.
10. See Chapter 5.
11. Author's interview with Salvador Sánchez Cerén, San Salvador, 30 May 2007.
12. Author's interview with Facundo Guardado, San Salvador, 30 May 2007.
13. Author's interview with Henry Ruiz, Managua, 13 December 2006.
14. Author's interviews with Jorge Soto (Pablo Monsanto) and Arnoldo Villagrán (Daniel Ruiz), Guatemala City, 28 May 2007; and with Alba Estela Maldonado (Lola), Guatemala City, 29 May 2007.

Appendices

1. See *Historia Del FMLN*: http://fmln.org.sv/portal/index.php?module=htmlpages&func=display& pid=1 (consulted 18 November 2006).
2. The Partido Guatemalteco del Trabajo-Núcleo de Dirección Nacional (PGT-ND) broke away from the PGT in 1978 under the leadership of Mario Sánchez. Other factions joined the UNRG as well, and together these factions constituted the Partido Guatemalteco del Trabajo-Comité Central (PGT-CR).
3. See Sichar Moreno, 1999, 2006 for a detailed history of the constituent factions of the URNG.
4. The EGP operated with the following *frentes guerrilleros*: the Frente Comandante Ernesto Guevara, in the north-western region and the Ixcán jungle; the Frente Ho Chi Minh, in the Ixíl region; the Frente Marco Antonio Yon Sosa, in the north-central region; the Frente Augusto César Sandino, in the central region; the Frente 13 de Noviembre, in the eastern region; the Frente Luis Turcios Lima, in the southern coastal region; and the Frente Otto René Castillo, in the surrounding region of Guatemala City.
5. The ORPA operated with two *frentes*, I and II, later renamed Frente Luis Ixmatá and Frente Unitario (formed by *guerrilleros* of the four constituent member organizations of the URNG); the comandante of this *frente* was Luis Santiago Santa Cruz.

References

Adams, R.N. (1993) 'Etnias y sociedades', in Héctor Pérez Brignoli (ed.), *Historia general de Centroamérica*, Vol. V: *De la posguerra a la crisis (1945–1979)*. Madrid: Sociedad Estatal Quintocentenario and FLACSO, pp. 165–243.

ADHAG (1998) *Guatemala nunca más*, Vol. II: *Los mecanismos del horror.* Guatemala: Oficina de Derechos Humanos del Arzobispado de Guatemala.

Alvarenga, P. (1996) *Cultura y ética de la violencia: El Salvador, 1880–1932*. San José: EDUCA.

Álvarez, E. (2003) *La Izquierda en Guatemala*. Guatemala: IDEM.

Anderson, J.L. (1997) *Che Guevara: A Revolutionary Life*. London: Bantam.

Andrade-Eekhoff, K. (2003) *Mitos y realidades. El impacto económico de la migración en los hogares rurales*. San Salvador: FLACSO.

Arias, P. (1981) *Nicaragua: Revolución. Relatos de combatientes del Frente Sandinista*, 2nd edn. Mexico: Siglo XXI.

Arias Gómez, J. (2002) 'Farabundi Martí y el comunismo', in O. Martínez Peñate (ed.), *El Salvador: Historia general.* San Salvador, Editorial Nuevo Enfoque, pp. 251–64.

Arnson, C.J. (ed.) (1999) *Comparative Peace Processes in Latin America*. Washington DC: Woodrow Wilson Center Press and Stanford University Press.

Artiga-González, Á. (2004) *Elitismo competitivo. Dos décadas de elecciones en El Salvador (1982–2003)*. San Salvador: UCA Editores.

Ávalos Trigueros, C., and Á. Trigueros Argüello (2005) *Inclusión social y competitividad urbana. Desafíos y oportunidades en el Área Metropolitana de San Salvador*. San Salvador: FLACSO.

Avendaño, N. (2007) *La economía y la pobreza de Nicaragua, 2006–2007. Una evaluación del desempeño económico en 2006 y un pronóstico económico para 2007*. Managua: 3H Comercial.

Baez Alvarez, G. (1979) *Pancasan. Convertir un revés en un triunfo revolucionario*. Managua: UNAN Editorial Universitaria.

Baires Martínez, Y. (1994) 'Origenes y formación del partido ARENA (1979-1982)', in G. Bataillon et al., *Centroamérica entre democracia y desorganización. Análisis de los actores y de los sistemas de acción en los años 1990*. Guatemala: FLACSO-CEMCA, pp. 29-49.

Balconi, J., and D. Kruijt (2004) *Hacia la reconciliación. Guatemala, 1960–1996*. Guatemala: Piedra Santa.

Bardini, R. (1984) *Edén Pastora, un cero en la historia*. Puebla y México: Departamento de Publicaciones de la Universidad Autónoma de Puebla y Editorial Mex-Sur.

Bardini, R. (1988) *Monjes, mercenarios & mercaderes. La red secreta de apoyo a los Contras*. México: Editorial Mex-Sur.

Barreto, P.E. (1980) *El repliegue de Managua a Masaya*. México: Editorial Cartago de Mexico.

Bataillon, G. (1994) 'Contras y recontras nicaragüenses: Reflexiones sobre la acción armada y la constitución de actores político-militares', in G. Bataillon et al., *Centroamérica entre democracia y desorganización. Análisis de los actores y de los sistemas de acción en los años 1990*. Guatemala: FLACSO-CEMCA, pp. 173-213.

Baud, M., and R. Rutten (eds) (2005) *Popular Intellectuals and Social Movements: Framing Protest in Asia, Africa, and Latin America. International Review of Social History*, Supplement 12. Cambridge: Cambridge University Press.

Baumeister, E., and E. Fernández (2002) *Análisise de la tenencia de la tierra en Nicaragua a partir del censo agropecuario 2001*. Managua: FAO-INEC-MAGFOR.

Becket, F.B. (1937) 'Lenin's Application of Marx's Theory of Revolutionary Tactics', *American Sociological Review* 2(3), pp. 353-64.

Beevor, A. (2001) *The Spanish Civil War*. New York: Penguin Books.

Béjar, R.G., and S. Roggenbuck (eds) (1996) *Partidos y actores políticos en transition. La derecha, la izquierda y el centro en El Salvador*. San Salvador: Konrad Adenauer Stiftung.

Belli, G. (2001) *El país bajo mi piel. Memorias de amor y guerra*. Barcelona and Managua: Plaza y Janés Editores and Anamá Ediciones.

Bendaña, A. (1991) *Una tragedia campesina*. Managua: Ediarte y CEI.
Benítez Mataút, R. (1989) *La teoría militar y la guerra civil en El Salvador*. San Salvador: UCA Editores.
Benítez Mataút, R., L. Lozano and L. Bermúdez (1987) *La guerra de baja intensidad en Centroamérica*. Madrid: Editorial Revolución.
Bethell, L. (1991) *Central America since Independence*. Cambridge: Cambridge University Press.
Biekart, K. (1999) *The Politics of Civil Society Building: European Private Aid Agencies and Democratic Transition in Central America*. Amsterdam: Transnational Institute.
Blanco, H. (1972) *Tierra o muerte. Las luchas campesinas en Perú*. México: Siglo XXII.
Boot, M. (2003) *The Savage Wars of Peace: Small Wars and the Rise of American Power*. New York: Basic Books.
Borge, T. (1983) *Apuntes iniciales sobre el F.S.L.N.* Managua: Ministerio del Interior-Dirección Política.
Borge, T. (1990) *La paciente impaciencia*, 4th edn. Managua: Editorial Vanguardia.
Boza Gutiérrez, F. (2002) *Memorias de un soldado. Nicaragua y la Guardia Nacional, 1928–1979*. Managua: PAVSA.
Brett, R. (2006) *Movimiento social, etnicidad y democratización en Guatemala, 1985–1996*. Guatemala: F & G Editores.
Brown, T.C. (2000) *When the AK-47s Fall Silent: Revolutionaries, Guerrillas, and the Dangers of Peace*. Stanford: Hoover Institution Press.
Brown, T.C. (2001) *The Real Contra War: Highlander Peasant Resistance in Nicaragua*. Norman: University of Oklahoma Press.
Cabarrús, C.R. (1983) *Génesis de una revolución. Análisis del surgimiento y desarrollo de la organización campesina en El Salvador*. Ediciones de la Casa Chata 16. Mexico: CIESAS.
Cabezas, O. (1985) *La montaña es algo más que una inmensa estepa verde*, 3rd edn. Managua: Editorial Nueva Nicaragua.
Cajina, R. (1997) *Transición política y reconversión militar en Nicaragua, 1990–1995*. Managua: CRIES.
Cardenal, E. (2004) *La revolución perdida*, 2nd edn. Managua: Anamá Ediciones.
Castañeda, J.G. (1994) *Utopia Unarmed: The Latin American Left after the Cold War*. New York: Vintage Books.
Castañeda, J.G. (1997) *Compañero: The Life and Death of Che Guevara*. New York: Alfred A. Knopf.
Castillo Guerrero, E. (1997) *Algo más que un recuerdo*. Managua: ANE-CNE-NORAD.
CEH (Comisión para el Esclarecimiento Histórico) (1999) *Guatemala. Memoria del silencio*, 12 vols. Guatemala: UNOPS.

Centro de Investigación y Asesoría Socio-Económica (1986) *La economía mixta en Nicaragua. Proyecto o Realidad (Una visión de académicos y políticos nacionales).* Managua: Centro de Investigación y Asesoría Socio-Económica and Friedrich Ebert Stiftung.

CEPAL (2007) *Panorama social de América Latina.* Santiago de Chile: Comisión Económica para América Latina y el Caribe.

CIA (1985) *The CIA's Nicaragua Manual: Psychological Operations in Guerrilla Warfare.* New York: Random House.

Ching, E. (1997) 'From Clientelism to Militarism: The State, Politics and Authoritarianism in El Salvador, 1940–1940'. Ph.D. thesis, Santa Barbara: University of California.

Close, D. (2005) *Los años de Doña Violeta. La historia de la transición política.* Managua: Grupo Editorial Lea.

Córdova Macías, R. (1999) *El Salvador: Reforma militar y relaciones cívico-militares.* San Salvador: FUNDAUNGO.

Corr, E.G., and C.E. Prisk (1992) 'El Salvador: Transforming Society to Win the Peace', in E.G. Corr and S. Sloan (eds), *Low-Intensity Conflict: Old Threats in a New World.* Boulder: Westview Press, pp. 223–53.

Cortés Domínguez, G. (1990). *La lucha por el poder. Revés electoral Sandinista.* Managua: Editorial Nueva Nicaragua.

CVR (2003) *Informe final.* Lima: Comisión de la Verdad y Reconciliación (www.cverdad.orp.pe).

CVR (2004) *Atún Willakuy. Versión abreviada del informe final de la Comisión de la Verdad y Reconciliación.* Lima: Comisión de la Verdad y Reconciliación.

Dalton, R. (1966) 'Los estudiantes en la revolución latinoamericana', *ARAUCO* 74, March, pp. 5–21.

Dalton, R. (1970) *¿Revolución en la revolución? Y la crítica de la derecha.* Havana: Casa de Las Américas (Cuadernos Casa 9).

Debray, R. (1999) *La guerrilla del Che*, 8th edn. Mexico: Siglo XXI.

De la locura a la esperanza. La guerra de doce años en El Salvador. Informe de la comisión de la verdad para El Salvador (1993). San Salvador: Comisión de la Verdad.

Degregori, C.I. (2008) *Qué difícil es ser Dios. El Partido Comunista del Perú–Sendero Luminoso y el conflicto armado interno en el Perú, 1980–1999.* Lima: IEP.

Diagnóstico socio-económico del personal incorporado de la Unidad Revolucionaria Nacional Guatemalteca (1997). Guatemala: Fundación Guillermo Torriello.

Diaz, N. [M.M. Valladares] (2005) *Nunca estuve sola*, 2nd edn. San Salvador: UCA Editores.

Dickey, C. (1985) *With the Contras: A Reporter in the Wilds of Nicaragua.* New York: Simon & Schuster.

Dirección Nacional del FSLN (1981) 'Comunicado oficial del FSLN sobre la religión', *ENVÍOS realizados por el Instituto Histórico Centroamericano* 1(4), pp. 52-6.

Doggett, M. (1993) *Death Foretold: The Jesuit Murders in El Salvador*. New York: Lawyers Committee for Human Rights.

Domínguez, J.L., and M. Lindenberg (eds) (1997) *Democratic Transitions in Central America*. Gainesville: University Press of Florida.

Dosal, P.J. (2003) *Comandante Che: Guerrilla Soldier, Commander, and Strategist, 1956–1957*. University Park, PA: Pennsylvania State University Press.

Dunkerley, J. (1985) *The Long War: Dictatorship and Revolution in El Salvador*. London: Verso.

Dunkerley, J. (1988) *Power in the Isthmus: A Political History of Modern Central America*. London: Verso.

Dunkerley, J. (1993) *The Pacification of Central America*. London: University of London, Institute of Latin American Studies, Research Paper 34.

Dunkerley, J., and R. Sieder (1996) 'The Military: The Challenge of Transition', in R. Sieder (ed.), *Central America: Fragile Transition*. London: Macmillan, pp. 55-101.

Dussel, E. (1979) *De Medellín a Puebla. Una década de sangre y esperanza (1968–1979)*. Mexico: EDICOL-Centro de Estudios Ecoménicos.

Eagleson, J. (1975) *Christians and Socialism: Documentation of the Christians for Socialism Movement in Latin America*. Maryknoll: Orbis Books.

Eich, D., and C. Rincón (1984) *The Contras: Interviews with Anti-Sandinistas*. San Francisco: Synthesis Publications.

'El Bloque Empresarial hegemónico salvadoreño' (2002) Special Issue of *Estudios Centroamericanos* (*ECA*).

Eugarrios, M. (1979) *Dos... Un ... Cero Comandante*. San José: Editorial Lehmann.

Ezcurra, A.M. (1983) *Agresión ideológica contra la revolución Sandinista*. México: Ediciones Nuevomar.

Fajnzylber, P., and J.H. López (2007) *Close to Home: The Impact of Remittances in Latin America*. Washington DC: World Bank.

Fitzgerald, E.V.K. (1982a) 'The Economics of the Revolution', in T.W. Walker (ed.), *Nicaragua in Revolution*. New York: Praeger, pp. 203-20.

Fitzgerald, E.V.K. (1982b) 'Agrarian Reform as a Model of Accumulation: The Case of Nicaragua since 1979', *Journal of Development Studies* 22(1), pp. 208-20.

Fitzgerald, E.V.K. (1985) 'Stabilization and Economic Justice: The Case of Nicaragua', in K.S. Kim and D.F. Ruccio (eds), *Debt and Develop-*

ment in Latin America. Notre Dame: University of Notre Dame Press, pp. 191–204.

Fitzgerald, E.V.K. (1986) 'An Evaluation of the Economic Costs of US Aggression against Nicaragua', in R. Spalding (ed.), *The Political Economy of Revolutionary Nicaragua*. New York: Allen & Unwin, pp. 195–213.

Fitzgerald, E.V.K. (1987a) 'Recent Developments and Perspectives of the Economy in the Sandinista Revolution', *Nordic Journal of Latin American Studies* 17(1–2), pp. 69–72.

Fitzgerald, E.V.K. (1987b) 'Notas sobre fuerza de trabajo y la estructura de clases en Nicaragua', *Revista Nicaraguense de Ciencias Sociales* 2(2), pp. 34–41.

Fitzgerald, V., and A. Chamorro (1987) 'Las cooperativas en el proyecto de transición en Nicaragua', *Encuentro* 30, January-April, pp. 21–71.

Flakoll, D.J., and C. Alegría (2004) *Nicaragua: La revolución Sandinista. Una crónica política, 1855–1979*, 2nd edn. Managua: Anamá Ediciones.

FMLN (1993) *Documentos políticos*. San Salvador: Ediciones Alternativa.

FSLN (1981) *Comunicación oficial del FSLN sobre la religion*. Managua: Frente Sandinista de Liberación Nacional.

Galeas, G. (2004) *Mayor Roberto D'Aubuisson: El rostro más allá del mito*. Special edition of *La Prensa Gráfica*, 7 November.

'Gastos de defensa, 1980–1987' (1987) *Envío* 6(76), August, p. 6.

Gleijeses, Piero (1992) *Shattered Hope: The Guatemalan Revolution and the United States, 1944–1954*. Princeton NJ: Princeton University Press.

Goffman, E. (1991) 'On the Characteristics of Total Institutions', in E. Goffman, *Asylums: Essays on the Social Situation of Mental Patients and other Inmates* [1961], 4th edn. Harmondsworth: Penguin, pp. 13–115.

González, L.A. (1994) 'Izquierda marxista y cristianismo en El Salvador, 1970–1992 (Un ensayo de interpretación)'. M.A. thesis, Mexico: FLACSO.

González, L.A. (2003) 'De la ideología al pragmatismo. Ensayo sobre las trayectorias ideológicas de ARENA y el FMLN', *Estudios Centroamericanos (ECA)*, pp. 351–68.

González, L.A. (2004) 'Estado, sociedad y economía en El Salvador (1880–1999)', in R. Cardenal and L.A. González (eds), *El Salvador: La transición y sus problemas*. San Salvador: UCA Editores, pp. 29–55.

Goodman, L.W., W.M. LeoGrande and J. Mendelson Forman (eds) (1992) *Political Parties and Democracy in Central America*. Boulder CO: Westview Press.

Gott, R. (1972) *Guerrilla Movements in Latin America*. Garden City NY: Doubleday.

Gramajo Morales, H.A. (2003) *Alrededor de la bandera. Un análisis praxiológico del enfrentamiento armado en Guatemala, 1960–1966*. Guatemala: Tipografía Nacional, 2003.

'Grandes Disparates' (2006) *La Prensa Magazine* 58, 7 May, pp. 21-7.

Guevara, E. (1972) *Guerrilla Warfare*, 3rd edn. Harmondsworth: Pelican.

Guevara, E. (1994) *El libro verde olivo*, 4th edn. Mexico: Editorial Diógenes.

Guevara, E. (2002) *Back on the Road: A Journey to Central America*, with an Introduction by Richard Gott and a Foreword by Alberto Granado. London: Vintage.

Gutiérrez, D. (1993) *La persona, la fé y la revolución*. San Salvador: ACJ-CJE.

Gutiérrez, D. (2004) *Nadie quedará en el olvido. Cuentos e la vida real*, 2nd edn. San Salvador: Ediciones Ven y Sigueme.

Gutierrez, P.G., et al. (1986) *Reflexión sobre la teología de la liberación*. Iquitos: CETA.

Hablan los desmovilizados de guerra. Nicaragua, El Salvador y Mozambique (1995) Managua: CEI-Programa de educación y acción para la paz.

Harnecker, M. (1981) *Los conceptos elementales del materialismo histórico*. Mexico: Siglo XXI.

Harnecker, M. (1984) *Pueblos en Armas*. Mexico: Era.

Harnecker, M. (1992) *Con la mirada en alto. Historia de las FPL. Farabundi Martí a través de sus dirigentes*. San Salvador: UCA Editores.

Henríquez Consalvi, C. (2003) *La terquedad del Izote. La historia de radio Venceremos*, 3rd edn. San Salvador: Museo de la Palabra.

Hernández Pico, J. (2005) *Terminar la guerra, traicionar la paz. Guatemala en las dos presidencias de la paz: Arzú y Portillo (1996–2004)*. Guatemala: FLACSO.

Historia del FMLN (2006) http://fmln.org.sv/portal/index.php (consulted 18 November 2006).

International Court of Justice (1984) *Case concerning Military and Paramilitary Activities in and against Nicaragua. Nicaragua vs. United States of America. Request for the Indication of Provisional Measures*. The Hague: ICJ, 10 May 1984, General List 70.

James, D. (2001) *Ché Guevara: A Biography* [1969], with a new introduction by Henry Butterfield Ryan. New York: Cooper Square Press.

Juhn, T. (1998) *Negotiating Peace in El Salvador: Civil–Military Relations and the Conspiracy to End the War*. London: Macmillan.

Kampwirth, K. (2002) *Women and Guerrilla Movements: Nicaragua, El Salvador, Chiapas, Cuba*. University Park, PA: Pennsylvania State University Press.

Kinloch Tijerino, F. (2006) *Historia de Nicaragua*, 2nd edn. Managua: Universidad Centroammericana-Instituto de Historia de Nicaragua y Centroamerica.

Klepak, H. (2005) *Cuba's Military 1990–2005: Revolutionary Soldiers during Counter-Revolutionary Times*. New York: Palgrave Macmillan.

Kornbluh, P., and M. Kornbluh (1993) *The Iran–Contra Scandal: The Declassified History*. New York: New Press.

Krauss, C. (1991) *Inside Central America: Its People, Politics, and History*. New York: Simon & Schuster.

Kruijt, D. (1999) 'Exercises in State Terrorism: The Counterinsurgency Campaigns in Guatemala and Peru', in K. Koonings and D. Kruijt (eds), *Societies of Fear: The Legacy of Civil War, Violence, and Terror in Latin America*. London: Zed Books, pp. 33–62.

Kruijt, D. (2000) 'Guatemala's Political Transitions, 1960s–1990s', *International Journal of Political Economy* 30(1), pp. 3–33.

Kruijt, D., and R. van Meurs (2000) *El guerrillero y el general. Rodrigo Asturias y Julio Balconi sobre la guerra y la paz en Guatemala*. Guatemala: FLACSO.

Kruijt, D., and E. Torres-Rivas (eds) (1991) *América Latina, militares y sociedad*, 2 vols. San José: FLACSO.

Lacayo Oyanguren, Antonio (2005) *La difícil transición nicaragüense. En el gobierno con doña Violeta*. Manaugua: PAVSA.

Le Bot, Y. (1997) *La guerra en tierras mayas. Comunidad, violencia y modernidad en Guatemala (1970–1992)*. Mexico: Fondo de Cultura Económica.

Leiden, C., and K.M. Schmitt (1973) *The Politics of Violence: Revolution in the Modern World*. London: Prentice-Hall.

Lenin, V.I. (1969 [1902]) *What Is To Be Done?* New York: International Publishers.

López Cuba, N. (1999) 'The Cuban People Remain Armed and Ready To Defend the Revolution', in M.A. Waters (ed.), *Making History: Interviews with Four Generals of Cuba's Revolutionary Armed Forces*. New York: Pathfinder Press, pp. 17–51.

López Vigil, J.I. (1991) *Las mil y una historias de radio Venceremos*. San Salvador, El Salvador: UCA Editores.

López Vigil, M. (2006) 'Cuando la memoria y la historia viajan en tren', *Envío* 25(295), October, pp. 21–5.

Lotton, I. (2002) 'Mémoire et identité des véterans de l'Armée Populaire Snsiniste et du Ministere de'l Interieur dans la Región de Somoto, Nicaragua'. Doctoral thesis, University of Paris-X (IHNCA/FN 972.850.54 L 884).

Loveman, B., and T.M. Davies Jr. (1997) *Che Guevara: Guerrilla Warfare*, 3rd edn. Wilmington, DE: Scholarly Resources.

Löwy, M. (1996) *The War of Gods: Religion and Politics in Latin America*. London: Verso.

Luciak, I.A. (2001) *Después de la revolución: Igualdad de género y democracia en El Salvador, Nicaragua y Guatemala*. San Salvador: UCA Editores.

Luján Muñoz, J. (2004) *Breve historia contemporánea de Guatemala*, 3rd edn. Mexico: Fondo de Cultura Económica.

Manwaring, M.G., and C. Prisk (1988) *El Salvador at War: An Oral History of Conflict from the 1979 Insurrection to the Present*. Washington DC: National Defense University Press.

Martí y Puig, S. (1994) *¿La última rebelión campesina? Revolución y contrarrevolución en Nicaragua, 1979–1987*. La Rábida: Universidad Internacional de Andalucía-La Rábida, 1987.

Martí y Puig, S. (1997) *La revolución enredada: Nicaragua 1977–1996*. Madrid: Los Libros de la Catarata, 1997.

McCleary, R.M. (1999) *Imponiendo la democracia: Las élites guatemaltecas y el fin del conflicto armado*. Guatemala: Artemio Edinter.

McClintock, M. (1985) *The American Connection*, Vol. I: *State Terror and Popular Resistance in El Salvador*. London: Zed Books.

Menjívar Larín, R. (1981) 'El Salvador: The Smallest Link', in *Revolutionary Staretgy in El Salvador*. London: Tricontinental Society, pp. 3–10.

Menjívar Larín, R., D. Kruijt and L. van Vucht Tijssen (eds) (1997) *Pobreza, exclusión y política social*. San José: FLACSO and UNESCO.

Menjívar Larín, R., and J. D. Trejos (1992) *La pobreza en América Central*. San José: FLACSO.

Menjívar Ochoa, R. (2006) *Tiempos de locura. El Salvador, 1979–1981*, 2nd edn. San Salvador: FLACSO.

Michels, R. (1911) *Zur Soziologie des Parteiwesens in de modernen Demokratie Untersuchungen über die oligarchischen Tendenzen des Gruppenlebens*. Stuttgart: Alfred Kröner Verlag.

Miguez Bonino, José (1979) *Doing Theology in a Revolutionary Situation*. Philadelphia: Fortress Press.

Millett, R. (1977) *Guardians of the Dynasty: A History of the US Created Guardia Nacional of Nicaragua and the Somoza Family*. New York: Orbis Books.

Montes, C. [J. C. Macías] (1999) *La guerrilla fue mi camino. Epitafio para César Montes*, 3rd edn. Guatemala: Piedra Santa.

Montgomery, T.S. (1995) *Revolution in El Salvador: From Civil Strife to Civil Peace*. Boulder CO: Westview Press.

Morales Carbonell, J.A. (1994) 'El suicidio de Marcial ¿Un asunto concluido?' *Estudios Centroamericanos*, June, pp. 653–89.

Morán, R. [R. Ramírez de León] (2002) *Saludos revolucionarios. La historia reciente de Guatemala desde la óptica de la lucha guerrillera (1984–1996)*. Guatemala: Fundación Guillermo Torriello.

Moroni Bracamonte, J.A., and D.E. Spencer (1995) *Stategy and Tactics of the Salvaroran FMLN Guerrillas: Last Battle of the Cold War, Blueprint for Future Conflicts*. Westport CT: Praeger.

Muñoz Guillén, M. (1990) *El estado y la abolición del ejército, 1914 –1949*. San José: Editorial Porvenir.

Murga Armas, J. (2006) *Iglesia católica, movimiento indígena y lucha revolucionaria (Santiago Atitlán, Guatemala)*. Guatemala: Impresiones Palacios.

Murillo, R. (1990) *Las esperanzas misteriosas*. Managua: Editorial Vanguardia.

Musset, A. (2007) *Hombres nuevos en otro mundo. La Nicaragua del ochenta en los diarios de campo de los brigadistas de la Cruzada Nacional de Alfabetización*. Managua: UCA-IHNCA.

NACLA Report on the Americas (1987) *The Israeli Connection: Guns and Money in Central America*, special issue, 21(2), March-April.

Nicaragua, The Economic Situation (1989). Managua: Secrataría de Planificación y Presupuesto, October-December.

Nuñez Soto, O. (1987) *Transición y lucha de clases en Nicaragua, 1979–1986*. México: Siglo XXI.

Nuñez Soto, O. (ed.), (1998) *La guerra y el campesinado en Nicaragua*, 3rd edn. Managua: CIPRES.

Olivier, A. (1939) *La commune*. Paris: Gallimard.

Orwell, G. (1977) *Homage to Catalonia* [1938]. London: Penguin.

Ortega Saavedra, H. ['Alberto'] (1978) *Sobre la insurrección*. Nicaragua: 'Algún lugar en Nicaragua'.

Ortega Saavedra, H. (1981) *Sobre la insurrección*. Havana: Editorial de Ciencias Sociales.

Ortega Saavedra, H. (2004) *La epopeya de la insurrección*. Managua: LEA Grupo Editorial.

Parkman, P. (2003) *Insurrección no violenta en El Salvador. La caída de Maximiliano Hernández Martínez*. San Salvador: CONCULTURA (Biblioteca de Historia Salvadoreña 13).

Payeras, M. (1987) *El trueno en la ciudad. Episodios de la lucha armada urbana de 1981 en Guatemala*. Mexico: Juan Pablos Editor.

Payeras, M. (1991) *Los fusiles de octubre. Ensayos y articulos militares sobre la revolución guatemalteca, 1985–1988*. Mexico: Juan Pablos Editor.

Payeras, M. (1992) *Los pueblos indígenas y la revolución guatemalteca. Ensayos étnicos, 1982–1992*. Guatemala: Magna Terra Editores.

Payeras, M. (2002) *Los días en la selva* [1981], 11th edn. Guatemala: Editorial Piedra Santa.

Pereira Gómez, M.A., and J.A. Bilbao Ercoreca (1991) *Recuerdos de una guerra en Nicaragua, 'Contras y FSLN'. Vida, historia y experiencias de tres comandantes de la resistencia. Intento de un estudio sobre la Nicaragua dividida.* Estelí: Archives of the IHNCA.

Pérez, J. (2004) *Semper Fidelis. El secuestro de la Guardia Nacional de Nicaragua.* Bogotá: Justiciano Pérez.

Pérez Baltonano, A. (2003) *Entre el estado conquistador y el estado nación: Providencialismo, pensamiento político y estructuras del poder en el desarrollo histórico de Nicaragua.* Managua: Universidad Centroamericana-Instituto de Historia de Nicaragua y de Centroamérica.

Pérez Brignoli, H. (1989) *A Brief History of Central America.* Berkeley: University of California Press.

Plan económico 1990. De la estabilización a la reactivación. Tomo I: Marco Macroeconómico y lineamientos de política (1989). Managua: Secretaría de Planificación y Presupuesto, November.

Preparación Política. Clases, Soldados y Marineros (n.d.). Managua: Dirección Política del EPS.

Ramírez, S. (1999) *Adiós muchachos. Una memoria de la revolución Sandinista.* Bogotá: Aguilar.

Ramonet, I. (2006) *Fidel Castro, biografía a dos veces*, 2nd edn. Barcelona: Random House Mondadori.

Ramos González, C.G. (1993) 'Solución política negociada y fuerzas sociales mayoritarias en El Salvador (1984–1990)'. M.A. thesis, San José: Universidad de Costa Rica and FLACSO.

Randall, M. (1999) *Las hijas de Sandino: Una historia abierta.* Managua: Anamá Ediciones.

Report on Guatemala. Findings of the Study Group on United States–Guatemalan Relations (1985). Boulder, CO: Westview Press.

RESDAL (2005) *Atlas comparativo de la defensa en América Latina.* Buenos Aires: RESDAL (www.resdal.org/libros/Archivo/atlas-libro.htm).

Renzi, M.R., and D. Kruijt (1997) *Los nuevos pobres. Gobernabilidad y política social en Nicaragua.* San José: FLACSO.

Rico Mira, C.E. (2004) *En silencio tenía que ser. Testimonio del conflicto armado en El Salvador (1967–2000)*, 2nd edn. San Salvador: Editorial Francisco Gavidia.

Romero, O.A., et al. (1979) *Iglesia de los pobres y organizaciones populares.* San Salvador: UCA Editores (series La Iglesia en América Latina 4).

Rosada-Granados, H. (1998) *El lado oculto de las Negociaciones de paz. Transición de la guerra a la paz en Guatemala.* Guatemala: Friedrich Ebert Stiftung.

Rosada-Granados, H. (1999) *Soldados en el poder: Prooyecto militar en Guatemala (1944–1990).* Amsterdam: Thela Thesis Publishers.

Rozenberg, T. (1992) *Children of Cain: Violence and the Violent in Latin*

America. Harmondsworth: Penguin.

Saldomando, A., C. Rosa de León, R. Ribera and C. Sojo (2000) *Diagnóstico de la investigación para la consolidación de la paz en América Central. A Review of Research for Peacebuilding in Central America* (www.idrc.ca/uploads/user-S/10226957630diagnostico.pdf).

Samayoa, S. (2003) *El Salvador. La reforma pactada*. San Salvador: UCA Editores.

Samayoa, S., and G. Galvan (1979) 'El movimiento obrero en El Salvador. ¿Resurgimiento o agitación?' *Estudios Centroamericanos*, pp. 591–600.

Sancho, E. (1991a) 'El Salvador frente a los desafíos del siglo XXI'. Parte I', *Estudios Centroamericanos* 510, pp. 295–318.

Sancho, E. (1991b) 'El Salvador frente a los desafíos del siglo XXI'. Parte II', *Estudios Centroamericanos* 511, pp. 431–53.

Sancho, E. [F. Cienfuegos] (1993) *Veredas de audacia*. San Salvador: Editorial Arcoiris.

Sancho, E. [F. Cienfuegos] (2003) *Crónicas entre los espejos*, 2nd edn. San Salvador: Editorial Francisco Gavidia.

Sancho, E., and D. Escobar Galindo (1996) *El venado y el colibri*. San Salvador: Ministerio de Educación-Dirección de Publicaciones e Impresos, Consejo Nacional para la Cultura y el Arte.

Sandoval, M.A. (1997) *Los años de la resistencia. Relatos sobre las guerrillas urbanas de los años 60*. Guatemala: Editorial Óscar de León Palacios.

Sanford, V. (2003) *Buried Secrets: Truth and Human Rights in Guatemala*. New York: Palgrave Macmillan.

Santa Cruz Mendoza, S. (2004) *Insurgentes. Guatemala, la paz arrancada*. Santiago de Chile, LOM Ediciones.

Schirmer, J. (1998) *The Guatemalan Military Project: A Violence called Democracy*. Philadelphia: University of Pensylvania Press.

Schirmer, J. (2002) 'The Guatemalan Politico-Military Project: Whose Ship of State?', in K. Koonings and D. Kruijt (eds), *Political Armies: The Military and Nation Building in the Age of Democracy*. London: Zed Books, pp. 64–89.

Selser, G. (1979) *Sandino, general de hombres libres*, 2nd edn. San José: EDUCA.

Sesereses, C.D. (1992) 'The Guatemalan Counterinsurgency Campaign of 1982–1985: A Strategy of Going It Alone', in E.G. Corr and S. Sloan (eds), *Low-Intensity Conflict: Old Threats in a New World*. Boulder CO: Westview Press, pp. 101–23.

Sichar Moreno, G. (1999) *Historia de los partidos políticos guatemaltecos. Distintas siglas de (casi) una misma ideología*, 2nd edn. Chimaltenango: Nojib'sa.

Sichar Moreno, G. (2000) *Masacres en Guatemala. Los gritos de un pueblo entero.* Guatemala: Grupo de Apoyo Mutuo (GAM).

Sichar Moreno, G. (2006) *Izquierda en Guatemala. Del levantamiento a la perdida del horizonte*, www.inisoc.org/sichar4.htm (consulted 19 November 2006).

Sieder, R. (ed.) (1996) *Central America: Fragile Transition.* London: Macmillan.

Sollis, P. (1995) 'Partners in Development? The State, Non-Governmental Organisations and the UN in Central America', *Third World Quarterly* 16(3), pp. 525-42.

Spence, J. (2004) *La guerra y la paz en América Central: Una comparación de las transiciones hacia la democracia y la equidad social en Guatemala, El Salvador y Nicaragua.* Brookline, MA: Hemisphere Initiatives.

Spencer, D.E. (1996) *From Vietnam to El Salvador: The Saga of the FMLN Sappers and Other Guerrilla Special Forces in Latin America.* Westport CT: Praeger.

Sprenkels, R. (2005) *The Price of Peace: The Human Rights Movement in Postwar El Salvador.* Amsterdam: CEDLA (Cuadernos del CEDLA 19).

Stanley, W. (1996) *The Protection Racket State: Elite Politics, Military Extortion, and the Civil War in El Salvador.* Philadelphia: Temple University Press, 1996.

Stevenson, D. (2004) *1914–1918: The History of the First World War.* London: Penguin.

Szulc, T. (1986) *Fidel: A Critical Portrait.* New York: William Morrow.

Taibo II, P.I. (1997) *Ernesto Guevara, también conocido como El Che.* Barcelona: Editorial Planeta.

Testimonios de cien días de sangre, fuego y victorias. Corresponsales de guerra/BARRICADA (1984). Managua: Editorial Nuevo Amanecer (2nd edn).

Tirado, V. (2007) 'El 19 de julio de 1979', *Nuevo Diario*, 21 July.

Toll, F. (2005) 'A Revolutionary Chess Game: The FMLN and Democratic Polities in the Salvadoran Post War Era'. M.Sc. thesis, Utrecht: Utrecht University, School of Cultural Anthropology and Sociology.

Torres, H. (2003) *Rumbo norte. Historia de un sobreviviente.* Managua: Editorial Hispamer.

Torres-Rivas, E. (1993a) *History and Society in Central America.* Austin: University of Texas Press.

Torres-Rivas, E. (ed.) (1993b) *Historia general de Centroamérica,* 6 vols. Madrid and San José: Sociedad Estatal Quinto Centenario and FLACSO.

Torres-Rivas, E. (1996) *Encrucijadas e incertezas en la izquierda cantroamericana (Ensayo preliminar de interpretación)*. Guatemala: FLACSO.

Trobo, C. (1983) *Lo que pasa en Nicaragua*. Caracas: Ediciones Centauro.

UN Secretariat (2003) *World Urbanization Prospects: The 2003 Revision*. New York. Population Division of the Department of Economic and Social Affairs of the United Nations Secretariat, http://esa.un.org/unpp (consulted 9 June 2006).

UN Secretariat (2004) *World Population Prospects: The 2004 Revision*. New York. Population Division of the Department of Economic and Social Affairs of the United Nations Secretariat, http://esa.un.org/unpp (consulted 9 June 2006).

US Assistance to Nicaraguan Guerrillas: Issues for the Congress (1988) (01-29-88, IB 84139).

van der Borgh, C. (1999) *Wederopbouw in Chalatenango, El Salvador. Ontwikkelingsorganisaties in een na-oorlogse maatschappij*. Amsterdam: Thela Thesis Publishers.

Vilas, C.M. (1994) *Mercado, estados y revoluciones. Centroamérica 1950–1990*. Mexico: Universidad Nacional Autónoma de México-Centro de Investigaciones Interdisciplinarias en Humanidades.

Villalobos, J. (1986) 'El estado actual de la guerra y sus perspectivas', *Estudios Centroamericanos*, pp. 169-204.

Villalobos, J. (1989a) 'A Democratic Revolution for El Salvador', *Foreign Policy* 74, Spring, pp. 103-22.

Villalobos, J. (1989b) 'Perspectivas de victoria y proyecto revolucionario', *Estudios Centroamericanos*, pp. 11-51.

Villalobos, J. (2000) *'Sin vencedores ni vencidos'. Pacificación y reconciliación en El Salvador*. San Salvador: INELSA.

Walter, K. (1997) *Las Fuerzas Armadas y el acuerdo de paz. La transformación necesaria del ejército salvadoreño*. San Salvador: FLACSO.

Walter, K. (2004) *El régimen de Anastasio Somoza, 1936–1956*. Managua: Universidad Centroamericana-Instituto de Historia de Nicaragua y de Centroamérica.

Weaver, F.S. (1994) *Inside the Volcano: The History and Political Economy of Central America*. Boulder CO: Westview Press.

Wellinga, K.S. (1994) *Entre la poesía y la pared. Política popular Sandinista, 1979–1990*. San José and Amsterdam: FLACSO and Thela Publishers.

Wer, C.E. (2003) *En Guatemala los héroes tienen quínce años*. Guatemala: Armar Editores.

Wheelock, J. (1990) *La Reforma Agraria Sandinista. 10 Años de revolución en el campo*. Managua: Editorial Vanguardia.

Wheelock, J. (1991) *La verdad sobre La Piñata. Los cambios en la propiedad agraria, julio 1979–abril 1990*. Managua: IPADE.

Wheelock, J. (1997) 'Revolution and Democratic Transition in Nicaragua', in J.I. Domínguez and M. Landenberg (eds), *Democratic Transitions in Central America*. Gainesville: University Press of Florida, pp. 67-84.

White, R.A. (1984) *The Morass. United States Intervention in Central America*. New York: Harper & Row.

Whitfield, T. (1998) *Pagando el precio. Ignacio Ellacuría y el asesinato de los jesuitas en El Salvador*. San Salvador: UCA Editores.

Wickham-Crowley, T.P. (1987) 'The Rise (and Sometimes Fall) of Guerrilla Governments in Latin America', *Sociological Forum* 2(3), pp. 473-99.

Wickham-Crowley, T.P. (1990) 'Terror and Guerrilla Warfare in Latin America, 1956-1970', *Comparative Studies in Society and History* 32(2), pp. 201-37.

Wickham-Crowley, T. (1992) *Guerrillas and Revolution in Latin America: A Comparative Study of Insurgents and Regimes since 1956*. Princeton NJ: Princeton University Press.

Williams, P., and K. Walter (1997) *Militarization and Demilitarization in El Salvador's Transition to Democracy*. Pittsburgh: University of Pittsburgh Press.

Wood, E.J. (2003) *Insurgent Collective Action and Civil War in El Salvador*. Cambridge: Cambridge University Press.

Zamora, A. (1990) '4000 Días de soberanía. La política exterior Sandinista', *Envío* 9(110), December, pp. 32–44.

Zamora, A. (1996) 'La piñata: Algunas reflexiones', *Envío* 171, June, pp. 12–15.

Zamora, R. (1997) 'Democratic Transition or Moderization? The Case of El Salvador since 1997', in J. Domínguez and M. Lindenberg (eds), *Democratic Transition in Central America*. Gainesville: University Press of Florida, pp. 165-79.

Zamora, R. (1998) *El Salvador: Heridas que no cierran. Los partidos políticos en la post-guerra*. San Salvador: FLACSO.

Zamora, R. (2003) *La izquierda partidaria salvadoreña: Entre la identidad y el poder*. San Salvador: FLACSO.

Zimmermann, M. (2003) *Carlos Fonseca Amador y la revolución nicaraguënse*. Managua: Universidad de las Regiones Autónomas de la Costa Caribe Nicaragüense.

Index